CLAIM YOUR BASIC RIGHTS

Create a Practical Partnership with Your Soul

About the Authors

JENNIFER PALMQUIST throughout her life has had the capabilities to perceive what most others cannot. As a small child her extrasensory capabilities remained open allowing her to experience the world in a split-minded manner. She witnessed the inconsistencies between a person's feelings and behaviors and their soul's intention and wisdom. Reconciling these discrepancies became essential to understanding the world within and around her.

For a time during adolescence she suppressed her gifts to a degree. When in college several experiences helped her to realize that her gifts needed further exploration. She recognized the need to increase her awareness, but the avenues to pursue were limited. She investigated psychology, dreamwork, breathwork, Reiki, yoga, shamanic healing, and other cross-cultural healing modalities. All the while, her spiritual helpers kept providing guidance and insight while she practiced meditation and refined her gifts.

Jennifer has taught classes in intuitive development, dreamwork, creativity, symbolism, and healing. For more than twenty-five years she has consulted with individuals to help them form a more practical partnership with their soul, assisting them on their path in life. Her life experience has allowed her to better appreciate and solidify the Basic Rights we are all endowed with and are in need of claiming consciously.

DANIEL COHEN received his BS degree from Penn State University in Science and his MD from Temple Medical School. He received his training in Neurology at the University of Minnesota Hospitals and Clinic and is a Diplomat of the American Board of Psychiatry and Neurology.

In 1982, Dr. Cohen co-founded CNS, Inc, was its CEO until 2001, and currently serves as Chairman of the Board. CNS developed innovative technology to monitor brain function during high-risk surgeries and Sleep disorders diagnostic equipment. The Company is best known for manufacturing and marketing the Breathe Right® nasal strip.

Dr. Cohen founded Round River Research, Corp. in 1996 to study the effects of sound, music, and vibration on states of consciousness and meditation. He is the inventor of the Infusion™ acoustic body pad and the BodySound™ system. In 1999, he began working with Jennifer to develop the Conscious Unfoldment™ course to assist individuals in creating a more practical partnership with their soul.

CLAIM YOUR BASIC RIGHTS

Jennifer L. Palmquist and Daniel E. Cohen, M.D.

Published by One Red River, Inc.
Eden Prairie, MN 55347

First Edition
First Printing, 2006

Library of Congress Cataloging-in-Publication Data
ISBN 0-9777577-0-6

Printed in the United States of America

Contents

PART V: TOOLS

Acknowledgements

We would like to acknowledge those closest to us who have helped shape our lives. They are Carl, Joanne, Sid, Betty, Kate, Tim, Cary, Tom, Ellen, Jason, David, Michael, Nicole, Whitney, Ali, Paul, and Audree. We would like to give special thanks to Patrick Delaney for his encouragement and helpful suggestions during the writing of this book. We would also like to thank Karen Karsten and Michael Hensley for their editing assistance, Donna Burch for her work on the layout of the book, Barry McMahon for his help with the cover's graphic design, and Ken Pavett for managing the printing of this book.

Cover artwork by Jennifer Palmquist

INTRODUCTION

The Path

Most of us have been exposed to words like soul and spirit in religious teachings. Our firsthand experiential knowledge, however, tends to be limited or nonexistent. We hunger for connection, but do not know how to go about it, or are too busy to think about it. Think about it now. Do you believe that you have a soul? Is it everlasting? How is your soul evident in your life today?

In this book, we outline Ten Basic Rights, Rights that we each have, but often do not acknowledge, accept, or exercise. These Rights are not rules, but instead are guidelines intended to help each of us create and travel our path toward enlightenment—unification with our soul and All That Is while living our daily lives.

The first three Basic Rights are covered in depth in this book. Becoming aware of these Rights and practicing them in your life forms a solid foundation upon which to deepen your communication with your soul and All That Is. When you are ready, the other Rights are also covered in depth in subsequent books.

What You Need to Know Before You Start

A human being consists of a soul and spiritual essence that is personal and transpersonal, respectively, joined with a personality that is based in our physical reality.

The teaching method for your path is that of an ongoing dialog between your soul and personality, combined with other information to aid in understanding. The soul coaches and enlightens the personality.

Your Soul

The word soul is used to identify your higher energetic self that is everlasting and evolving. Similar to your personality, which also has an energetic component, your soul has qualities that are unique. Your soul is personal to you—part of your personal self—and is your conduit to All That Is, referred to by many as God, Creator or by many other names.

Spiritual Essence

The aspect of All That Is that resides within and flows throughout you is referred to in this book as your spiritual essence, which exists in a state of perfection. Your soul is your connection to All That Is through that spiritual essence. Spiritual essence is beyond the limits of ego and personality and represents a consciousness that is not personal or limited to self. Spiritual essence is connected to all.

Personality

The personality is a vehicle for the soul and is the part of us that has free will and acts in the manner of its choosing within self-imposed limits. The personality uses subconscious coping strategies developed in response to violations of its Basic Rights. These coping mechanisms cause the personality to act in ways that restrict its ability to work in partnership with the soul. Learning to listen to the soul can lessen the need to rely on coping strategies and help resolve those violations in a conscious, spiritual way.

What if you could better communicate with your spiritual side? Would you follow the guidance you receive? If you did, would you do it because you think you should or would you do it because you want to? What is the payoff for following spiritual advice?

Timeframe

Most of us are largely unaware of our spiritual side. Learning to listen to your soul and have it be a part of you in the present moment takes time. How much time depends on you. You need to be willing to spend the time it takes to benefit from your spiritual connection.

Tools

To help you in your search for connection to your spiritual side, we provide tools you can use to speed your way to listening to your soul.

- Observation
- Forgiveness
- Compassion
- Hope
- Relaxation
- The Feel, Deal and Let Go Process

- Meditation

- Love, Truth and Will

As in any path there is a long way and a shorter way. Would you like to learn a shortcut? We invite you to read on with an open heart and a smile. We also encourage you to consider the questions that are posed at the end of the chapters. We've left space for journaling or note taking, but please, write on. Most of all, we wish you well on your path.

chapter one

OUR MINDS

I was in a hurry and running late for a class that I was teaching. My mother always taught me never to be late and inconvenience others. I found myself caught in traffic on the highway, feeling pressured and angry. How frustrating! Another traffic jam precipitated by peoples' endless curiosity to gawk at a car on the side of the road. Traffic finally eased and I was able to exit. One block before my destination I was cut off by a driver whose look of disdain suggested that I was at fault. I found a parking space and began to back into it, but another driver behind me kept inching forward preventing me from parking. My angry stare caused her to relent and I parked my car, sat back, closed my eyes, and asked myself why the world was so crazy.

The answer came immediately. "It's all about you." Then in my mind's eye I saw an image of a hurricane with large circular storm clouds surrounding the calm eye at the center and I realized that I had to calm myself. The following week on my way to class I again found myself in a traffic jam at about the same location. I imagined that I was as calm as the eye of the hurricane and I spread that feeling throughout and around me causing the storm clouds to dissipate. I realized that I was doing the best I could to be on time. I let go of my feelings of guilt and I stopped feeling pressured. Traffic eased. Nobody cut me off or prevented me from parking and I arrived on time. Had the world changed in a week? I don't think so, but my world was different because at that moment I was different.

It's hard for us to accept that many of the events in our lives, even those that seem trivial, are created in response to our own attitudes (our beliefs, feelings, and behaviors). If this is so, then why is it not commonly acknowledged and taught, so that we can remedy these situations and make our lives better? What external force is at work that prevents us from doing so? There is none, it's all about you. We prevent ourselves from perceiving the nature of our reality. How can this be? Why would I deny myself this awareness? We do it all the time, and furthermore, we do it purposely.

We have given this phenomenon a name. It's called our subconscious (below or out-side of our conscious awareness). It's that part of our mind that our personality chooses not to be consciously aware of because it contains many of our fears and old painful be-liefs. Despite our diminished awareness of this information, our subconscious fears and beliefs continuously influence our conscious beliefs, feelings, and behavior and can cause the events in our lives to develop. As a result, we remain largely unaware of why things happen the way that they do.

There is more. I know what I know (conscious) and I know that there are certain things that I don't want to know (subconscious). However, I also don't know what I don't know, which therefore, is also subconscious or outside of my conscious awareness. How vast is that which is unknown to me, and is some part of that my soul?

Does your soul have a mind or is it an aspect of your mind? Are you aware of this mind? Is it different from the mind of your personality? Imagine that you are in your car driving to or from work or on any drive that is part of your routine. You are on autopi-lot, operating mindlessly. You come to a stoplight or stop sign and you catch yourself hav-ing a conversation in your head. Who are the conversants? Is this the dialogue between the mind of your personality and the mind of your soul? Which conversant are you most identified with?

How can your conscious mind sort all of this out? You are constantly being influenced by subconscious fears, old beliefs, and your soul. Your conscious mind is the gatekeeper, allowing in only that which it is willing to consider. The scope of your awareness is self-de-termined. You have access to your subconscious mind and to the mind of your soul. In fact you have created these seemingly separate minds by controlling your access and thereby limiting your conscious awareness. You have focused your conscious awareness in response to fear and as a result, blinded yourself to that part of you which makes you feel bad. This narrowed focus, unfortunately, also diminishes your ability to perceive your spiritual side and your spiritual connectedness.

Your conscious mind has free will, the ability to choose. At the time of your choosing you can have greater access to that which you have been denying yourself. What will you find when you access more of your mind? That will depend upon what is on your mind because your mind is responsive, reactive to the thoughts that you wish to consider. The same thought may evoke a fearful response from your subconscious mind and an entirely different perspective from the mind of your soul. Your conscious mind has the ability to withstand any fear and to perceive the mind of your soul. To understand yourself more completely it is therefore necessary to engage every aspect of your mind.

What thoughts would be best to consider in order to engage more of your mind and expand your awareness? It's all about you. Why do you feel and therefore act in the ways that you do? What do you believe that triggers your feelings? Why do you believe what you do? The Ten Basic Rights address our physical, emotional, mental, and spiritual natures.

Considering these Rights physically, emotionally, mentally, and spiritually will enable you to better understand why you and others believe, feel, and act the way that you and they do. It will alter your conscious awareness about yourself, others, and your world.

We each have the ability to feel physically, emotionally, and intuitively. Our feelings can help us probe our beliefs. Our mental capabilities provide us with the ability to think, reason, and understand ourselves, others, and the world around us. By directing these innate capabilities you can expand your conscious awareness to include more of your subconscious mind and your spiritual side. Do you wish to expand your conscious awareness? Are you prepared to change?

---
chapter two

CHANGE

Sᴏᴍᴇ ᴘᴇᴏᴘʟᴇ ᴀʀᴇ ᴇxᴄɪᴛᴇᴅ by the concept of change, but most fear it. Most often, change is perceived as the devil we don't know. Consequently, the majority of people opt for the status quo. Some people are actually happy with how they and their lives are progressing. Many are in denial about themselves or their present circumstances or they fear how things might turn out if they proactively make a change. Despite the barriers that we erect to avoid change, it happens nonetheless. Change is as inevitable as the passage of time.

Why do we struggle with a proposition that can lead to improvement in our circumstances and ourselves? How often do we ask that things be different? After all, if we want something to be different, then aren't we asking for change? Of course we are, but it always comes back to who must do the changing.

Soul: It appears as though you have had a difficult day.

Personality: Many of my days seem like this. I feel like I'm stuck in the fast lane, but going nowhere.

Soul: Why?

Personality: My life seems like an endless cycle of repetition and each cycle ends badly. I've been told that the problems I experience relate to my own attitudes about life, but that's how I was raised. I am what I am. I learned to be this way from my parents mainly and some others.

Soul: I am sure your parents raised you as best they could. Blaming them at this time in your life does not seem to be productive.

Personality: It might make me feel better.

Soul: How will it help with your understanding?

Personality: There's nothing to understand. They could have done so much better. I would be a completely different person if they had raised me with more compassion and empathy so that I was allowed to become the kind of person that I would like to be. Instead they molded me into the kind of person that they thought I should be and it's not working for me.

Soul: What kind of person do you want to be?

Personality: I don't want to worry about everything the way they did. I want to be able to trust that things will work out for the best as long as I do my part. I don't want to feel guilty and pressured to do more when I think that I'm being fair and honest. Most of all I just want to feel good about myself and not worry about how others judge me.

Soul: Is that all?

Personality: I can create a longer wish list, but this would be a great start. Wait a minute. Who are you anyway? I've just realized that this conversation has been going on inside of my head. You wouldn't happen to be a genie would you? I could use a few wishes.

Soul: I have been called worse, but, no, I am not a genie.

Personality: I'm not having a nervous breakdown, am I?

Soul: No. You have just decided to pay attention to me. You do so every once in a while.

Personality: I don't remember ever having this kind of experience.

Soul: Do you remember when you were very ill five years ago and you thought you were going to die? You started to question whether or not it was your time and whether you had accomplished what you had set out to do.

Personality: I don't remember it quite like that. I remember being scared to die and worried that I wouldn't go to heaven. Now that you mention it though, I do remember feeling reassured at one point, but that was different.

Soul: Remember when you were a small child and your parents were arguing? You were frightened that you would be left alone and that whatever they were arguing about was your fault.

Personality: Yes I do remember that and you told me that it would be okay. You told me that they loved me and that their argument wasn't about me. Where have you been all these years, on vacation?

Soul: I have never left you. I have been here all along waiting for you to become more receptive, more attuned to me.

Personality: That's ridiculous. I've always been a good listener.

Soul: Great. That will make my job much easier.

Personality: What job would that be?

Soul: Providing input that will increase your understanding about why things are the way they are in your life. I am here to offer you my love and wisdom.

Personality: I'll be the judge of that.

Soul: Certainly. I am only here to help. You do not have to take what I offer.

Personality: You still haven't told me who you are. I'm not likely to take input from strangers.

Soul: I would rather be considered a genie than a stranger.

Personality: Make up your mind.

Soul: I am your soul, not a genie, but I do respond to you when you call.

Personality: How so?

Soul: I try to help you feel connected and assist you in understanding yourself and your circumstances.

Personality: Who sent you here, my parents?

Soul: I am always here. You are just better able to appreciate me right now.

Personality: Why?

Soul: Because you are trying to understand yourself. You are searching for answers.

Personality: I think I've figured it out. My problems stem from my childhood and the way I was raised. It's not my fault.

Soul: It may not be your fault, but your problems exist nonetheless and they are your problems.

Personality: That's not fair. I didn't cause them. I was a victim.

Soul: It appears as though you are feeling and thinking like a victim.

Personality: Well I am. I am the way I am because of the way I was raised, the way I was told to be. I feel stuck with me and I don't like it.

Soul: So change.

Personality: Sure, I'll just snap my fingers and assume a new identity. I don't think you understand. Changing yourself is nearly impossible.

Soul: I have noticed. People tend to make changes only when there is no other option or when they are forced to change as a result of the actions of others.

Personality: That's right. That's how it is.

Soul: Then I presume you will continue to feel stuck with yourself the way that you are and remain victimized by your past. Continuing along in this way must have its pay-offs, otherwise you would opt for a change.

Personality: What kind of payoffs?

Soul: Self-pity for one. In your mind that justifies your sad mood, particularly when you do not feel like doing chores or other tasks that you consider menial. You often use your mood as an excuse to receive unnecessary help from others. You have friends and family that are sympathetic to your plight. When they see that you are sad, they reach out to you and support you, which reinforces your attitude of victimization.

Personality: They're just being kind.

Soul: They are often being manipulated.

Personality: I help them when they need it.

Soul: Yes you do. They have their issues to deal with as well.

Personality: That's simply the nature of our lives. We all have our problems and we have to help each other out the best we can so we can get by. What's wrong with that?

Soul: There is nothing wrong with that. You and they are simply choosing to get by rather than dealing with the underlying issues that are causing your problems. There is a difference between treating symptoms and understanding the cause of the problem. You can keep adding water to a leaky radiator every time your car's engine starts to overheat, or you can replace the faulty radiator, to fix it once and for all.

Personality: People are more complicated than cars.

Soul: You can acknowledge and accept your circumstances in life and yourself as you are right now and from this time forward be consciously accountable for your beliefs, feelings, and actions. Take responsibility for your life and yourself here and now and live with that awareness, consciously.

Personality: Why should I have to take ownership of problems that I didn't create?

Soul: If you inherited a million dollars would you accept the inheritance?

Personality: Of course.

Soul: So, you would take ownership of the inheritance?

Personality: Yes, but that's different. I don't deserve my problems.

Soul: Did you earn that money?

Personality: No.

Soul: Then why would you accept it?

Personality: Because I would want to. I'm entitled to some good fortune.

Soul: To make up for your misfortune, as you perceive it, the way that you were raised?

Personality: That would help.

Soul: Would you then be more accepting of your problems?

Personality: Probably not.

Soul: How would you use the money?

Personality: After paying taxes, we would probably take a vacation. Then we would most likely pay down our second mortgage, buy a new car, put some money into college funds for the kids, and invest the rest.

Soul: Why not spend some for therapy to better understand your issues?

Personality: I don't need therapy.

Soul: Then you do not view your issues as being all that troublesome, do you? After all, you would consider buying a new car and there is nothing wrong with the one that you drive now.

Personality: After a vacation, having less debt and some investments I'm sure that I would feel better.

Soul: Would you feel good enough to not blame your parents for your upbringing?

Personality: I would feel better about my current circumstances, but my parents are still to blame.

Soul: What would allow you to forgive them and move on with your life?

Personality: What's done is done, but not forgiven. They can't make it better at this point in my life.

Soul: Only you can do that.

Personality: You keep coming back to me having to do something, even though it's not my fault.

Soul: You said it yourself, they can't make it better at this point in my life. It's up to you. They had their own issues to deal with from their parents. They did the best they could raising you just as you are doing your best with your children.

Personality: You're right I am, but I can already see some aspects of me that I don't like beginning to show up in my kids. This is how some of our prejudices and peculiar thinking gets passed from generation to generation, isn't it? I don't want my kids to have the same problems that I have. How can this process be changed?

Soul: You are a role model for your children. If you want them to become different than you are now, you must change.

Personality: I don't want to have to change. I wouldn't even know where to begin or how to attempt it. What would I change into?

Soul: You have a wish list.

Personality: Yes, I would like to feel better about myself and to not worry so much, but how do I become that way? Isn't there something you could do to transform me?

Soul: I cannot impose upon your free will, but I can help you in the process of changing.

Personality: How so?

Soul: Insight and opportunity.

Personality: I don't understand how you help me with opportunity.

Soul: For now, just consider that things happen for a reason and that I am part of that reason, assisted by All That Is.

Personality: So you are a genie.

Soul: Not in the way that you would like me to be. I am not here to grant the kind of wishes that you have in mind, but I will facilitate your experiences and development to the best of my ability.

Personality: I'm willing to consider a few small changes for the sake of my kids, but I don't know if I want to go through a development program. What do you think I'm signing up for?

Soul: Life is a development program and you have been enrolled since before you were born. It has just been hard for you to recognize the nature of this classroom because most teachers do not seem to know any more than the students. Every once in a while a very good teacher comes along and a few students take the time to learn. However, with the passage of time and the spread of knowledge by the less learned there is dilution in understanding. Successive generations may hear or read some parts of the message, but much of the practical significance is lost.

Personality: Are you here to teach me?

Soul: I am here to offer insight and to assist in providing opportunities for you to develop. You may consider that teaching, but it is entirely up to you to learn.

Personality: So what insight do you have for me so that I can get out of my seemingly endless cycle of going nowhere?

Soul: Consider making some changes.

Personality: We've been through this already. What do I change and how do I do it?

Soul: What do you want for yourself above all else?

Personality: That's a hard question. I want a lot of things. I want to be different than I am. When I think of what I want for myself I feel selfish and guilty.

Soul: What do you desire? If I were a genie and I could grant you one wish, what would that wish be?

Personality: I would want to feel good about myself. Can you do that for me?

Soul: No, but you can do that for yourself.

Personality: I've been unsuccessful so far. What makes you think this time will be any different?

Soul: You are ready.

Personality: How do you know that?

Soul: You have identified what you want and you have begun to seek greater understanding.

Personality: Is it that easy?

Soul: It is that easy to initiate the process.

Personality: And then it gets harder, right?

Soul: If you believe that learning is a hard process then it will be. If you view obstacles as opportunities to learn then it will not be hard. It is entirely up to you. Your attitudes greatly influence your perceptions. Accept and embrace the opportunities that are presented to you. Make your choices and be accountable for them. Accept the outcomes, regardless of your judgements about them. That is how you can learn from life more effectively and with greater ease.

Personality: I would have to change a lot in order to approach life that way.

Soul: A shift in your awareness would facilitate that change.

Personality: Maybe I should just snap my fingers.

Soul: Are you a genie?

Personality: No. Are you going to help me?

Soul: Are you going to allow me to help you?

Personality: What do you mean?

Soul: Are you ready to change?

Personality: I might be ready to change a little.

Soul: Being willing to change may not be enough. What is stopping you from committing to change?

Personality: I want to better understand what I will get out of it, and I want to be in control of the process. This is my life and I'm going to do what I want with it.

Soul: I understand that you have free will and that you do not need to consider what I have to say, but if you knew what I know you might think differently.

Personality: Why, what's in it for me?

Discuss and/or Journal

Time passes, events in our lives occur, and we change or react to change. We may not initiate those events, but change happens regardless.

1. Are you more often the recipient of change or the initiator?

   _____

   _____

   _____

   _____

2. Have the changes you've initiated worked out better or worse than the changes that have befallen you?

   _____

   _____

   _____

   _____

3. Are you presently committed to making some changes in your life or circumstances? Why or why not?

   _____

   _____

   _____

   _____

4. What is your wish list?

   _____

   _____

   _____

   _____

   _____

chapter three

AWARENESS

Most of us observe the world around us with our five senses and analyze what we perceive to a limited extent. We pay considerably less attention to our inner landscape. We tend to notice when we are in pain or emotional discomfort. However, we rarely understand why we feel the way that we do or understand the motivations that underlie our actions. We generally do not question our lack of self-awareness. The lack of curiosity in this regard is further testimony to our lack of awareness. How can we develop greater insight about ourselves without greater self-awareness?

It is insight about ourselves that we choose to avoid. Why? Might we learn things about ourselves that we would not like or approve of? If so, we would be responsible for either changing them or acknowledging our failings and judging ourselves accordingly. It is no wonder that we practice avoidance. We choose to exist in a state of reduced self-awareness for this reason. We are not aware of the benefits that greater self-awareness would confer and the insights about ourselves that would develop. As a result, the payoff of avoidance outweighs the potential benefits that we remain unaware of.

Personality: Why would I want to become more aware?

Soul: You would learn what is true, experience real love and the simple things in life that can bring you much joy. These things are eluding you at present. That is why the limited happiness and joy that you experience is so transient. For you to appreciate these things you must become more aware.

Personality: Aware of what?

Soul: Aware of me, your soul, and your connection to All That Is, in a practical way with the knowledge that I am a part of you. Embody me by merging with me to a greater extent and your awareness will grow.

Personality: I have begun to hear you. Some of your messages are getting through.

Soul: They are your own messages. I am a part of you.

Personality: What do you mean?

Soul: I am a part of you, but you do not identify me as such. You were taught to view me only as a faith-based intellectual concept. On rare occasions, you acknowledge me as a thought or an idea that is in your mind, seemingly a part of you. Most often however, you view me as something that actually does exist, but in your way of thinking I remain separate from you. In general I remain subconscious because my influence rarely reaches your conscious awareness. I am not real to you because you do not perceive me with your five senses. I do not have nearly the impact that an attractive member of the opposite sex has on you. For that matter I am not even as important to you as your next meal.

Personality: Well maybe that's how it should be.

Soul: It has been that way for most of your life, but that time is over. It is time for you to move forward with your life.

Personality: In what way?

Soul: It is time for you to become more aware of who you are in total.

Personality: You mean to become more influenced by you. I like the control that I have now.

Soul: You will remain in control. It could not be any other way. I can only work in partnership with you, but for me to do so requires your permission.

Personality: Tell me again why I would want to do this.

Soul: You will learn more of what I know. My awareness can become your awareness. I am your connection to All That Is. When your awareness expands, you become more connected. You will not feel as isolated as you do now. You will be happier.

Personality: Are there any penalties if I start and then stop this process?

Soul: The only penalties, as you put it, are those that you impose upon yourself. That is always the way things are.

Personality: That's not true. Bad things happen to people that I wouldn't wish on my worst enemy.

Soul: You will understand differently when your awareness has grown.

Personality: I don't see any reason not to give this a try, but first I want to know why I couldn't have had greater awareness earlier in life or for that matter, when I was born?

Soul: You did have much greater awareness when you were born. You identified much more strongly with me at first, but to accomplish what you set out to do in life you had to learn how to function in the physical world. You had to learn how to meet the needs of your physical body and personality. That process consumed much of your energy and your focus. You concentrated on the needs of your body and personality and you developed coping strategies in order to meet those needs.

Personality: Aren't coping strategies like defense mechanisms?

Soul: Coping strategies, defense mechanisms or any means by which you attempt to control events, people or outcomes, are all the same. It is your way of trying to get what you want or avoid what you do not want. It is generally the way that the personality operates in order to meet its needs.

Personality: Aren't coping strategies a bad thing?

Soul: Rather than judging things as good or bad, think about actions and reactions or consequences of your actions or lack of actions. You have free will. You have the right and ability to learn. Making a choice that results in a reaction that you would judge as bad is simply a way to learn what not to do in the future if you wish to avoid that reaction. When someone adds the label bad or wrong to an action, it is typically done in an attempt to control or criticize another or yourself. That is just another coping strategy.

Personality: Okay, I get it. So then, what are the consequences of coping strategies?

Soul: Coping strategies are ways of believing, feeling, and acting in order to get what you want or avoid what you do not want.

Personality: What do you mean?

Soul: For example, if you believe that you require the approval of another in order for you to believe that you are deserving of love or to avoid the fear of abandonment, you will take actions that please that person. Learning and using that coping strategy will have taught you how to please another. However, every time that you use it, your belief will be reinforced that you require the approval of another instead of believing that you are deserving of love regardless of their approval. It will also reinforce your belief that you must act in this way to feel connected, when in fact, you are already connected through me. Using coping strategies limits your awareness to only those beliefs, feelings, and actions that you impose upon yourself. Also, because you use coping strategies in your attempt to achieve a specific outcome, you will not easily perceive other potential outcomes and alternative ways of being.

Personality: In my way of thinking, it seems like there is more bad than good to them.

Soul: Although they constrain your awareness to only that which you are willing to believe, feel, and do, they provide you with a set of tools to use in the physical world. As you become more aware of your coping strategies and the reasons you have developed them, you can shed them, while retaining the capabilities that you have developed. You can achieve your objectives without using coping strategies, but to do so requires that you face your fears.

Personality: I don't think I have too many fears.

Soul: You have more fears than you are aware of. That is why you have developed a subconscious mind so that you are less consciously aware of them. You have buried many of those fears in your subconscious mind along with your coping strategies, which you have used so regularly that you are no longer consciously aware of them.

Personality: Why did I create this?

Soul: Throughout your life, but particularly early in life, you did not have your needs met in the way that you had wanted. You also had some of your Basic Rights violated. That is a part of the human experience. As a result, you developed beliefs about yourself and the world that caused you to feel pain. In an attempt to protect yourself from revisiting these painful beliefs you have developed other ways of believing, feeling, and acting. These are your coping strategies. The painful beliefs that you work so hard to avoid were for the most part formed in early childhood. If you could view those beliefs in the light of your present knowledge you would dismiss many of them. Instead, you have developed strongly ingrained patterns of believing, feeling, and acting that deflect your attention and make it difficult for you to inspect these deeper painful beliefs. You use your coping strategies to avoid revisiting your painful beliefs and feeling bad about yourself and your situation in life.

Personality: How can I become more aware of my coping strategies and my painful beliefs if I have programmed myself to avoid them?

Soul: That is where I can help you. It is hard for you to perceive yourself, unless you can devise a way to do so from another viewpoint. I can offer you a different perspective.

Personality: Does that principle work in reverse? Am I the way in which you can perceive yourself?

Soul: Only to the extent that your awareness grows to perceive more of me.

Personality: So what do you get out of this relationship?

Soul: You and I are not separate so, what you get I get. We only seem to be separate to you. You as your personality are based in the physical realm. I as your soul am based partly in your realm and partly beyond the physical. I can perceive you in the physical realm as well as what is occurring outside the physical realm. My awareness is broader than yours. You can perceive the physical realm and as you become more adept at identifying with me, then you can perceive more of what exists beyond the physical through me.

Personality: So how can you help me perceive my coping strategies and painful beliefs?

Soul: I can only help you to the extent that you wish and allow it. Remember that you have free will.

Personality: Yes I have free will, but in this instance I'm not sure I know what to do with it.

Soul: Since I am an extension of you, all you need do is identify with me. I am that part of yourself that can observe you better.

Personality: How do I do that?

Soul: When you say I, consider me as well. You may wish to accept me as a practical part of you.

Personality: It's that simple?

Soul: If changing your beliefs is simple then it is as easy as changing your beliefs about me. Accepting me means that you truly believe in me, my existence, and my purpose. Become accountable for who you are in total by embodying me. This is how you bring all of yourself into this life. It is not quite as simple as you would like to believe.

Personality: I'm not very fond of change and I know myself well enough to know that changing my fundamental beliefs doesn't come so easily.

Soul: It rarely happens all at once. This shift in your attitude about me is a process that typically takes years, not days.

Personality: Why must it take so long?

Soul: Because you have free will. As you accept me into your life you begin to see the need to make changes in how you operate. You begin to realize that your coping strategies limit you. As you begin to shed them, you may become fearful and that can slow or sometimes stop the process.

Personality: Why would I become fearful if I want this to happen?

Soul: You have decided that you want this at a conscious level, which is a start, but it is only a start. You are not aware that your subconscious fears will be triggered. When they are, you will have a tendency to retreat back into the safety of ignorance instead of moving forward and confronting your fears. Many of these subconscious fears are the fears of your childhood. They often do not respond rationally to your present-day conscious decisions regarding your new approach to life. Your subconscious mind can work to prevent you from making changes that could potentially trigger your fears. It may create the sensation of fear or other negative emotions such as shame, anger, sadness, and so on in an attempt to make you look away from your painful beliefs because you have programmed yourself to do so. That may cause you to retreat.

Personality: And so what can I do?

Soul: Despite feeling fearful, feel your emotional feelings more fully by staying present with them. Understand the beliefs that cause these feelings to arise, but do so with the knowledge that you exist as more than your personality. By embodying me and allowing me to be present with you, you will be able to observe yourself more completely. In the process you may not be caught up in the drama to the extent that you are now or experience as strong a need to flee these feelings. You can still be the active participant in life and in control. Your awareness can encompass more of the underlying reasons for your feelings and actions as long as you are earnestly seeking the truth. Your resultant understanding can lessen the grip that your coping strategies have on you. You can shed these strategies like peeling the layers of an onion, until you reach the core. Then you may encounter your painful beliefs and with my help you can bring comfort and understanding to those childhood fears.

Personality: This sounds like a lot of work.

Soul: It is no more work than what you are doing now, but it is more rewarding. Instead of hiding from your fears, you will begin to experience and understand them, while feeling less fearful. The process makes life much more interesting. Each encounter with your coping strategies becomes an opportunity to learn the truth about yourself rather than short-circuiting the process by fearfully retreating into the realm of your subconscious. That is why this process is an awakening, because you consciously awaken to the truth about your life. This is how you develop greater conscious awareness and mastery of your life.

Personality: Give me an example as to how this works.

Soul: Can you think of one yourself?

Personality: I'm not that smart.

Soul: Thank you. That is an excellent example.

Personality: What do you mean?

Soul: The way that you demean yourself. There is no reason to do that.

Personality: Are you saying that my not being smart is a coping strategy?

Soul: Your intelligence is not an issue, but you claim not to be smart to avoid criticism. If others believe that you are not smart enough then they will not ask or expect much of you. When you do make a mistake you already have provided an excuse. In this way you believe that you are not disappointing others or yourself and as a result, you will not be criticized.

Personality: But I'm not all that smart.

Soul: That is the coping belief that you have adopted. You created that belief in response to the criticism you received as a child, particularly from your father. You are smarter than you give yourself credit for. You avoid trying and potentially making mistakes in order to avoid experiencing your deeper painful belief that would be triggered by criticism. That is one of your payoffs, avoidance.

Personality: But I do believe that I'm not very smart.

Soul: Of course you do, but that does not make it true. It is nothing more than a pattern of thinking that is deeply ingrained, automatic, and embedded in your subconscious mind. What happens when you challenge this coping belief?

Personality: It makes me feel anxious. Why do I feel anxious when you tell me that I'm smarter than I think I am? That's a compliment.

Soul: Why do you think you feel anxious?

Personality: I don't know, but I want it to end.

Soul: That is why negative feelings are so effective as an element of coping strategies. That feeling motivates you to suppress or otherwise alter this line of thought because you do not want to revisit your painful beliefs.

Personality: Why don't we stop this process?

Soul: The feeling will not hurt you. Persist and you will understand. You are feeling anxious because if you changed this particular coping belief of not being smart enough, then you would become more vulnerable to criticism. That is what you fear because criticism triggers your underlying painful belief.

Personality: Nobody likes to be criticized.

Soul: Some like it less, especially when it triggers painful beliefs.

Personality: I see your point.

Soul: Not entirely.

Personality: Why do you say that?

Soul: You are still avoiding the issue.

Personality: No, I get it. I can see how my excuse of not being smart enough helps me avoid criticism.

Soul: But why did you develop a coping strategy to avoid criticism in the first place?

Personality: Now I'm feeling even more nervous.

Soul: When you understand why, the nervousness will fade.

Personality: Fine, tell me.

Soul: If I simply tell you then you will not receive the full impact and the full benefit. You must feel it.

Personality: I don't know if I'm willing to do that.

Soul: That's fine. You can wait.

Personality: Until when?

Soul: Until you are ready.

Personality: How much will it hurt?

Soul: Not enough to warrant all of this avoidance.

Personality: Okay, what do I have to do to understand?

Soul: Remember what it felt like when your father criticized you as a child? Revisit an episode. How do you feel?

Personality: I feel hurt. He doesn't like me when I make a mistake.

Soul: Why do you say that?

Personality: He is angry with me. I don't mean to make him angry.

Soul: How do you know he is angry with you?

Personality: He is looking at me and yelling at me in a way that makes me feel like I'm bad.

Soul: Are you bad?

Personality: I'm not trying to be. I just made a mistake.

Soul: Is your father angry with you or angry at the mistake that you made?

Personality: I can't tell the difference.

Soul: Does your father still love you?

Personality: I think he does. He's nice to me later after all of the yelling.

Soul: Now think about that event from your present-day adult perspective. Did your father love you?

Personality: Yes, but he acted in a harsh manner when I made mistakes.

Soul: Do you see why you work so hard to avoid criticism?

Personality: I hated that feeling of disappointing him and feeling rejected whenever I made a mistake. When he did that I felt and believed that I was worthless.

Soul: That is why you developed a coping strategy to avoid recreating those feelings and revisiting that painful belief, which makes you feel bad about yourself.

Personality: I don't feel nervous anymore. I could get used to this.

Soul: Not if you practice avoidance.

Personality: You're right, all of the avoidance isn't warranted, but for a while there I started to feel really anxious.

Soul: But that passed and now you have a greater understanding about why you act the way that you do in certain circumstances.

Personality: I'm glad it's over and I don't have to reexperience that.

Soul: You have only begun to work through this issue. You have a new understanding about it, but an issue this deeply embedded is not so easily dismissed. It will continue to crop up in your life until you more completely understand how it impacts you in your everyday life. However with greater understanding you will lessen the effect that this issue has on your beliefs, feelings, and behaviors. Then there will come a time when you are able to deal with it more completely, but realizing that the issue exists and being willing to work through it is substantial progress.

Personality: I can see how I benefit by identifying with you. I can observe myself better, but how do you benefit from this process?

Soul: As you develop greater awareness I am able to perceive myself through your perceptions because I am also you.

Personality: Why do you need to perceive yourself through me?

Soul: It is the nature of learning and growth, witnessing yourself from another perspective. It is how knowledge is exchanged and truth is experienced. This is why we are in relationship.

Discuss and/or Journal

Curiosity and a strong desire to know what is true about yourself can help you overcome your fears. With that mindset, you can choose to not use your coping strategies and not practice avoidance. As a result, you will become more self-aware. Your soul is your partner —always available to assist you in this process and provide a different perspective.

1. Do you wish to become more self-aware? Why?

\
\
\
\
\
\

2. What benefits would you derive by becoming more self-aware?

\
\
\
\
\
\

3. Do you believe that your soul can assist you in this process?

\
\
\
\
\

chapter four

TEN BASIC RIGHTS

Developing greater awareness about ourselves and our lives requires a means of evaluation. We need a framework that we can use to better understand ourselves and our lives. Since we, as individuals are multi-faceted, it would be beneficial to see ourselves through various lenses that would reveal our physical, emotional, mental, and spiritual nature. This would allow us to perceive the different aspects of ourselves more specifically and with greater depth.

It would also be helpful for each of us to be able to evaluate ourselves within the context of our lives because no two lives are the same. We are individuals and we learn, grow, and make progress at our own pace. However, we all have a purpose and are on a path. We interact with others and the world around us. Therefore, it would be beneficial to choose a framework that not only allows us to evaluate our characteristics, but one that also allows us to evaluate our interactions with others and the world around us.

We, as multi-faceted individuals, travel paths of great diversity, and so, the framework that we choose must have sufficient breadth. It must allow us to evaluate our basic tendencies and our highest goals. Since we, as individuals, are also part of a larger community, this framework must allow us to evaluate ourselves within a context that reveals our inter-relatedness as well.

The framework that we choose can be universal if it describes something that is intrinsic to all life. The framework proposed is a collection of Rights that we are all endowed with. These Rights can serve as a means of self-evaluation and also to chart a path in life to achieve our potential.

Personality: So what do I have to do in order to learn more about myself and help myself grow as a person?

Soul: Claim your Rights so that you can achieve your potential.

Personality: What rights are you referring to?

Soul: The Rights that every living being has.

Personality: Where are they written? Who can I write to so that I can get a copy or can I download them from a website?

Soul: These Rights are very basic. They apply to everyone. They are intrinsic to all life on Earth. They also apply to all collectives such as businesses, institutions, and even governments and nations although they are rarely acknowledged and adhered to.

Personality: If they are so basic, why haven't I ever heard of them?

Soul: They are not routinely taught. You have been exposed to certain aspects of them in different ways. However, you have not integrated them into a cohesive framework that you can use to help you learn, grow, and accept yourself more completely. Understanding the degree to which you accept and observe these Rights will enable you to understand why you believe, feel, and act in the ways that you do, physically, emotionally, mentally, and spiritually.

Personality: I certainly can't acknowledge, accept, and observe something that I'm not aware of.

Soul: Let's start at the most basic level. When you were born you were helpless and defenseless, but by accepting this life you had the Right to exist as a human being in the physical world. You had the Right to be fully present in the physical. Obviously you were not capable of sustaining your own life at that time. You had to be cared for and nurtured. As you were growing you had to be kept safe and secure and your material needs had to be met by others. As you developed during early childhood you began to understand that you existed as an individual. You could explore your physicality and physical surroundings and you had the opportunity to understand your connection to your physical surroundings. You started to recognize that there were boundaries between yourself and others and that you had the opportunity to develop self-acceptance —acceptance of yourself that is not based upon the approval of others. Would you agree that these Rights are yours?

Personality: I guess so, but simply acknowledging and accepting them isn't going to change the way that I feel about myself.

Soul: It is just the beginning. It is a gradual process, but consciously understanding your Rights will initiate the process. Then you can become more aware of how you violate your own and other's Rights and how you allow others to violate your Rights. You have many Rights that you are not consciously aware of. As a result, you do not consider them and you do not take advantage of the understanding that they would bring to you about yourself, others, and your world. Some of these Rights pertain primarily to your personality and some pertain to the deepening relationship between you and me. The highest Rights describe what you and I can do together as one.

Personality: So tell me what these rights are.

Soul: There are Ten Basic Rights and each of the Rights is further defined by their elements. The first three Rights pertain to your personality.

I. **The right to exist as a human being in the physical world.**

II. **The right to experience physical sensations and to feel and express emotional and intuitive feelings.**

III. **The right to think, choose, and create beliefs about yourself and the world around you.**

Personality: They seem pretty reasonable.

Soul: Do they apply to you?

Personality: I think so.

Soul: Do you feel that you observe these Rights and that you prevent others from violating them in regard to yourself?

Personality: For the most part.

Soul: As you become more aware of your subconscious beliefs, fears, and coping strategies you may think otherwise.

Personality: How so?

Soul: You will see that you violate your own Rights and that you allow others to violate them quite regularly. Also, consider how you may violate the Rights of others.

Personality: We'll see.

Soul: Recognize that these Rights build upon each other. When you do not acknowledge, accept, and observe the earlier Rights, you will have greater difficulty accepting and enforcing your higher Rights or even other elements in the same Right. For instance, if you do not accept and respect yourself, you are unlikely to operate with healthy boundaries, express emotional feelings fully and honestly, act with confidence, and so on.

Personality: I can see how that would be a problem.

Soul: In this way, by understanding the patterns of how you allow these Rights to be violated you can more easily trace your difficulties to your more primary, Basic Right One issues. You can then perceive your more basic tendencies. By understanding these Basic Right One violations more thoroughly you will be able to seek improvement in all of your Rights more quickly.

Personality: This seems like just another set of labels that I can apply to myself.

Soul: These Rights are not labels. They describe and enable your potential. You can use them to characterize how you presently function, which is directly related to the beliefs that you hold about yourself. These Rights are aspirational. You have a number of beliefs about each of the elements of these Rights whether you are conscious of them or not. The beliefs that you hold about them in the broadest sense create your reality because your beliefs dictate how you feel and behave. Therefore, by consciously understanding your beliefs about these Rights, you will be able to consciously understand why you feel and act in the ways that you do and how that impacts your potential.

Personality: Even if I do accept these Rights, then how can I be sure that others would accept that I have them?

Soul: Once you explain and enforce them with others, they will have a higher likelihood of accepting these Rights too. Would you deny another person Rights that you claim for yourself?

Personality: No.

Soul: Then is it reasonable that others would deny you?

Personality: I guess not.

Soul: Learn your Rights and apply them to your life to achieve your potential. To do so, however, requires that you use them as a framework to evaluate your present beliefs about yourself and your circumstances. First, evaluate yourself in relation to these Rights which apply more to your personality. Then you will be better positioned to evaluate yourself with regard to the Rights that relate to the deepening relationship between you and I.

Personality: What are those Rights?

Soul: They are

IV. The right to bring love into the world, to accept it for yourself, and to give it to others.

V. The right to have personal truths and to test those truths for Truth

VI. The right to envision the purpose of your love in the world.

VII. The right to know and manifest your soul's wisdom.

Personality: I have a fairly good understanding about love and truth, but I'm not too sure I want to venture beyond that.

Soul: If you understood me better, then you would perceive the difference between your version of love and truth and mine.

Personality: Do you think you have a monopoly on love and truth?

Soul: I do not seek a monopoly. I have been trying to share these values with you, but it is you who resist.

Personality: I understand and possess these things on my own without you.

Soul: You understand and possess only limited aspects of these values that survive your filters. You do not allow them to shine through unfiltered. To do so would require that you accept and identify with me more completely. At this time you only accept yourself in a limited manner. Greater self-acceptance is necessary before you will be willing to more significantly accept and identify with me. You will understand why that is as we progress.

Personality: I don't know why I should believe you.

Soul: I am not asking that you believe me. If you simply believed me without having a basis to form your own beliefs, then you would not develop a deeper understanding of your beliefs, and you would be unable to successfully evaluate and change them. I am encouraging you to experience these things for yourself and make your own decisions.

Personality: I can't argue with that.

Soul: You can and you do.

Personality: You're pretty critical of me.

Soul: I am not passing judgement on you. I am expressing my observations based upon my perceptual capabilities. You are applying judgements to my observations and ascribing them to me. This is part of your own self-critical nature, not mine.

Personality: Maybe so.

Soul: There are still three more Rights. Would you like to know of them?

Personality: Why not.

Soul: Here they are.

VIII. The right to accept yourself beyond space and time.

IX. The right to accept yourself as part of an evolving greater whole.

X. The right to spiritualize matter and manifest the higher purpose of humanity.

Personality: These seem like Rights for you, not me.

Soul: These are Rights for you and I to accomplish together after we have made more progress on the earlier Rights.

Personality: Do you mean that I don't need to be functioning perfectly in the earlier Rights in order for me to work on these Rights?

Soul: All of these Rights are aspirational because we can always progress further.

Personality: Then why don't we start on these later Rights? They seem a lot more interesting.

Soul: Many people attempt to do just that, but it is less effective. It frequently takes the form of a coping strategy that most people would not regard as such.

Personality: How can working on a person's Rights be considered a coping strategy?

Soul: Being focused on their higher Basic Rights without a strong acceptance and adherence to their lower Rights can be a form of escapism. That person may be attempting to convince themselves and others of their spirituality without having an understanding of their coping strategies and the reasons behind them. They often take this path in an effort to avoid their underlying painful beliefs and their coping strategies.

Personality: I see that on Sundays quite often. Now I can call them spiritual escapists—I like it.

Soul: Why do you enjoy labeling people in this way?

Personality: They make themselves out to be better than others. They are not as pure or as high and mighty as they think they are.

Soul: They may be attempting to better themselves, but because they have not dealt with the reasons underlying their coping strategies, they will still be heavily influenced by them. That will manifest in the ways that they feel and behave. However, it is just another path to take. Everyone can choose for themselves.

Personality: I choose to start at the beginning. I've always believed that you can build a better house if it is built on a strong foundation

Soul: Then we will start at the beginning.

Discuss and/or Journal

Can your life be better? Accepting and enforcing your Rights and not violating the Rights of others may make a dramatic difference in you life.

1. What Rights do you acknowledge and accept as your own?

_____

_____

_____

_____

_____

_____

2. Do you enforce your Rights?

_____

_____

_____

_____

_____

_____

3. Do you violate the Rights of others?

_____

_____

_____

_____

_____

_____

Our Ten Basic Rights

I. The right to exist as a human being in the physical world.

II. The right to experience physical sensations and to feel and express emotional and intuitive feelings.

III. The right to think, choose, and create beliefs about yourself and the world around you.

IV. The right to bring love into the world, to accept it for yourself, and to give it to others.

V. The right to have personal truths and to test those truths for Truth.

VI. The right to envision the purpose of your love in the world.

VII. The right to know and manifest your soul's wisdom.

VIII. The right to accept yourself beyond space and time.

IX. The right to accept yourself as part of an evolving greater whole.

X. The right to spiritualize matter and manifest the higher purpose of humanity.

Part II

Basic Right I

I. The right to exist as a human being in the physical world.

Accept and Respect Yourself	Be Grounded in the Physical	Feel Safe and Secure	Meet Your Material Needs in a Reasonable Manner	Operate with Healthy Boundaries	Feel Vital, Participate in Physical Activities, and Nurture Yourself

II. The right to experience physical sensations and to feel and express emotional and intuitive feelings.

III. The right to think, choose, and create beliefs about yourself and the world around you.

IV. The right to bring love into the world, to accept it for yourself, and to give it to others.

V. The right to have personal truths and to test those truths for Truth.

VI. The right to envision the purpose of your love in the world.

VII. The right to know and manifest your soul's wisdom.

VIII. The right to accept yourself beyond space and time.

IX. The right to accept yourself as part of an evolving greater whole.

X. The right to spiritualize matter and manifest the higher purpose of humanity.

chapter five

ACCEPT AND RESPECT YOURSELF

Most people believe that they accept themselves. After all it seems that way to our conscious mind, but is it really so? Unfortunately, it is not. If we did accept ourselves, our subconscious minds would not be cluttered with painful self-beliefs, which cause us to act defensively or feel insulted or uncomfortable. For most of us this is a daily occurrence. Our feelings and behaviors reveal what we truly believe about ourselves in our subconscious mind, the stronghold of self-denial.

When was the last time someone said something to you that caused you to take offense or feel bad? If you accepted yourself at the time why did it bother you? What did it feel like? Did you feel sad, depressed, hopeless, helpless, angry, or bitter? Did it feel like you were literally retreating into yourself, as though you had lost the ability to reach out into the world and connect with others? You may have closed yourself off from others and the world and probably without the awareness that you were doing so. Or you may have displaced your anger by blaming and attacking others.

Do you accept yourself now? Do you feel fulfilled? Are you hopeful and positive? Do you feel energized with an open heart and an accepting mind? Are you accepting of and connected with others, the world around you, and making life-affirming decisions?

Do you truly accept yourself? This question typically prompts a yes or no response, but self-acceptance is not an all or none characteristic. We may accept certain things about ourselves, but not others. Some days we are more accepting of ourselves than on other days. Why? We tend to accept ourselves more on days when things are going well or at least, not too badly. Our feelings about self-acceptance generally represent what is happening in our lives rather than an intrinsic feeling about ourselves that has greater constancy. Why?

It is that part of us that is fickle and changes its mind often and quickly that decides how accepting of ourselves we are. The decision is based more upon activities and outcomes and less on who we are. We rarely take time to investigate our true nature because our mind deems us too unworthy, further demonstrating our lack of self-acceptance. And what of self-respect? How much can we respect ourselves if we do not accept ourselves all that much? Very little. Before we can care for and nurture ourselves we must accept ourselves to a greater extent—it is a prerequisite.

If on a self-acceptance scale from one to ten, you are a two today, is it possible for you to become a six tomorrow? How can you learn greater self-acceptance? The simple and seemingly mindless answer is, through greater acceptance. Self-acceptance does not result from being right or being the best. It does not result from having more material possessions or by having a more powerful job. It does not result from adulation or even acceptance by a loved one. It can only occur when you allow it to occur and it can only grow when you nurture its growth. Self-acceptance does not result from a job well done unless that job is to create greater self-acceptance.

How can you proceed? Where does one start? Consider your Basic Rights. Acknowledge, accept, and enforce them for yourself and in turn do not violate the Rights of others. The choice of greater self-acceptance is yours alone.

Soul: So many of your problems exist simply because you do not love yourself.

Personality: Loving myself makes me feel vain or egotistical. I don't like it when people act that way. I don't think people should be that way.

Soul: If people are that way, what do you believe they should do?

Personality: They should change. It's not right to love yourself. It's selfish!

Soul: Maybe we should discuss love another day. For now let's talk about acceptance. Are you able to accept yourself as you are?

Personality: In what way?

Soul: In every way. Can you accept your body the way that it is?

Personality: My body isn't too bad. I weigh more than I would like to and my belly is a little too flabby, but otherwise it's okay for a person my age.

Soul: Can you accept your attitudes—the ways that you believe, feel, and act?

Personality: I think I accept what I'm consciously aware of. However, I now realize that I have a problem accepting some things, so I place them in my subconscious mind. I admit that my subconscious mind operates when something causes me to feel bad. When that happens I suppress my feelings as quickly as I can to avoid feeling any more discomfort and to avoid thinking about whatever is causing me to feel bad. I would rather leave those topics buried in my subconscious.

Soul: Can you accept the relationships and the other situations that you have created in your life?

Personality: I get along fine with most people, especially my family and close friends. We have our good and bad times, but we stick together and work things out when we need to. Sometimes though, it's better for me to ignore some things and not push the people I love away. I ignore even more of what bothers me at work, but I do what I have to do in order to get by.

Soul: Now that you have had a chance to think about acceptance a little more, do you believe that you truly accept yourself and your situation in life?

Personality: I think that for the most part I accept things the way they are, but I don't always like it.

Soul: Not liking something generally means that you do not accept it because you do not take responsibility for it.

Personality: Well maybe I don't accept myself as much as I think I do. There are a number of things I don't like about my life and myself that I avoid thinking about.

Soul: Why not take your own advice and change those things about your life and yourself that you do not like?

Personality: I do make some changes here and there, but the truth of the matter is that as long as the people who are important to me feel okay about me, then I don't feel much of a need to change.

Soul: Does it matter to you if you compromise yourself in the process of having others feel good about you?

Personality: In what way?

Soul: What if someone close to you does something that you disapprove of, such as act selfishly? They regularly make demands on your time in order for you to help them, which prevents you from completing what you need to do. In addition, they almost never reciprocate and help you get your work done. In this situation you probably believe that they approve of you because everyone is getting along, but how would you be feeling?

Personality: I would feel angry.

Soul: Would you show your anger?

Personality: I would feel guilty if I did that.

Soul: If this situation kept repeating itself would you become resentful?

Personality: Yes, I feel that way about some people now, but then I feel guilty about feeling resentful. They shouldn't act that way. It's their fault and they should change.

Soul: How can they come to know their effect on you if you say or do nothing?

Personality: I don't want to be the one to tell them and cause any problems.

Soul: Are you allowing the problem to persist?

Personality: I guess so.

Soul: Are you afraid that if you tell them how you feel that they will no longer accept you?

Personality: I don't want to risk losing their approval, their acceptance of me.

Soul: So, if they approve of you, then you approve of yourself, is that it?

Personality: Sure, that means that I'm getting along with everyone and that means that they accept me and everything is fine, so I accept myself.

Soul: Can you accept yourself if others do not accept you?

Personality: I don't think I can.

Soul: Why is their acceptance of you more important than your acceptance of yourself?

Personality: What's the point of accepting myself if I'm alone?

Soul: Even if others accept you, when you do not accept yourself you are alone.

Personality: How so?

Soul: When you do not accept yourself, you close yourself off more than you realize because you feel unworthy. You retreat into a state where you are less open to receive, even from me. When that occurs you are less connected to life. Even if others accept you as you are, you are not open to receive what they have to offer because you have developed an attitude that you are undeserving or not good enough. That is why you sometimes refuse their help or you feel awkward when they offer you a gift or a compliment.

Personality: You certainly aren't making me feel any better.

Soul: I cannot help you solve a situation that you do not acknowledge or perceive. Once you become aware of something, you are more likely to accept it and then do something about it.

Personality: You probably think I'm a coward for not sticking up for myself or for what I think is right.

Soul: Fear gets the better of you in those circumstances. I am not suggesting that you place yourself above others. However, you do have equal Rights and you are just as entitled to those Rights as everyone else. You may believe that you are making sacrifices in the name of love, but if you were really doing so you would feel love and not anger, guilt or resentment.

Personality: I do love those close to me.

Soul: Yes, I love them as well, even when you are angry with them. Do you feel love towards them at the same time that you feel angry, guilty, and resentful or do you know deep inside that you still love them even though you feel angry about their behavior?

Personality: I guess I believe that I still love them even when I'm not feeling that way. How can you feel one way and I feel another?

Soul: I am that part of you deep inside that still loves them. When you do not accept yourself you also cannot accept the love inside of you and that is why you do not feel it when you feel angry or resentful. You would feel more like I do if you accepted yourself.

Personality: You mean if I accepted you.

Soul: You cannot accept me if you do not accept yourself first, but you do not even have to cross that bridge to feel better about yourself. I am just referring to you being able to accept your Rights as an equal and enforcing those Rights. When you do so and you better accept yourself in that way you will find that you are more accepting of others because you have become more accepting of yourself.

Personality: I do accept others.

Soul: If you really accepted them, you would respect them enough to be honest and let them know how you feel. That would demonstrate that you not only accept and respect them, but that you also accept yourself and your feelings.

Personality: But then they might not accept me anymore.

Soul: They do not fully accept you now. If they did then they would not violate your Rights. Why do you believe that they accept you now? Must they become overtly abusive towards you in order for you to understand? If you permit their violations by not taking action, your circumstances could worsen. Would a worsening of your circumstances help you to perceive and understand your situation more clearly?

Personality: Are you working for me or against me?

Soul: My hope is that you become more aware so that you will accept me into your life in a more meaningful partnership. That is how you and I will make the greatest progress. I am always working on your behalf to increase your awareness and understanding. I am here to assist in providing opportunities that can help you learn as quickly as possible with the least amount of hardship.

Personality: Why must learning be painful?

Soul: It need not be. The discomfort that you experience depends upon your willingness to perceive and accept the need to make changes in yourself that will lead to greater self-acceptance. Your resistance to change creates the pain that you experience. At times, your life's circumstances become even more difficult, but even that occurs to help you perceive the consequences of your choices more clearly. In that way the results you have created are less subtle and easier to perceive.

Personality: More bad luck.

Soul: If you view the worsening of your circumstances as simply bad luck rather than accepting responsibility for your role in creating them, then you are unlikely to learn in this process. Furthermore, the pain will persist. However, by becoming accountable for your life and yourself and proactively making the necessary changes, you will free yourself from your false feelings of victimization and the associated pain. It is your choice.

Personality: From what you're saying it feels like everything is my fault.

Soul: I am not blaming you, but realize that you and your circumstances in life are mostly of your making. Regardless, I accept you as you are and I wish you would do the same. I love you unconditionally. I do my best to assist in presenting you with opportunities to exert your free will and learn. I am optimistic that you will make choices that will benefit you. I am always available to provide you with guidance, but you need to listen, perceive it, and choose to use that guidance for me to have any impact on your life. My guidance to you is offered as a gift. It is yours to accept or reject. Either way I will always remain with you to offer guidance with no strings attached.

Personality: Do you approve of me?

Soul: I have unconditional love for you.

Personality: Why?

Soul: That is my nature.

Personality: What do you have to gain?

Soul: In partnership with you I can evolve more fully, as can you.

Personality: Will you disapprove of me if I don't work with you?

Soul: My love, and therefore my support, for you is unconditional.

Personality: But you have an outcome that you wish to achieve. If you don't achieve it, won't you become angry and disapprove of me?

Soul: I do have a purpose to accomplish by living in partnership with you and I do wish to achieve it, but if I do not, then I will still have learned much from my endeavors. I will still grow and evolve and regardless of how much or how little you evolve, I will not disapprove of you. You have free will and therefore your decisions are your decisions. If things do not work out in the way that I would like them to, then I also must be accountable for my role in our affairs. I chose to work with you and I have tried to provide guidance in as meaningful a way as I can.

Personality: So you're not perfect either.

Soul: I am evolving too, but I accept myself as I am now even though I am evolving toward what I aspire to become. It is because I accept myself that I am able to grow. If I did not accept myself then I would not deem myself worthy of becoming more.

Personality: I think it is easier for you to accept yourself because you're more evolved than I am.

Soul: We can discuss pity later, but as for now please understand that everybody can accept themselves and their circumstances by simply choosing to do so. Choosing not to only delays their progress until they decide that they have waited long enough. Accepting yourself is not an endpoint, it is a beginning because it positions you to accept opportunities to grow. Looking to others for acceptance may temporarily make you feel secure, but in doing so you will only develop a dependence on them.

Personality: But at least they will accept me.

Soul: You may believe that they accept you because you are willing to accept your relationships and circumstances the way that they are. You are closing your eyes to the compromises that you have been making in order to maintain the status quo. The truth is that most people will not accept you until you accept yourself. You must enforce your Rights in order for others to respect you and your Rights.

Personality: You're saying that I must make the first move and only then will I get what I want.

Soul: It usually works that way.

Personality: I guess I knew that, but I didn't want to admit it.

Soul: Yes, you did not want to accept it because by accepting it you would begin to feel responsible for your actions. That responsibility or accountability—accepting responsibility—is a privilege and not an obligation. It allows you to determine if your choices and the consequences of your actions are meaningful to you. By being accountable you can more quickly learn about yourself and the world around you. When accountability replaces avoidance and a state of victimization, growth ensues.

Personality: Then I would have to accept my failures.

Soul: They are simply undesirable outcomes that refine your ability to produce desirable outcomes.

Personality: Yes, but learning all of this can be painful.

Soul: That is the beauty of acceptance. Accepting what you have been resisting out of fear no longer creates fear. The more you practice acceptance and accountability, the more accomplished you become. That leads to confidence and soon you begin to view obstacles for what they really are—lessons or guidance.

Personality: This is all very contradictory to the way I was raised. Criticism begets change and lack of criticism maintains the status quo. It wasn't a matter of lessons or guidance.

Soul: The way you were raised and the way that you have been operating are all too common. It is understandable that as a child you submitted to the will of your caregivers, but you are no longer a child. You have Rights and it is up to you whether or not you choose to acknowledge, understand, and enforce them. You need not allow others to dictate how you or your life's circumstances should be. You have free will. It is your life and you have the right to live it in the manner of your choosing.

Personality: Unfortunately those thoughts keep playing in my head and I act accordingly.

Soul: It is still your choice. Be aware, choose wisely, and accept the outcome.

Personality: I'll take it under advisement, but I feel as if I'm on shaky ground.

Discuss and/or Journal

Our lack of self-acceptance and respect exists because we are strongly anchored in our personality. Without the ability to achieve a higher perspective from our soul we each are likely to have little acceptance or respect for ourselves.

1. Does self-acceptance seem like something that you must strive for rather than a Right that you already possess?

_____

_____

_____

_____

_____

_____

2. Do you believe that your soul accepts you?

_____

_____

_____

_____

_____

_____

3. What must happen for you to accept yourself more completely?

_____

_____

_____

_____

chapter six

BE GROUNDED IN THE PHYSICAL

GROUNDEDNESS IS A STATE of being during which our energetic self is present throughout our physical body and we are observant of ourselves, our relationships to others, and our surroundings. A person, consciously in this state, is referred to as being grounded. Alternatively, not being in this state is being ungrounded, which is the state that most of us are in most of the time. Being in an ungrounded state is so common in fact that it is our norm, which is why groundedness is so poorly understood. When we are not grounded we tend to be easily distracted, scattered, or preoccupied with thoughts of the past or future. We may be lethargic or hyperactive. We may lack focus or be so focused inwardly or outwardly as to be unaware of our immediate surroundings. We may even be present, but so involved in a situation, as to not be self-observant. Most people experience groundedness too infrequently to have an experiential knowledge of what it is actually like.

When grounded, our energetic self—those energies that comprise our emotional, mental, and spiritual side—is evenly distributed throughout and around our entire physical body. Groundedness, like acceptance, is not an all or nothing trait. For many who are not grounded most of the time, their energetic structure surrounds their head. They think much more than they feel or they may not feel at all. This all too common energetic distribution is reinforced by a society that rewards thinking more than feeling. For some people, most of their energetic structure is located from their heart up. They feel to a greater extent, but still not completely. Very few people have their energies evenly distributed from head to toe most of the time.

Our state of groundedness is a direct reflection of our intention to be fully present in our bodies and consciously aware of ourselves, our situations, and the world around us. Being grounded is a manifestation of our will to do so. Being grounded narrows the gap between our personal life on Earth and our spiritual life. Our body is the juncture between the two. It is the meeting place between the matter of form and the energy of spirit.

Our body can be viewed as a bar magnet, made of matter. Moving through and around our body is our energetic self, akin to a magnetic field. Imagine that the South Pole of the magnet is more identified with the Earth and the North Pole more identified with the spiritual realm. Our bodies are formed from matter, of the Earth and sustained by the Earth, while our energetic selves originate from the realm of spirit bringing forth consciousness. The two poles create a magnetic force of attraction binding spirit to form, energy to matter. Our free will determines the strength of attraction and thus, how well our energetic self is grounded in the physical. Being more grounded has its payoffs. It increases the likelihood that we will feel more peaceful and fulfilled, enjoy work and life, and have deeper more satisfying relationships because our personal lives will be more impacted by our spiritual nature. However, there is a price to pay.

Very few people are willing to confront their conscious and subconscious fears. Therefore, they remain in an ungrounded state. Why? Living in a grounded state increases our conscious awareness. This results in our being more present in our physical bodies, which causes us to more completely feel our physical body, our emotions, and become aware of our painful beliefs when they are triggered. How often are you willing to feel fearful or experience other negative emotions and encounter beliefs about yourself that are unpleasant?

In order to avoid these experiences we remain in an ungrounded state. It serves that purpose. Avoidance is our payoff. We move into a reactive, subconscious mode and utilize our coping strategies to avoid feeling our fears and confronting our issues. This perpetuates our ungrounded state. We avoid a more grounded state because we do not wish to stay present with our feelings and thoughts. We purposefully loosen the forces of attraction between consciousness and form, energy and matter. It is our choice to do so. When was the last time you intended to be completely grounded? Have you ever done so in the face of your fears?

Soul: You are not very grounded today.

Personality: I've got a lot on my mind right now. My new boss expects me to do things differently than we've been doing around here. He views me as part of the company's past and I wouldn't be surprised if he's looking to replace me. With the added payments on my second mortgage, now wouldn't be a good time for me to lose my job.

Soul: What are you feeling?

Personality: I'm trying to figure out where I can get another job if I get fired.

Soul: What are you feeling?

Personality: I'm feeling like I need to start looking for that job pretty soon.

Soul: That is not a feeling I am familiar with.

Personality: Of course not, you don't need a job. I'm the one who has to worry about practical matters.

Soul: Now we are making some progress. Worry, that is a feeling. Are you feeling worried?

Personality: I have reason to worry.

Soul: I am not asking whether or not your fear is justified. I am simply asking you to identify what you are feeling. Do you know why it is so hard for you to get in touch with your feelings?

Personality: I don't think much about my feelings.

Soul: It is not about thinking. It is about feeling.

Personality: I don't want to dwell on my feelings. I just need to figure out how I'm going to find another job.

Soul: Why are you avoiding your feelings?

Personality: Feeling my feelings won't get me another job.

Soul: If you could feel more completely, then it might be easier for you to find your next job assuming that you actually do need another job. Feeling your feelings may in fact make it easier for you to keep your present job if that is what you want. You presume that your boss is searching for a replacement for you, but you really do not know how he feels about you or your employment situation. Do you?

Personality: I've never asked him how he feels about my standing in the company or me, if that's what you mean.

Soul: If you are worried about losing your job, then why not consider asking him these questions?

Personality: For a moment last week it occurred to me to do just that, but then I put it out of my mind.

Soul: Do you know why you avoided doing so?

Personality: Fear.

Soul: Fear of what?

Personality: I'm afraid that my fears are justified.

Soul: If your fears are justified then so be it. Confront them and your boss. Accept it, move on, and find another job if that is what you need to do. If they are not justified then you can more easily focus on what you are doing at work and not be distracted by your worries. In either case learn about yourself in the process and what is and is not working for you on the job. There is another big lesson for you to learn about your current approach to this matter.

Personality: You mean my lack of approach.

Soul: Yes, I mean your avoidance.

Personality: I already told you that I'm afraid to find out whether or not I'm going to lose my job. It's embarrassing. When you lose your job, people look down on you. When you lose your job you're not keeping up your end of the bargain. I'm supposed to be employable. How will my kids view me? What if no one else will hire me?

Soul: Do you feel a little better now that you have gotten some of these issues out in the open?

Personality: A little better, but I still may need to find another job.

Soul: Do you know why you feel a little better?

Personality: Probably because I'm addressing some of my fears.

Soul: Yes, you are also becoming a little more grounded.

Personality: That's the second time you've used that word. What are you talking about?

Soul: Why didn't you ask the first time?

Personality: I was too preoccupied with my dilemma.

Soul: Yes, you were not grounded enough to respond to me in the present moment, but at least the word registered with you. What do you think it means?

Personality: I hope we're not talking about the six feet under groundedness.

Soul: It is not your time.

Personality: Then I assume it's about being grounded in reality. If we are, then I can tell you that you're certainly not grounded in my reality otherwise you would be concerned that I might be losing my job.

Soul: If I was grounded in your reality then you would have no worries.

Personality: Would you worry for me?

Soul: No. There would be no reason to worry. You would see the truth of things more clearly and you would better understand why you worry.

Personality: Well, come on down.

Soul: I know you better than that. Your invitation is half-hearted. As soon as our separateness narrows and your awareness grows, your fears begin to surface and you reject me. You do not reject me directly, but it occurs as a by-product of your coping strategies.

Personality: Maybe this time it will be different.

Soul: It will not be any different until you learn to deal more directly with your fears. When you ask me to participate more meaningfully in your life you are asking me to become more grounded in the physical. I can participate to a greater extent in your physical reality in partnership with you, but when I do so, I bring with me values that are in conflict with your coping strategies. When you use those strategies instead of the values that I bring with me, you reject me.

Personality: Does that make you feel angry or sad?

Soul: I understand why you make the decisions that you do. As a result of my understanding and my very nature I do not respond in the same ways that you do.

Personality: What are these values that you speak of?

Soul: Love and truth. They are in conflict with your coping strategies. Where there is love there cannot be fear and where there is truth there cannot be avoidance. It also works in reverse. When you use your coping strategies you are fearful and you take steps to limit that feeling by avoiding your deeper painful beliefs. Remember that you have free will. When you choose your coping strategies you are simultaneously rejecting my values of love and truth. That is how you reject me, indirectly, out of fear.

Personality: Well, I can admit that I'm fearful and that I sometimes act out of fear, but I come by my fears honestly. What's untruthful about that?

Soul: The dishonesty lies in your avoidance. When you cut off your feelings you avoid understanding why you feel the way you do. Do you ever allow your feelings of fear to persist and then, while experiencing them, ask yourself why you feel the way that you do?

Personality: It's too uncomfortable. Why would anyone want to experience those feelings longer than they have to?

Soul: In order to get to the root of those feelings. That is how you can learn to deal with your fears more directly. Your most significant memories, those that you have used to form beliefs about yourself, are emotionally laden. By allowing yourself to feel those emotions more completely you are able to gain access to those memories and your subconscious beliefs about yourself. Some of those beliefs, such as unworthiness, are painful to you and that is why you have constructed coping strategies to avoid revisiting your painful childhood beliefs and concerns. For instance, even though you thought to, you never wanted to ask yourself the question, "Am I really unworthy of receiving love?" What would you have done if your answer was yes? You stopped yourself from asking this question by using avoidance tactics, such as the negative emotional feelings of your coping strategies. However, these beliefs and that question were formed when you were very young and very inexperienced. If you could inspect these secretly held beliefs, you would see that they are untrue, but your coping strategies prevent you from doing so. Using them confines your fears, old beliefs, and concerns to the realm of your subconscious mind so that you remain unaware of them at a conscious level. However, because your coping strategies are regularly triggered and employed, those fears and old beliefs continue to influence your feelings and actions to a great extent even though you remain largely unaware of them.

Personality: I guess some of my beliefs are not truths either.

Soul: You adopted many of your early beliefs at a time when you were not well equipped to evaluate them. That is why it is so important to revisit them. You are able to change those beliefs, but first you must become aware of them and how they play out in your life. Once you recognize how many of your beliefs limit you, you will become motivated to change them.

Personality: So when I choose to avoid rather than deal with these issues then I am less grounded.

Soul: When you practice avoidance, you are using a coping strategy. Your coping strategies are like computer programs that you have created. They are just like your responses while you are driving and the traffic light turns red. You do not spend time consciously thinking about your response. You automatically take your foot off the gas and press down on the brake. Your coping strategies run at the same speed and also work automatically when they are triggered by something that you fear at a subconscious level. When your coping strategies are operating you are functioning from your past because you are responding to a trigger that resembles a fear created in your past. As a result, you lose touch with the present moment and with me. You are less consciously aware and instead you are operating more from your subconscious.

Personality: If I do what you suggest and I stay with the fear, then won't I still be experiencing my past?

Soul: When you stay in the moment with your feelings as they are in the present you are not engaging a coping strategy. If you take this suggestion and also ask yourself why you feel the way that you do, you can identify what it is in the present that is triggering your feelings. Once you can do that, it is helpful to ask yourself when in the past have you felt similarly? In that way you can begin to understand why you have created your coping strategies.

Personality: If you're remembering your past, then haven't you lost touch with the present moment?

Soul: No because, you are looking at the past from the perspective of how the past is influencing your present moment. You are holding your present moment feelings and the knowledge of your current situation. The same feeling state, which you are experiencing in the present and that which you have experienced in your past creates a link that transcends time, but you can still remain present-centered and grounded. Your feeling state, now and then, will help you unlock your past memories. In this manner you will be recalling them rather than reliving them subconsciously, as long as you stay grounded in the present, while you are asking questions of yourself.

Personality: In this situation, what does groundedness have to do with you?

Soul: I enable you to observe yourself in the present moment. When you invite me to be grounded in the physical it becomes easier for you to switch your frame of reference to me. When you do so to a greater extent than you normally do, you can better observe yourself without being caught up in your circumstances and reliving the past.

Personality: Switching my frame of reference sounds like another form of avoidance.

Soul: I practice truth not avoidance. When you identify with me and better witness your personality, your understanding about yourself grows. I do not take you out of your circumstances or out of the present moment. Through me you can see your actions and beliefs more clearly. You can also begin to see the payoffs that you receive by acting, feeling, and believing in the ways that you do.

Personality: I should have you visit more often.

Soul: You prefer the payoffs of your coping strategies to the truth. That is why you continue to use your coping strategies and in so doing reject me.

Personality: Maybe these payoffs are simply better or more fun than the truth.

Soul: At times your payoffs can provide you with what you want, but most often your payoff is nothing more than the avoidance of something you fear. You will never know if your payoffs are preferable to the truth until you try the truth and compare.

Personality: Yes, but the truth hurts sometimes.

Soul: The pain that you experience is born of ignorance, which is perpetuated by your coping strategies. You use them in your attempt to hide from the pain, but the pain persists and all you accomplish is a partially reduced awareness of it. Learning the truth behind the pain cures it. You believe the truth hurts because in this process you feel what has been hurting you, but as you understand the truth the pain dissipates and it will not hurt you anymore. You will also come to realize that some of the pain that you experience is the fear associated with avoidance, which goes away when you no longer practice avoidance.

Personality: It all sounds so simple provided I allow you to become more grounded in the physical.

Soul: Which in turn allows you to become even more grounded in your reality as opposed to avoiding it.

Personality: How does this process of groundedness begin?

Soul: You must first intend for it to happen. You must choose this path of your own free will.

Personality: That's easy enough.

Soul: Very simple in fact, but in doing so you will begin to experience yourself more completely. You as a human being are the juncture of heaven and Earth, the meeting place between these dimensions. This is where you can experience opposing forces at play. Often that will precipitate fear in you and cause you to abort the process. However, if you keep trying you will become better able to accept rather than avoid your feelings.

Personality: What else can be done to facilitate this process?

Soul: Your ability to perceive me has been limited. You are responsive to your five senses and although I can be perceived in a similar way, my impressions on your senses are considerably more subtle than what you are accustomed to experiencing from physical stimuli. Therefore, it is easy for you to be unaware of my presence. My substance vibrates faster than the physical matter of your body and its associated energy fields, but even so, I can interface with you to a greater extent.

Personality: How can this interface be improved?

Soul: There are many ways, but the best results can be achieved when the alignment of our energies takes place throughout your entire body and energy system. This requires that your energy system is functioning well.

Personality: I'm not aware of my energy system.

Soul: If you were more aware of it, then you would be more aware of me because I am an extension of it. Suffice it to say your energy system functions better when you have reduced the need to use coping strategies and when you are able to confront your subconscious fears, old beliefs, and concerns. However, it is also important to understand your relationship to the Earth.

Personality: I live on the planet.

Soul: Your relationship to the Earth is more significant than that. Part of you is of the planet. The Earth has provided you with the substance of your physical body. The Earth also nourishes you by providing you with a source of food and by bathing you in its energy. The Earth is alive and it has its own energy system, of which you are a part. Your actions affect the Earth and its energy system, which in turn impacts you and everyone else. In time you will appreciate the importance of understanding your relationship to the Earth in order to better know yourself in total.

Personality: What does this have to do with groundedness?

Soul: Your ability to live in greater harmony with the Earth and all life is improved by being better grounded. Groundedness is a conduit or connection that allows you to deepen all of your relationships. Remember that you are the link between heaven and Earth. You can visualize groundedness as a series of connections. The Earth provides the substantive and energetic grounding for your body, which provides the grounding for your personal energy fields, which provides the grounding for me. I can become better grounded to the Earth to the extent that your energy system flows more completely through your physical body and as a result, is better grounded to the Earth.

Personality: Why is this important to you?

Soul: This is how I can become more fully present in the physical. By doing so, it allows me to be more effective in spiritualizing matter. That enables more of my purpose to manifest on Earth through my partnership with you.

Personality: How do I know how well I'm grounded to the Earth?

Soul: You are capable of feeling the Earth's energy. The more that you are grounded, the greater you are able to feel the Earth's energy throughout your body. Can you feel it?

Personality: Where?

Soul: It is all around you. You are bathed in it constantly. Try to feel it in your feet. Sit down in a comfortable position with your feet resting on the floor and imagine that there are roots growing from your feet deep into the Earth. Imagine the Earth's energy moving up those roots and try to feel that energy in your feet. You can feel it with any part of your body.

Personality: I can sort of feel some tingling. Is that it?

Soul: That is how most people feel it at first. With practice the feeling grows stronger and can be perceived as soon as you turn your attention to it. As the energy of your personality becomes more aligned with the Earth's energy and my energy, then you can perceive me as well. The better I am grounded in the physical, the better you will be able to perceive my presence. That is one way for you to know how engaged you have allowed me to become.

Personality: Do I feel you in my feet too?

Soul: You can although our strongest point of connection is in your heart region. However, when our connection is more complete after you permit me to merge with you more fully, you will feel me throughout all of you, including your feet.

Personality: All of this connectedness is alien to me. I have always viewed myself as a separate being.

Soul: That is why you often feel alone. Your mindset of separateness keeps you from experiencing how connected we truly are—you to the Earth, to me and through me to All That Is.

Personality: Plug me in.

Soul: Do you feel safe enough?

Discuss and/or Journal

Take a moment, sit back, close your eyes, and relax. Place your attention on the soles of your feet. Imagine the Earth's energy being pulled into the soles of your feet and travelling up your legs and throughout your body. Stay with this image and relax.

1. What do you feel in your feet, legs?

   _____

   _____

   _____

   _____

2. Take another moment and allow more of the Earth's energy to move throughout your body. Allow more of your soul's energy to enter the top of your head and move throughout your entire body. Relax.

   _____

   _____

   _____

   _____

3. What do you feel?

   _____

   _____

   _____

   _____

4. Are you more relaxed?

   _____

   _____

   _____

   _____

chapter seven

FEEL SAFE AND SECURE

For MOST OF US there was a time in our lives when we felt safe and secure. It was a simpler time. We were aware of a less complicated world with little fear. This time in our lives did not last long, but it did leave an indelible imprint upon our psyche. It was so powerful that today we continually strive consciously and subconsciously to reproduce the feelings of peacefulness we had then. We had little responsibility other than to experience our environment. We were warm, nourished, and well supported. Our senses were protected from bright lights, loud sounds, and rough edges. We were connected, enveloped, and cared for. We were safe and secure in our mother's womb.

Our birth was an event of cataclysmic proportion that few of us consciously remember or care to explore. Yet for most of us it exists as a gaping wound in our subconscious minds. It remains with us every day of our lives, influencing us more than we choose to acknowledge. How does it impact us? Our birth was a monumental change, physically, emotionally, mentally, and spiritually. With that as one of our earliest exposures to change in the physical world, is it any wonder that we are resistant?

What were our perceptions like at that time? How aware were we? We were in transition, moving from one way of life to another, from one world to another. In the womb we were physically dependent upon our mothers and generally well cared for. We were intimately connected to her emotional environment, infused chemically, and permeated energetically. Our mental capabilities were in early development, but not devoid of activity. We could perceive motion, sound, and touch. Events occurred and we were influenced, creating a growing level of awareness. We could sense that we were not alone. We were literally attached to and dependent upon another life to sustain our own and fulfill our needs. With changes taking place in our environment we began to develop preferences and in time wants. All the while we remained connected to and comforted by spiritual forces. Our spiritual support system was ever present and for us then it was more prominent than the mortal life at hand. And then it happened.

What is happening to me, my world? I'm being crushed. The pressure is enormous. It's painful. I have no control. What's happening now? Bright lights, loud sounds, cold, and pain. This is overwhelming. Where's my support? Help! There's no relief. What is this? This is familiar—this voice and this energy. I'm being held and rocked. I feel warmer. This is different. It helps. I'm not alone.

Our world is different. We struggle and are forced to take action in order to meet our needs, which are all too pervasive. This is the harsh reality of our early life. Our independent existence requires us to work to survive. It is not easy and at times it is not pleasant. We continue to be dependent on others, but we are not as closely connected as we once had been. This process is a part of our human experience that shaped our beginnings and has influenced us ever since. We have been conditioned.

Every perceived threat to our safety and security triggers these traumatic memories, which causes us to feel as we do. It happens far below our conscious awareness, buried so deeply in our subconscious minds that we remain in total denial of the existence of these long forgotten memories. We respond to these threats in a reactive, unconscious manner and we do not feel safe and secure because the traumas of our past are still with us and remain active. We work hard to insulate ourselves from potential threats in a unceasing effort to re-create the feelings of safety, security, and peacefulness we once had very long ago in a place we do not consciously remember.

Soul: I hope you realize that I do appreciate your efforts to maintain a safe and secure environment in the physical realm.

Personality: It's about time you thanked me for doing all of the work that I do.

Soul: I have thanked you many times, but you were not listening.

Personality: I'll take your word on that, but I would appreciate a little help in this area.

Soul: I would like to help you to not feel as fearful as you do, but there is only so much you will allow me to do.

Personality: I think you enjoy using my free will as an excuse for not helping me more. I would be happy to give you greater access to me if you would do more of the work.

Soul: Okay.

Personality: Really?

Soul: Sure. Go ahead. Drop your guard, relax, and accept whatever comes into your life without feeling as fearful as you do.

Personality: That's so unrealistic. There's a lot to be afraid of. This world can be a dangerous place. I don't think you've been paying attention to what's going on down here.

Soul: Where do you think I have been all these years?

Personality: You live up in heaven and I've been left to deal with the hell on Earth.

Soul: I have never left you.

Personality: Well it certainly seems that way.

Soul: I am sure that it does. This is a big part of your safety and security issues.

Personality: I don't think so. You're not really a part of my world. There is a lot of crime and senseless violence that happens here. It's on the news every night and I even have friends that have been personally affected.

Soul: I do not deny the reality of the world as it is or the wisdom in taking reasonable precautions. However, the fears you hold regarding safety and security are of a deeper nature.

Personality: Why must everything be so deep and mysterious to you. The things I worry about happen everyday and are cause enough for fear.

Soul: How is being fearful of benefit to you in this regard?

Personality: It causes me to take action to provide a safe and secure environment.

Soul: After you have taken the actions you deem necessary, why do you continue to be fearful?

Personality: Because bad things can still happen.

Soul: Why do you fear the unknown?

Personality: Because it may be bad.

Soul: It may be good.

Personality: Then I would be positively surprised, but things can then still turn bad.

Soul: Is that what you are hoping for?

Personality: Of course not. Why would you suggest such a thing?

Soul: It would justify your fears.

Personality: I guess it would, but I still don't want to have to live through it.

Soul: As you have done in the past?

Personality: I don't remember having anything bad like that ever happen to me.

Soul: Nevertheless, events have happened in your life that you have perceived negatively.

Personality: What are you talking about?

Soul: There have been times in your life when you have felt loss. You have experienced separation from a loved one on more than one occasion. You do not remember all of these events at this time, but that does not mean that they did not happen.

Personality: Everyone experiences loss at one time or another. It's part of life, but life goes on anyway.

Soul: Yes it does, but your experiences continue to shape your feelings and actions because you created fearful beliefs as a result of those experiences. That is why you believe that bad things may happen to you because they have in the past.

Personality: I'm not aware of the fearful beliefs you are referring to and their impact on me.

Soul: You will understand more when you become more willing to revisit your fears.

Personality: Why would I want to do that?

Soul: So that you can lessen the grip that your fears have on you.

Personality: In what way?

Soul: For starters, if you better understood the nature of your fears you could allow yourself to feel more safe and secure.

Personality: How so?

Soul: Many of your fears stem from past events that resulted in separation from loved ones. As a result, you fear the potential of loss, which gives rise to safety and security concerns.

Personality: What do you mean?

Soul: Your past experiences have left you with a fear about feeling separated and alone, which causes you to not feel safe and secure. You are not aware of the love and support that is ever present around you and as a result, you fear loss and the potential that some of your needs will not be met.

Personality: I have learned that I am responsible for getting my own needs met.

Soul: You must do your part, of course, but realize that you are also dependent upon others to meet many of your needs. And for that matter, who do you think helps to arrange for the people that you encounter in life? Your actions do not occur in a vacuum.

Personality: Are you going to take credit for my good luck?

Soul: I am not only going to take some credit for your good luck, but also for your bad luck and I will continue to do so until you realize that there is no such thing as luck.

Personality: Well I like to think that luck has a lot to do with things.

Soul: You can continue to think that way for as long as you like. However, as long as you do, you will not be accountable for your life. You will not realize that each of us creates our reality through our attitudes, our soul's purpose, and our connectedness to one another.

Personality: Wait a minute. What if someone is out at night and they are attacked by someone that they don't even know. Are you saying that they caused the attack to happen?

Soul: The word "caused" from the personalities reference point implies that the personality had complete control over the event. Remember that there is more to you than your personality and therefore, the personality can only control certain things. The person that was attacked, as well as the attacker, may have had something to learn from the process.

Personality: Is this about karma?

Soul: Karma is a limited way of viewing action and reaction. It is as limited as an eye for an eye. In your example it is possible that the person attacked had wanted to learn about injustice or rehabilitation, while the attacker may have been struggling with ways of dealing with suppressed anger from childhood. They will both have to deal with the consequences of their actions related to the event and all that follows. In that way they each can learn more about accountability.

Personality: That's speculation. This is the kind of event that makes people feel unsafe because the reasons underlying the event are not well understood. It seems random and purposeless. I like to know why things happen.

Soul: Then you must understand more about the person in question, including their soul.

Personality: Why do I have to understand their soul? You told me that their reality results from their beliefs, feelings, and actions. What does that have to do with their soul?

Soul: If your thoughts of self included me too you would be more aware of my purpose, which remains largely unknown to you as long as your awareness is limited to only your personality. I experience all the events that occur in your life as well. I exist at its center, whether or not you notice me, but I have an effect on your life even if you do not acknowledge me. I have a lot to do with creating your path.

Personality: Why don't you get your own life? And while you're at it, please make sure that you can be completely in control of it so that you won't feel the need to interfere with mine.

Soul: When you perceive life more completely, you will understand the fallacy of control. You believe in luck in order to believe that you are in control most of the time. You equate the unseen forces that are at work in your life with luck so that you can dismiss the idea that other sentient influences play an important role. You conjure up beliefs to feel deserving when you receive good luck and to rationalize away bad luck. Are you beginning to appreciate the illusion of control?

Personality: But I thought you said that my free will gives me control over my beliefs, feelings, and actions. Do I have that control or don't I?

Soul: Of course you have control over your beliefs, feelings, and actions, but the flow of your life is dictated by more than your personality. Your life is also my life. I have desires as well.

Personality: What are they?

Soul: I am here to learn and evolve through my participation in your physical reality.

Personality: What is my involvement in that regard?

Soul: You are a mixture of heaven and Earth. You experience and connect with All That Is through me. You are also of matter from the Earth with your own life force and free will. I have been working with you from the beginning of your life so that we can co-operate in life. It is your choice as to whether you wish to assist me in fulfilling my purpose or accomplish something else of your own design or some combination of the two.

Personality: You are making me feel separate from you.

Soul: That is because you have free will to choose. The extent to which you feel alone and separate, signifies the degree to which you choose to isolate yourself from me. When this life is over, all that you have become as a result of your choices and experiences remains with me. That is why I am accountable for your choices, because in my reality, you and I are one and have never been separate. The separateness that you experience conforms to your sense of reality. However, when you perceive more, including me, your sense of reality will change.

Personality: Now I'm confused. Are you part of me or not?

Soul: I am a part of both you and All That Is. Through me, the spiritual essence that permeates us both sustains your very life. I am always with you and I experience physical life through you. The degree to which I participate in life with you and the manner in which you experience your connectedness to All That Is, depends upon how much you allow it to happen. Therefore, even if you do not allow me to participate more fully, I am still present and a part of you and you are always a part of All That Is. It is your choice as to whether or not you wish to acknowledge me and allow me to participate more significantly.

Personality: Choosing to acknowledge you seems to diminish me.

Soul: The human experience creates this enigma. Acknowledge me and you seem to be nothing more than a link in a chain even though you are an important part of the evolving whole. Do not acknowledge me and you are able to magnify your personality through egocentrism. However, the falseness of that presumption will ultimately erode any sense of connection that you have and cause you to feel alone. You make this choice in every moment. How do you choose?

Personality: I want to be important.

Soul: You are. I could not experience the physical world without you.

Personality: I want to be alive for my own purposes.

Soul: You are and that is also important.

Personality: Why?

Soul: All life evolves. As I am a part of you, you are a part of me. To the extent that you evolve, so do I.

Personality: Then why do I need you?

Soul: I can help you evolve more effectively. Your perceptions are limited, but they need not be. The more that you learn about the life that you have, the faster, and more completely you can evolve. The more that your attitudes are aligned with mine, the more you can perceive through me. As that occurs to a greater extent, the more safe and secure you will feel, which will more easily allow you to deal with your fears. That is important for us both.

Personality: That is exactly my point. Safety and security benefits you, but I have to do all of the work. Why can't you help more?

Soul: I can help you to the extent that you will allow me to be more grounded in you. That can help you address your fears. However, you are always directly responsible for taking the necessary physical, emotional, and mental steps to feel safe and secure.

Personality: So the bulk of the effort falls on my shoulders.

Soul: That is part of your job, but your body has a number of built in mechanisms to assist you. Unfortunately, some of them are engaged far too often because you feel isolated and as a result, you fear dealing with your painful beliefs about yourself and the world around you. With my help you could use these mechanisms with greater discernment, feel more at peace, and even use them to learn how to deal with your fears.

Personality: What are you referring to?

Soul: Your body has a very sensitive, but relatively non-specific, early warning system to help you with life-threatening situations. This system is designed for emergencies—such as if you are standing in the middle of the road and a car is bearing down on you. This system allows you to react automatically. Realistically however, life-threatening occurrences are rare, but you allow less dangerous circumstances to trigger these same mechanisms. Your coping strategies trigger them when you fear that someone will criticize you or not approve of you. Clearly these are not life-threatening circumstances, but you often act as though they are. If you allow me to be more grounded in the physical in partnership with you, then I could help you short-circuit this mechanism when no real threat exists. You could even learn to use this mechanism to your advantage. You would feel safer because you would be more aware of what is actually happening in the present moment.

Personality: I'm not aware of this warning system.

Soul: You can be. This system is active and it causes you to experience a heightened level of stress reaction. Most often this happens below your level of conscious awareness. It is how you have programmed yourself neurologically, psychologically, emotionally, and spiritually and it has resulted in an elevated level of tension in your body and mind. You have become accustomed to this level of tension to the point that you consider it to be the norm for you. You could be experiencing a much more relaxed state. You can change your programming.

Personality: Would I still be able to deal with life-threatening events?

Soul: Even better than you can now, because you would remain more consciously aware. You would be able to perceive more options.

Personality: Why wouldn't I want your help in this area?

Soul: Fear. To be able to consciously discern which fears are life threatening and which are not requires a willingness to experience your fears as they emerge rather than avoiding them.

Personality: That doesn't sound like fun.

Soul: You would be less on guard and more relaxed as your attitudes about your fears change. Recognize that if you do not explore them, then to a large extent your feelings and actions result from fears that you are not very aware of. For someone who likes control, how do you like that?

Personality: I like avoiding fear more than being in control.

Soul: You are often fearful, but you do not fully appreciate why. When those close to you become angry with you and you back off from some of your requests, which by the way are often reasonable, are you not feeling fearful and acting out of fear?

Personality: Now that you mention it, I do become frightened when they get angry with me.

Soul: Is this a life-threatening situation? Are they going to hurt you?

Personality: No I don't fear that.

Soul: Then what are you afraid of?

Personality: I think I'm afraid that they won't love me as much and I will lose them.

Soul: Do you think that is likely?

Personality: Not really.

Soul: But you act as though you will lose them. You retreat from your position so that you will not upset them, even when what you are asking of them is reasonable. Even simple things like asking your children to clean up after themselves. So what is the fear really about?

Personality: I don't know. I've never taken the time to figure it out.

Soul: That is because when the fear arises you quickly take steps to subdue it so that you will not have to feel afraid. The feeling of fear will not hurt you. The feeling is just a barrier that you have created for yourself as part of your coping strategy in order to avoid confronting a painful belief. It is part of the early warning system. You are afraid to stay with the feeling and face the underlying belief that you could lose them and be left alone. You fear that your need for love will be unmet if that happens.

Personality: You're probably right.

Soul: I too remember your childhood experiences. I remember when your parents used to argue and one would threaten to leave. I remember how you feared separation. Those experiences have reinforced even older fears and beliefs that you hold deep in your subconscious mind. All of these fears are triggered when a family member becomes angry with you. The fear that you will be alone causes you to compromise yourself. It causes you to do things for others to win their approval and affection. Unless you confront and reevaluate some of these fears and painful beliefs they will continue to play out in your life.

Personality: I have a hard time believing that these deep seated memories, that I never think about, are influencing me to the extent that you say they are.

Soul: Yes, I am aware of that.

Personality: Is that all you're going to say?

Soul: I could repeat myself if that would be of benefit to you.

Personality: Don't you feel the need to convince me?

Soul: I perceive needs only through you.

Personality: And you don't have any?

Soul: Correct.

Personality: Everyone has a need to be safe and secure, feel loved, and be connected to others. Why don't you have some of those needs?

Soul: Feeling safe and secure and being safe and secure are different. Being is the state that you exist in from moment to moment. You cannot guarantee that you will remain in that state regardless of whatever actions you have taken. Therefore, striving to always be safe and secure is a goal that can never be attained. Feeling safe and secure, on the other hand, is having a sense that whatever happens to you, you will be okay.

Personality: What about love and connection?

Soul: I am aware of my connectedness and the source of all love. You can also have that awareness. It would reduce your sense of separateness and as a result, allow you to feel more safe and secure, even in the physical world.

Personality: You just want me to be more connected to you.

Soul: And to everyone and All That Is. You are never alone.

Personality: It often feels that way.

Soul: That is because you believe that you are alone. Your beliefs and fears drive your reality. This even happens in regards to more trivial matters.

Personality: What are you talking about?

Soul: I am referring to some of your beliefs about germs and how you have chosen to deal with them.

Personality: Nobody likes germs. They can make you sick. Everyone has their own routine to keep things clean and sanitary.

Soul: How many times do you wipe the kitchen counters each day and why do you clean the counter, then sweep the floor and then feel the need to clean the counter immediately thereafter?

Personality: My grandmother used to do it that way. She told me that was the only way to make sure that the germs that have fallen on the floor and then are swept back into the air won't contaminate the counter again and end up in the food.

Soul: Then why not simply sweep the floor before wiping the counter the first time?

Personality: Okay, I get your point, but this is just a silly habit, although if I did as you suggest the crumbs that I wipe off the counter would fall on the floor. Anyway, this habit doesn't hurt anyone.

Soul: This demonstrates how your underlying fears and beliefs create habits that get passed on from generation to generation in a mindless way. You are always complaining that you do not have enough time. Changing this simple behavior will save you a little. For that matter, why not have some other members of the family help clean up after meals? It seems to me that you must like things the way that they are.

Personality: I don't. I want help just like everyone else. Why should I have to do everything?

Soul: Then ask for some help. Would others be there to help you?

Personality: I guess so.

Soul: But you are not sure, because others have not always been there for you in the past.

Personality: That's right. At least I can count on myself.

Soul: Anyone else?

Personality: I would like to be able to count on you, but you're not very practical.

Soul: I am more practical than you realize. After all, to a significant degree I am responsible for your opportunities or good luck, as you like to refer to it.

Personality: How do I know that you would come through for me?

Soul: Your feelings of safety and security benefit me too, remember?

Personality: So I can count on you to pull me through, is that it?

Soul: Not exactly.

Personality: Make up your mind, which is it?

Soul: I cannot help you if you are unwilling to help yourself. If you desire life and you work to make progress along the path of your choosing then I can assist in providing opportunities that you can perceive. When you are not interested in life or progress, then I will still provide opportunities, but you may not perceive them or act upon them. I cannot act on your behalf.

Personality: I guess that would violate my free will.

Soul: Precisely.

Personality: So then inevitably it is up to me.

Soul: You wanted to be important.

Personality: Yes, but everyone has their limits.

Soul: Everyone also has their unique talents, including those close to you. You can count on others as well as yourself.

Personality: Why are you so sure I can count on others?

Soul: What do you think?

Personality: There is safety in numbers. Is that what you mean?

Soul: That kind of tribal mentality is certainly a factor and it usually does manifest when times get tough. We souls are in much greater demand when there is a mass response to seemingly unavoidable happenings that invoke substantial fear.

Personality: During really tough times or tragedies?

Soul: Yes. During those times people no longer dismiss the unseen forces. They begin to search for answers at a deeper level.

Personality: There is nowhere else to turn.

Soul: Does that make you feel more safe and secure?

Personality: That's why we do it.

Soul: Why wait for times to be tougher? Why not search within yourself when times are not so tough?

Personality: Avoidance. Ignorance is bliss.

Soul: Ignorance is ignorance. Why wait until tomorrow to accomplish what you can today?

Personality: I guess you have been around listening to my mother all these years.

Discuss and/or Journal

Safety and security concerns are an ever-present issue for your personality. Your soul, without physical form, does not have this fear. However, your soul desires to participate in your life in the physical realm and is available to assist with your fears.

1. What safety and security fears do you have (fear of physical harm, disease, germs, loss of loved ones, abandonment, inadequate support system, etc.)?

_____

_____

_____

_____

_____

_____

2. How do you deal with these fears?

_____

_____

_____

_____

_____

_____

3. Do you ever call upon your soul to assist you with fears concerning your safety or security?

_____

_____

_____

_____

_____

---
chapter eight

MEET YOUR MATERIAL NEEDS IN A REASONABLE MANNER

T HERE IS A DIFFERENCE between our needs and our wants. We do have clear material needs that when satisfied help us live from day to day. How we define those needs however, is a matter of choice that many people struggle with. Determining the reasonableness of our needs in a world of deprivation for some and excesses for others is not so simple, as we each have different roles to play in life. Attempting to satisfy our material requirements for some people creates an obsessive or hoarding mentality and for most of us becomes a burdensome preoccupation. Why? Could it be that we do not understand how the process of satisfying our needs works?

Although we have true material needs, our wants may not be aligned with our real needs. Wants are typically substitutes, distractions, or an easy fix for what we truly need, and they tend to result in only temporary gratification. Many of our material wants only obscure different unmet physical or emotional needs that do not become satisfied even when our wants are achieved. We cannot come to understand the difference between our needs and our wants unless we take the time to consult our hearts and with due consideration determine what we truly desire. Our needs will then become clearer. Satisfying those needs is then of paramount importance and will likely result in genuine feelings of gratification and gratitude.

When friends or relatives give us a gift we can direct our gratitude accordingly if we so choose. When we are the beneficiary of good fortune beyond our understanding and control, what then? Do we thank our lucky stars or assume that we deserve it for reasons unknown to us? Does our good fortune obligate us to do good for others? Do we feel guilty and undeserving and become unable to accept it or do we squander what has been gifted to us? Many of us would be eager to find out how we would feel and respond in this situation.

Far too often we have experienced loss rather than gain. How has that conditioned us? Many of us have created a mindset of scarcity and a sense that there are not enough resources to go around. We feel that we must look out for ourselves first and foremost and only when we have enough consider assisting others. Or we do give to others, but cling to what we have left for fear that it will be taken away. This mindset leaves us wanting, not grateful for what we have and thus we fear not having enough. Our fears in fact obstruct the path to greater abundance because fear precludes an openness to receive. Why?

When we are fearful we attempt to control our path to meet our perceived needs, our wants. In so doing we are not open to receive whatever comes our way. We are only willing to have what we want. We therefore close ourselves off from being receptive to whatever may come our way for fear that what may come may be unwanted. Gratitude on the other hand, signifies thankfulness for already having received and results in an open heart capable of receiving more. People with this attitude are grateful regardless of what is received. Do such people remain grateful even when they receive what they do not want?

How often do we receive something that we do not want, yet need? Some of our best gifts in hindsight were disguised as loss, hardship, or tragedy. Only with the passage of time or a higher perspective can we perceive the significance of all the gifts we receive, provided we are open to that understanding. And only with the belief that this understanding will be forthcoming can we be open to receive whatever may come our way. For most of us this requires a significant shift in attitude because of our difficulty in believing that our true needs can always be met.

Soul: It will work out for the best.

Personality: What are you talking about?

Soul: Your finances.

Personality: Easy for you to say. You don't need to eat or put a roof over your head or send your kids to college.

Soul: I too want to see that your needs are met. However, for that to occur more naturally and easily there are some important concepts to be understood.

Personality: I'm not in the mood for another lesson. I'm tired of worrying about these issues and I would rather not have to.

Soul: Please, do not worry. There is no need.

Personality: Do you expect me to simply stop feeling what I'm feeling?

Soul: Not at all, but do you know why you worry? How did you learn to feel this way?

Personality: What do you mean learn to feel this way? I feel this way because I struggle to make ends meet.

Soul: Just as your parents did when you were young?

Personality: They worked hard to keep a roof over our heads and food on the table. It wasn't easy for them.

Soul: Did they worry?

Personality: All the time. My father worked long hours while my mother raised us and stretched every penny. They always told us that it was their hope that we would have it easier.

Soul: Do you?

Personality: I don't work the long hours that they did. I take some time for leisure activity that they wouldn't have dreamt of doing, but I still worry as much as they did.

Soul: Why?

Personality: I already told you. It's tough making ends meet. I have a lot of responsibilities to live up to.

Soul: Are you living up to them?

Personality: So far, but that could change in an instant. I could lose my job or get sick and not be able to work. My insurance wouldn't cover all of our expenses. The price of living never seems to go down and it could go up even faster. I feel sick to my stomach every time I evaluate the college funds for our kids. I could buy a nice new car each year for what we will pay in tuition. And what about retirement? All of this weighs on my mind. I'm reminded of my obligations all the time.

Soul: How so?

Personality: I'm reminded when I look at my retirement plan, when my kids get their report cards, when I pay my bills, and when everyone else talks about their financial problems.

Soul: It sounds like quite a preoccupation.

Personality: That's what I've been telling you. This is what my life is all about, but you can't seem to relate to it.

Soul: I simply have a different perspective.

Personality: And that is?

Soul: How did your parents work through it?

Personality: What do you mean?

Soul: Financially, how has everything worked out for them?

Personality: They kept us fed and in clothes with a roof over our heads. They couldn't afford to send us to college, but some of us were able to get a college education by working or taking out loans. I guess we did okay.

Soul: How are your parents doing now?

Personality: My dad is retired and getting a check from social security. When the kids got older my mother got a part time job and they were able to put a little money aside. We kids buy them some things that they can't afford or that they wouldn't buy for themselves.

Soul: Do they still worry?

Personality: That's a good question. I don't know for sure, but they don't seem to be worried when I visit them.

Soul: Why do you think that is?

Personality: Most of their worries were about taking care of our needs and now we're no longer with them. They don't seem to have any problems dealing with their own needs.

Soul: When you and your siblings were living with your parents what expectations did you have of your parents?

Personality: I didn't have any expectations of them. I was just a kid. When I got a little older I realized that they were doing all they could to take care of our needs. It made me feel a little guilty that I hadn't done more to help. I was on the receiving end for the most part.

Soul: Do you think your parents understood how you felt?

Personality: Probably not. I don't think it would have mattered if they realized that I didn't have any specific expectations and that I understood that they were doing the best they could. They kept telling us that it was important to make things better for the next generation and they expected us to do the same.

Soul: Your parents were worried that they would not live up to their own expectations about how to help you have a better start in life. How did they come by those expectations?

Personality: Their parents were immigrants who had even less. They gave of themselves in order for my parents to have a better life so that they could make an even better life for us.

Soul: When does it end? When does one of their descendants finally have a good enough life?

Personality: When they feel that they have made enough.

Soul: Made enough of what?

Personality: When they have enough money so that they won't have to worry.

Soul: That seems to be a moving target.

Personality: Why do you say that?

Soul: You have a nicer home than your parents did and you have your own cars. You have many other material possessions and it appears as though you may even be able to send your children to college with some supplemental loans. What is driving your expectations?

Personality: I want my kids to have the opportunities that other kids have so that they can get ahead in the world. The workplace is very competitive and I want them to be able to get a good-paying job and be able to raise a family.

Soul: So that they can worry?

Personality: If they get a really good paying job then maybe they won't have to worry as much as I do.

Soul: Then they will move to a nicer neighborhood with bigger mortgage payments and then they may feel the need to own more expensive cars and send their children to more expensive schools and on and on and on. When does it end?

Personality: Why should it end? We're all striving to be better off.

Soul: Better off in what way?

Personality: Financially.

Soul: Why?

Personality: So that we don't have to worry about finances and we can do what we want in life.

Soul: How much money do you need in order to do what you want in life?

Personality: I guess that depends on what you want to do in life.

Soul: I certainly have a purpose to fulfill in life, but it does not require a lot of money. However, if you are so preoccupied with financial matters, then I do not know that you will ever realize what my purpose is all about, which is ultimately your purpose.

Personality: I'm frankly less concerned with your purpose than I am with making ends meet.

Soul: If you were more concerned with my purpose then you would not need to be concerned about your finances.

Personality: You don't relate to practical matters very well. It is you who require me to look after these things. It's no different than our safety and security issues. Even you thanked me for taking care of those needs.

Soul: I told you that I appreciated your actions, but I also informed you that I assist in the creation of your opportunities. You need only act on them when they appear.

Personality: Fine, but I am still the one that has to take action.

Soul: That is always the case and to the extent that you are moving in a particular direction then I can help arrange for the necessary opportunities to appear. Presently your actions related to your financial worries are motivated by the expectations that you have created for yourself. However, these expectations have been influenced primarily by your family, friends, co-workers, and society, but not by me. As such, they lack deeper meaning for you.

Personality: My expectations seem meaningful enough.

Soul: Are they really your expectations? They are motivated by factors outside of yourself and as such they do not reflect your deeper plan. That is why they seem like obligations to you.

Personality: They do weigh heavily on me and even when I continue to make my payments and save for the future I don't feel gratified. I simply feel that I'm getting by.

Soul: That is because what you are accomplishing does not have real significance to you. The goal of trying to achieve financial security or independence so that you can do what you want in the future is a delusion. If you are travelling down the path that reflects your true purpose then isn't it reasonable to expect that everything you need will be provided along the way?

Personality: That seems like a fairy tale. How can I believe that you will keep your end of the bargain?

Soul: It is a matter of faith, a trust in me, and All That Is.

Personality: I would like to see a sign that it will work.

Soul: You would like to win the lottery.

Personality: That would convince me.

Soul: That would only make you believe that the path you are currently on is the right one for you.

Personality: How do I know that it isn't?

Soul: You feel that you are simply getting by. You are not grateful for what you have. If your goal were to be on a path consistent with your purpose rather than chasing some ill-defined financial target, then you would be feeling grateful that you have what you need in order to move forward toward your goal. The sign that you seek is within.

Personality: I was hoping for something more solid, something that I can perceive more easily.

Soul: You are that part of us that manifests what is real to you.

Personality: I don't know what my purpose in life is and therefore I don't know what steps to take.

Soul: You simply need to move in the direction that feels right for you. It does not have to be a big step. I will help you to know what steps to take when the time is right and then it is up to you to take action. As you progress along this path you will encounter opportunities that will allow you to meet your financial needs and possibly more.

Personality: I like the more part, but that doesn't seem to fit with your spiritual nature.

Soul: Why not?

Personality: Being spiritual means that you have risen above materialism.

Soul: Spiritualizing matter is what I do on Earth. If in that process greater wealth results, then so be it. I am not advocating that my purpose seeks that result, but rather if it is a by-product, or it serves as a means to an end then I would accept it and be grateful.

Personality: Why would you be grateful? You have no need for material possessions or financial wealth.

Soul: From your perspective you see money and objects. From my viewpoint I perceive a greater flow of energy. The current of what is moving through me is magnified in this situation. I would be grateful for the ability to participate in this manner.

Personality: How does your gratitude impact me?

Soul: You may perceive it as a sense of fullness, anticipation, or excitement. Those feelings may inspire you to be generous with what you have and delight in the prosperity.

Personality: What if I want to use these new financial resources only for my own purposes?

Soul: That is your choice. It is yours to do with as you please.

Personality: Maybe I can learn to be grateful.

Discuss and/or Journal

Your personality has true needs and perceived needs—wants. Your soul has desires. Some people believe that if you are on your path, your true needs will be met along the way. Those people also would be grateful for what they have and have an open heart, willing to receive more of whatever was needed.

1. Do you believe that your true needs are being met?

_____

_____

_____

2. Are you grateful for what you have?

_____

_____

_____

3. What do you want now?

_____

_____

_____

4. What is it that you need now?

_____

_____

_____

5. What do you desire now?

_____

_____

_____

_____

chapter nine

OPERATE WITH HEALTHY BOUNDARIES

Boundaries take many forms. We create personal boundaries concerning our physical bodies. We each define a zone of personal space that we are comfortable with. We allow some people to get closer to create greater intimacy, while we keep others a certain distance away. We create boundaries around possessions labeling them as mine, yours, or ours so that we can dictate who can and cannot use them. We create boundaries concerning our time by making time for work, errands, play, and time for others and ourselves. These boundaries help us manage our personal lives. We also create boundaries, which delineate physical sensations into self-defined categories, such as warm versus hot and pain versus pleasure and many others. These boundaries are useful aids helping us learn and communicate. Boundary considerations also extend into later Basic Rights in terms of differentiating our own feelings from those of others and our own thoughts from those of others.

Some boundaries, by their very nature, divide things, people, acts, etc. These boundaries exist as a result of our beliefs about ourselves, the world around us, and our relationships. They are defined by our choices and they play out in our behaviors. These boundaries are often formed as a result of our judgements. We make judgements as to what is good or bad and right or wrong. We make rules for ourselves and others in terms of things that should be done and things that should not be done. How we experience life depends upon the boundaries that we choose to create and maintain and those that we choose to dismantle. We build fences, walls, and barriers to keep some people inside and some people outside. We form friendships, clubs, and groups, including some people and excluding others. Why do we create boundaries?

We do so because we feel the need to. Our free will allows us to determine how we choose to view ourselves, the world around us, and all of our relationships. Boundaries compartmentalize our world and our experiences, providing us with reference points for taking action and at times to further our understanding. We have chosen to act and to learn in this manner. We also form boundaries in an effort to protect ourselves. Many of the boundaries we have formed are windows into our hearts and minds and define our current state of being. Some of our boundaries, however, limit us because we often create boundaries where none truly exist.

How often do we create boundaries out of fear? We have every Right to protect our physical bodies from harm by another and in turn respect the Rights of others. If we have been violated in this way in the past then we are likely to have a heightened level of awareness of our need to protect ourselves. Fortifying this boundary may be prompted by fear. It may also demonstrate self-love in the form of self-protection. Which boundaries are healthy and which are not? Although we may feel a need for greater self-protection, fortifying this boundary may not serve us as well as we would like. It may isolate us and limit intimacy. It may preoccupy us. It may even signal weakness and predispose us to further violation. Boundaries created out of fear may result from a natural reaction of self-preservation and be beneficial in the short run. However, would we do better long-term by addressing our underlying fears and recasting our boundaries? How often do we evaluate the boundaries that we have created?

How difficult is it for us to cross the line of one of our own boundaries? Doing so reflects change. It signifies that we have decided to operate differently, along new lines or erase them completely. How do we go about changing or dismantling our boundaries? First we must come to recognize the boundaries that we have created. To do so does not require a deep exploration into our subconscious minds. It only requires that we become aware of our actions. Our behaviors demonstrate the boundaries that we have created and maintain, predominantly at a subconscious level. As we become consciously aware of our boundaries we can witness their effects upon ourselves and others. We can then decide how well they serve us.

Soul: Take today off and have some fun.

Personality: I would love to, but I've got to go to work.

Soul: You work most days. You could use some time for yourself. What is the harm in taking one day off?

Personality: No, I should go to work. They're expecting me.

Soul: What are your expectations about time for yourself?

Personality: When everything else gets done, then I can take some time for myself.

Soul: That time never seems to come. After work, you take care of chores and family needs. On weekends, more chores, errands, and other family needs.

Personality: Well that's just how it is.

Soul: I guess that is just how you want it to be.

Personality: No I would like some personal time.

Soul: Why? What would you do with it?

Personality: There are lots of things.

Soul: Go on.

Personality: I have some reading I would like to catch up on and I would like to get back into my exercise routine on a regular basis and I'm sure I can think of some other activities.

Soul: Then schedule some time for yourself.

Personality: I've done that in the past and then something comes up.

Soul: Every time?

Personality: It's happened enough that I never seem to get back to whatever it was that I was doing.

Soul: I guess your needs are not very important.

Personality: I just have a lot to do.

Soul: There are other busy people that can make some time for themselves. I do not believe it is because you are too busy.

Personality: Maybe they're just more selfish than I am.

Soul: What does selfishness have to do with it?

Personality: They probably take time for themselves at the expense of doing what needs to be done for others.

Soul: Do you ever do that?

Personality: Rarely.

Soul: Why not?

Personality: It's selfish and I don't want to appear that way.

Soul: What do you call it when you always put the needs of others before your own?

Personality: Giving of yourself.

Soul: When is it your turn to receive?

Personality: When others give to you.

Soul: What if they do not?

Personality: They will. It's just a matter of time.

Soul: How long are you prepared to wait?

Personality: I don't know. I've never thought about it that way.

Soul: Consider setting a deadline for yourself to see if it happens.

Personality: That's silly.

Soul: Why?

Personality: What's the point in setting a deadline?

Soul: By doing so you would be deciding how long you are willing to wait before you would act differently.

Personality: What would I do differently?

Soul: If no one is going to help you so that you can have some time for yourself, you can simply take some time for yourself rather than doing for others. They are not helpless.

Personality: I would feel guilty if I did that.

Soul: How do you feel now? You are doing more than your share and nobody is reciprocating. It does not seem equitable to me.

Personality: I do become a little angry at times and sometimes I'm sad that no one seems to appreciate what I do. Everyone just takes it for granted.

Soul: Then why would you feel guilty if things were more balanced and you had some time for yourself?

Personality: My current situation doesn't make a lot of sense does it?

Soul: That is my point, but that is how you have allowed it to be.

Personality: Are you saying that it's my fault because I'm being charitable with my time and nobody helps me?

Soul: I would call it a choice with consequences, action and reaction. Are you willing to be accountable for the consequences of your actions or lack of actions?

Personality: I am and I would like a little recognition and cooperation for being as charitable with my time as I am. Is there anything wrong with that?

Soul: Your frustration is beginning to show. If giving of yourself in this way were truly charitable, then you would not be angry about it. Being charitable implies giving unconditionally, which means that you are not expecting anything in return. If you truly expected nothing in return you would not be disappointed, sad, or angry. Some of your giving is charitable, but the remainder is motivated by other factors.

Personality: Like what?

Soul: There are several reasons. You have already mentioned one of them.

Personality: I don't have time for a guessing game. I've got important things to attend to.

Soul: That is another one.

Personality: Stop being so cryptic.

Soul: Make yourself a priority for a change. Taking some time for yourself is not selfish.

Personality: It often appears that way.

Soul: The appearance of selfishness is a significant concern for you, is it not?

Personality: Shouldn't it be?

Soul: That word should also causes you great hardship. Do you know how many times you have made statements like, "I should be more charitable"? How can you obligate yourself to give unconditionally? Unconditional giving cannot be derived from guilt because you would be giving to alleviate feelings of guilt. However, that would not matter if your giving were only intended for appearance sake. Most people cannot tell the difference and if you are only interested in appearances then you can keep giving out of guilt, while maintaining a charitable appearance for yourself and others.

Personality: I don't do that.

Soul: You do not want to accept your behavior, but it was you who said that you did not want to appear selfish and you are the one feeling sad and angry. These feelings are not accompaniments of charitable giving. It is often difficult to realize that our actions are not as pure as we would like them to appear.

Personality: This is tough to swallow. I like the appearance of being charitable. If you are correct about my motives, then my appearance isn't always truthful.

Soul: Still finding it hard to accept?

Personality: Yes, I don't want to be selfish.

Soul: How did you jump from not wanting to appear selfish to being selfish?

Personality: You're either one way or the other.

Soul: Is there nothing in between?

Personality: People are typically thought of as being selfish or being unselfish.

Soul: What ever happened to being equitable?

Personality: When I have done things that I considered to be fair in the past, I got the distinct feeling that I was being judged as selfish, although nobody said anything out loud.

Soul: Judged by whom?

Personality: By my family, friends, and co-workers.

Soul: Why do you think that happened?

Personality: They just felt that way. People get pretty annoyed with people who are selfish.

Soul: Especially the people who have been on the receiving end of the relationship.

Personality: What do you mean?

Soul: If you are the one that is worried about being perceived as selfish you are going to go out of your way to appear generous. Obviously those around you are going to be the beneficiaries. When you pull back and attempt to interact in a more just and balanced way, then those same people are going to receive less from you than they had in the past. As a result, they will resist the changes that you are making in the relationship. It was easy for them to fall into the habit of taking from you and not reciprocating when you so willingly kept giving.

Personality: They shouldn't have taken advantage of me in that way.

Soul: They simply accepted what you were willing to give.

Personality: They should have noticed that the situation was unfair.

Soul: Did you notice?

Personality: Sort of.

Soul: If you felt that your situation had become imbalanced, then you could have stood up for your Rights.

Personality: I told you. I didn't want to appear selfish.

Soul: Selfishness is being concerned for yourself more than for others. It means that you will endeavor to get what you want even if it compromises another. Fairness may look like selfishness to those who were previously on the receiving end, but it is not selfishness. I do not think you are really confusing selfishness and fairness. I believe that you do not want to consider why you have been so willing to play the role that you have been playing.

Personality: Can't a person just be charitable?

Soul: Sure, and at times you are, but for the most part you like feeling needed. By always giving and having others become accustomed to receiving you have created a situation where you fill the needs of others.

Personality: What's wrong with that?

Soul: I never suggested that there was anything wrong with giving or feeling needed or anything else for that matter. I am just curious as to your awareness about not taking some time for yourself.

Personality: So you think that it's fine that I keep giving of myself?

Soul: Certainly, keep giving. Give to your heart's content although I think you already have.

Personality: What do you mean by that?

Soul: You are past the point where you are giving from your heart. Much of your giving is out of need. You have a need to be perceived in a certain way, a need for approval and self-respect, and a need to be needed in order to hold onto those around you. Your giving is a habit for the most part, conditioned by your fears.

Personality: I think you need to be a little more charitable. A few kind words would be appreciated.

Soul: I have tried gentler persuasion, but you are having a difficult time accepting what is truly motivating you when giving of yourself.

Personality: Why do you think this issue is so hard for me?

Soul: Because there are so many strong influences that cause you to believe, feel, and act in the ways that you do. Your parents, teachers, and religious and societal values all have influenced you in this regard. The pressure to remain this way is very strong. I just want you to take an open-minded look at the boundaries that you have imposed around yourself so that they can be redrawn with greater equality if you so choose. You are not being fair to yourself or to me.

Personality: Sooner or later I knew the truth would come out. I knew this was all about you.

Soul: I certainly would like more of your time dedicated to my pursuits, but I will not try to make you feel guilty so that you will comply with my requests.

Personality: My religious affiliations have already done that.

Soul: For starters I want you to recognize why you take so little time for yourself. I want you to realize why you are reluctant to stand up for your Rights and why you believe that you cannot operate in an equitable and balanced way.

Personality: I do for the most part.

Soul: Like the time when your neighbor returned your lawn mower broken after two weeks? How high was your lawn when you finally got it back in working order?

Personality: Well at least I didn't have to mow the lawn for a month.

Soul: How about all the times that some of your co-workers do not accomplish all they need to and you fill in for them? You are always the last in line it seems.

Personality: Somebody has to pitch in and get the job done.

Soul: Why does that somebody always have to be you?

Personality: I feel that it's expected of me.

Soul: Do you know how to say no?

Personality: Not really. I take it upon myself to get everything done.

Soul: Why?

Personality: Because it's always been that way.

Soul: Why?

Personality: Because I allow it to be that way.

Soul: Why?

Personality: So that others will approve of me and they will stay with me.

Soul: Why will they approve of you and stay with you?

Personality: Because I do things for them. I make their lives easier.

Soul: What of fairness?

Personality: I guess it's a compromise I've been willing to make.

Soul: Is that the example you want your children to learn from?

Personality: No, I would like their lives to be better.

Soul: Then maybe you should lead by example.

Personality: But that would make their lives harder.

Soul: They are capable of doing more for themselves. They need to develop the skills that will allow them to function independently. They also need to understand that it is important to do their share and learn how to meet their own needs.

Personality: Maybe it's time. Even my kids tell me to get a life.

Soul: They probably realize that you are not as happy as they would like to see you be because you have so little time for yourself.

Personality: There was a time when I was happier and I enjoyed life more.

Soul: Being that way is the best example for those around you. If everyone emulated that behavior the world would be a happier place. People would have more to give of themselves in a truly charitable manner.

Personality: I think I'll take today off and plan some activities for myself.

Soul: Now that you have the extra time, please consider my desires.

Personality: When I have time.

Discuss and/or Journal

Our personalities (not our souls) create many boundaries and over time we forget about them at a conscious level. However, they play out in our behaviors because they remain active in our subconscious minds.

1. Have you evaluated any of the boundaries that you have formed? If so, which ones?

   _____

   _____

   _____

   _____

2. Do you have enough time for yourself?

   _____

   _____

   _____

   _____

3. Are you selfish? Do you give more than you receive? Are you concerned about being perceived as selfish by others?

   _____

   _____

   _____

   _____

4. What insight does your soul give you regarding your boundaries?

   _____

   _____

   _____

   _____

chapter ten

FEEL VITAL, PARTICIPATE IN PHYSICAL ACTIVITIES, AND NURTURE YOURSELF

THIS BASIC RIGHT ELEMENT at first glance seems relatively mundane and simplistic. However, evaluating our adherence to this element underscores one of our most profound inclinations—do we love ourselves enough to nurture ourselves and choose life or instead, choose death? Notwithstanding the dramatic nature of this question, we each have a responsibility to our mortal body. It requires care and maintenance. If we do not attend to this task we will undoubtedly experience the consequences of our behaviors. It is easy to take our vitality for granted when we are young, but with age it must be earned. How much effort are we willing to expend in order to maintain ourselves in optimum health? This after all, is the foundation for our life on Earth and a prerequisite for us to be able to feel more fully, think and reason clearly, and have healthier relationships.

For most of us, the feeling of vitality that accompanied our youth is a distant memory. Instead we often experience weariness and fatigue, even after a night's sleep. We supply our bodies with that all too familiar antidote, caffeine in order to compensate. Many of us in developed countries meander through life, seemingly unconcerned about the foods we devour, the drinks we consume, and our sedentary lifestyle. We cannot escape the consequences of our actions so we make resolutions to change.

Unfortunately, many of us do not follow through and instead only can take comfort in the growing normalcy of our condition. We take pharmaceuticals, when lifestyle changes would effectively treat our high cholesterol, diabetes, blood pressure, etc., because we have been labeled with a diagnosis rather than an attitude. We make excuses for our lifestyle, claiming that we do not have enough time or money or the support of others, but again our condition results from our own actions or lack thereof. Many of us are killing ourselves, however, we have not yet come to the realization that we are slowly committing suicide.

Or have we? We really do understand what we are doing. We have watched friends and family members become less active, succumb to illness, deteriorate, and finally die. We truly do comprehend the consequences of overeating, smoking, alcohol, and lack of exercise. Why then do we act in this manner? We do not begin this process with a conscious proclamation to ourselves and to others, but our actions, nonetheless, declare our intentions. The primary issue is not what we eat or drink or our activity level. These are only manifestations. Our beliefs and feelings underlie our behaviors. How do we feel and what do we believe about our lives and ourselves that prompts us to act as we do?

Do we feel the excitement that we did during our youth, when so many possibilities existed in our future? Are we energized at the start of each new day? The undeniable yet unspoken truth, given our actions, is that many of us believe that what we have to live for is no better than our next over-indulgence. We believe that our best days are behind us and now we must simply pass the time. When we choose to believe in this way we begin to die.

Isn't this the way of life? We are born, grow and develop, peak, grow older, then old, become ill, and finally die. This is the way of things because this is what we have witnessed generation after generation. Must it be this way? There are some who defy this path of their own free will. They certainly do grow older and finally die, but they do not grow old, nor must they suffer the infirmities of old age. They do not encounter these states of existence because they choose life over death each and every day.

Their activities are life affirming not death-defying, because it is not death that they fear, but life that they love. They accept what life has to offer and they love it and themselves enough to stay and receive love as life provides. They meet life fully engaged, physically, emotionally, mentally, and spiritually. They understand the need for nurturance by taking the necessary time for themselves and participating in physical activities that allow them to maintain as healthy a lifestyle as they are capable of. It is their Right to remain vital and yours as well. How do you choose to exercise it?

Soul: That felt good, didn't it?

Personality: I like the feeling of body fatigue after a hard workout. It helps me relax.

Soul: When you feel this way you have an easier time being grounded in the physical.

Personality: Yes, I can more easily feel my body.

Soul: The sensation that you are feeling is muscle fatigue throughout your body. It brings greater awareness to your body and triggers your desire to relax. Muscle fatigue in and of itself is a sensation derived from the body alone. Feeling more of yourself throughout your body includes feeling more of your energy system and me, interfacing with the physical matter of your body. This sensation is derived from more than your physical body.

Personality: Why would I want to feel myself in that way?

Soul: It helps you to understand the present state of your physical health.

Personality: I already get an annual physical exam. My EKG and cholesterol level are normal. I try to eat enough fiber and calcium and not too much red meat. I only occasionally drink alcohol, I don't smoke, and I exercise a couple of times a week. Isn't that enough?

Soul: You do more than most people to care for your body. You have tried to follow the recommendations of experts, but the level of knowledge is limited in terms of how to care for the physical body and prevent and cure disease. Many people visit their doctors again and again for treatment of their illnesses and only a fraction of them are cured.

Personality: Doctors are doing the best that they can.

Soul: Of course they are and the medical sciences are beginning to recognize not only the importance of the relationship between mind and body, but also the interplay between health and positive thinking, meditation, and prayer.

Personality: So what's wrong with the system?

Soul: Far too often the patient looks to the doctor for treatment instead of making the necessary lifestyle changes recommended. The health system accommodates this attitude despite the attendant costs and side effects of the treatments because it is what people want. Pharmaceutical companies lure consumers into believing that they do not have control over their own bodies, feelings, and even their own mental health. They advertise directly to consumers and force doctors to respond to the consumer's requests to fix their ills with pills. With all of the focus on pharmaceuticals and other external treatments there is lack of appreciation for the importance of our spiritual essence and the impact that it has on the body.

Personality: I can understand that health care is a profit driven business, which creates some pretty big conflicts of interest, but you can't possibly make me believe you have any real impact on my body. You're not part of the physical world. At best, you're a passenger and for that matter I often think that you're just a freeloader in the physical world.

Soul: Our situation is a matter of your choice. I could manifest in the physical realm more easily if you realized that my presence is actually quite essential in maintaining the healthy functioning of your body.

Personality: You said that you are always with me, so then I'm sure I'll be fine. Right?

Soul: I am with you, but you do not fully embody me to the extent that you can.

Personality: What does that mean?

Soul: I am with you to the degree that you allow it. You have recently become more accustomed to having me around ever since we have begun our dialogue. However, you maintain many areas in your body and energy system that are off limits to me and so my level of integration throughout your physical body and personality is limited. We are not well merged.

Personality: That's not true. I let you into my mind.

Soul: That is my point. You are willing to communicate with me on a mental level, but you are unwilling to embody me more completely.

Personality: Why do you need access to my body?

Soul: So that I and through me, All That Is, can be grounded in all of you including the rest of your personality and physical body. Our ability to work well together is dependent upon a closer working relationship.

Personality: I don't like the idea of turning over my body to you. It sounds like you want to possess me.

Soul: I am not asking you to turn your body over to me. I need you to be a partner in life. I cannot work alone in the physical realm. I am simply stating that if we are better integrated physically, emotionally, and mentally, then we will be in a better state of communication and your body will be in a better state of health. You are the one with free will when it comes to your body. At any time you can reject me, which you do quite often.

Personality: How will your presence throughout me help my body?

Soul: For starters, realize that it is our spiritual essence that truly animates your body. Our spiritual essence maintains life because it is life. Your body is matter that is no longer alive when our spiritual essence withdraws. As your soul, I am your conduit to our spiritual essence and All That Is. If you limit my access to areas of your body then you are depriving.yourself of our spiritual essence in those areas. You are depriving those areas of life.

Personality: So what if our spiritual essence doesn't make it to my liver or kidney. What does it matter as long as I have good blood supply to that area and whatever else is needed for physical existence?

Soul: It matters a great deal. An organ deprived of our spiritual essence will deteriorate over time and be more predisposed to disease.

Personality: If that were the case then I would expect people would be dying before my eyes.

Soul: They are, but the process is slow, which in part is why so many people have chronic diseases such as high blood pressure, asthma, diabetes, arthritis, and the list goes on.

Personality: These diseases are being effectively treated with medications that effect the physical body, not their spiritual essence and those treatments cause people to get better.

Soul: How are they better?

Personality: Drugs working on the physical body help control blood pressure, decrease asthma attacks, maintain normal blood sugar, and decrease pain and inflammation of joints. They're a big help.

Soul: They do help, but the underlying disease persists. Why?

Personality: I guess modern medicine can only treat them at this point, but in time they may be able to cure them.

Soul: How?

Personality: With all of the genetic research taking place I'm sure that in time there will be therapies that cure these diseases.

Soul: What is wrong with your genes?

Personality: Different people are genetically predisposed to certain diseases and that is why they get sick.

Soul: For the most part, those are only predispositions. Those illnesses may not materialize. Why do some people that are similarly predisposed remain free of the disease?

Personality: I guess that they eat better or exercise more.

Soul: That can certainly be beneficial for a person's health. Lifestyle changes for many can make the difference as to whether or not a disease manifests physically. Lifestyle changes can also replace medications in many instances, but there are also other factors that play a significant role in optimizing health.

Personality: What lifestyle changes are you talking about?

Soul: Meaningful dietary changes can dramatically alter a number of metabolic conditions of the body, especially when associated with an exercise regimen. Relaxation, meditation, and other stress-reduction practices can also significantly affect health and wellness, more than you are presently willing to appreciate.

Personality: Why do you say that?

Soul: You would rather focus on physical causes and treatments for physical ailments. You perceive little or no connection between bodily processes and our spiritual essence.

Personality: What do you mean?

Soul: Some people do not make lifestyle changes and despite being genetically predisposed they still remain without those diseases.

Personality: Are you saying that illness isn't affected by how we treat our bodies?

Soul: That is not what I am saying. All of those factors are important in maintaining normal functioning of the body. People may derive substantial health benefits by nurturing themselves to a greater extent by taking the necessary time to care for themselves through lifestyle changes. However, the presence of our spiritual life force is also required to maintain life and health. Without it there will be an increasing predisposition to disease as you age.

Personality: That's an easy argument for you to make when it can't seem to be proven either way.

Soul: Some scientists are already proving it. They have shown the positive impact of meditation and prayer, which increase the acceptance and presence of our spiritual essence. The results of their efforts would be even more dramatic if a person's spiritual essence could more easily make its way throughout the physical body.

Personality: Are you suggesting that all a person needs to do is allow their spiritual essence to heal their illnesses?

Soul: That is possible for those people whose personalities have become well integrated with their souls providing that maintaining the illness does not serve a higher purpose. People who are very well integrated in this manner do not limit their souls access to their bodies and personalities and healing is greatly facilitated.

Personality: If someone is ill and they believe what you are saying, then why would they limit access?

Soul: Even if they allow access, the emotional and mental blocks established by their personality and maintained at a subconscious level, prevent the normal flow of spiritual energy throughout their body.

Personality: What are these blocks you are referring to?

Soul: It is hard for you to perceive that you are in essence a spiritual being with a physical manifestation, because your conscious awareness is rooted at the level of the physical. It is difficult for you to appreciate yourself in total, including the energetic self of your personality, me, and the rest of our spiritual essence. If you could perceive more, you would appreciate the blocks and constrictions that you have created in your energetic self, based upon the ways in which you deal with your emotional feelings and beliefs. That is how your coping strategies manifest energetically. You actually do configure your energetic self by how you think and feel. In this way you create the lower part of the pathway that our spiritual essence must traverse in order for it to get to the physical body.

Personality: Draw me a clearer picture or talk to me like I'm five years old, because I don't get it.

Soul: Imagine a sphere. Now imagine another smaller sphere inside of the first and another smaller sphere inside the second and so on. The smallest sphere in the center is your physical body. The next several larger spheres comprise your energetic self most closely associated with your personality. The next several larger spheres have greater association with me.

Personality: You're talking about auras aren't you?

Soul: Some people perceive these auric bodies as energy layers surrounding the physical body, but in fact they are bodies or fields of energy that all overlap in and around the space of your physical body. These energetic bodies intermingle with the physical and extend a variable distance beyond it and the smaller bodies or fields contained within them. For instance your first auric body is most closely associated with your physical body, the next body is most associated with your emotional processes and extends beyond the first auric body. The third auric body, which extends beyond the second auric body, is most associated with the mental processes of your personality. Your emotional and mental fields are dynamic and reflect your state of being, emotionally and mentally. These states in turn influence the energetic body closest to your body, which in turn most directly influences your physical body.

Personality: How do these fields interrelate?

Soul: There is a very rich and dynamic interplay between these energetic bodies. Specific functionality is difficult to ascribe to any one part since they are each a part of a functioning whole. Imagine that all of these concentric bodies have thousands of channels or conduits that traverse them. If the channels from one body to the next are aligned and not blocked then energy can flow easily. If they are blocked or not aligned then the energy of our spiritual essence cannot flow unimpeded to your physical body. Unblocking these channels can be accomplished by ridding yourself of your coping strategies.

Personality: How can these channels be better aligned?

Soul: When your attitudes, which are comprised of beliefs, feelings, and behaviors are more in tune with my attitudes, then these channels are better aligned. The more that you and I are attuned the more we are aligned. You are in control of this process to the extent that you choose to align your attitudes with mine. Working through your coping strategies not only removes the energetic blocks, but also serves to increase our alignment.

Personality: How do I know how well I'm aligned?

Soul: From the perspective of your physical body you can feel it when you are better able to appreciate the finer vibratory sensations that results from the interplay of your energetic self with your physical body. When you are better integrated and well aligned you can feel these vital energies throughout your entire physical body.

Personality: I don't feel anything.

Soul: You will in time.

Discuss and/or Journal

Feeling vital and optimally caring for your physical health requires substantial involvement and commitment from your personality and greater integration of your spiritual side.

1. Do you feel vital throughout the day?

_____

_____

_____

_____

_____

_____

2. Are you eating, sleeping, and exercising enough?

_____

_____

_____

_____

_____

_____

3. Do you have a spiritual practice that assists you to better merge and align your personality with your soul and All That Is?

_____

_____

_____

_____

_____

Part III

Basic Right II

I. The right to exist as a human being in the physical world.

| Accept and Respect Yourself | Be Grounded in the Physical | Feel Safe and Secure | Meet Your Material Needs in a Reasonable Manner | Operate with Healthy Boundaries | Feel Vital, Participate in Physical Activities, and Nurture Yourself |

II. The right to experience physical sensations and to feel and express emotional and intuitive feelings.

| Experience and Enjoy Sensual Activities | Feel Full Range of Emotional Feelings | Express Emotional Feelings Fully and Honestly | Create Healthy Sexual Relations | Know and Trust Inner Guidance from an Intuitive Feeling Sense |

III. The right to think, choose, and create beliefs about yourself and the world around you.

IV. The right to bring love into the world, to accept it for yourself, and to give it to others.

V. The right to have personal truths and to test those truths for Truth.

VI. The right to envision the purpose of your love in the world.

VII. The right to know and manifest your soul's wisdom.

VIII. The right to accept yourself beyond space and time.

IX. The right to accept yourself as part of an evolving greater whole.

X. The right to spiritualize matter and manifest the higher purpose of humanity.

chapter eleven

EXPERIENCE AND ENJOY SENSUAL ACTIVITIES

WHY DO SOME OF us feel more than others do? Some people feel awestruck by a breath-taking view or are moved to tears or rapture by a musical score, while others in the same surroundings remain altogether uninspired. Some people have strong emotional feelings with little provocation, while others remain callous in the midst of an emotionally charged event. Some people have strong intuitive abilities, while others cannot recall having ever had a hunch. Is there a common denominator that underlies these different types of feelings? What is at the center of our feelings?

It is our feeling nature, directed by our intention to sense and experience our world, its inhabitants, and All That Is including ourselves. Our feeling nature comprises our five senses, our full range of emotional feelings and our energetic system, which in total provides us with a broad sensory capability. What is it that determines the breadth and depth of our feeling nature? Each of us determines this for ourselves, based upon our past experiences and what and how deeply we are willing to feel. We experience life through self-imposed filters because we have chosen to perceive in a certain way. Our perceptions and the impact that they have on us are uniquely personal, regulated, and self-fulfilling, tailored to our needs, wants, and expectations.

Although we may see the same sunset, hear the same music, and touch the same substance, we experience and enjoy them differently. Does it matter? It is our choice to experience these phenomena as we do. However, to the extent that we diminish the potential fullness of our physical sensibilities we reduce our level of interaction with our world and others. This occurs to some degree because we do not appreciate the degree to which we can experience the sunset, music, or touch to the extent that we might. This is an unfortunate accompaniment of muting any of our senses and just as importantly it reinforces the limits we have placed on expanding our feeling nature in general. Our diminished perceptions signify the degree to which we have isolated ourselves from our surroundings, others, and the world at large. We feel what we are willing to, which is far less than what we are capable of.

This self-imposed dampening of our feeling nature is done intentionally to avoid our deeper painful emotional feelings. Our emotional feelings, physical sensibilities, and intuitive feelings all emanate from our feeling nature. To avoid some of our deeper emotional feelings we reduce our feeling nature and as a result, everything that we feel. Unfortunately, this reduces our sense of connectedness and inter-relatedness, which results in less happiness and fulfillment. Why? When we are fully immersed in the reality of connectedness, we feel accepted, we have no safety and security issues, our needs are met, and we have no boundaries. This is a state that typically only occurs briefly during physical life, but can become a more constant state of being if we choose.

We experience brief moments of this state during sensually rich activities such as love-making, when gazing deeply into the eyes of a loved one, or whenever we creatively express our spiritual side. For a moment we enter timelessness and our focus shifts to our connectedness. For that moment our personal perspective is transformed into an experience of unity and connection. This is in stark contrast to the feeling state that we experience when we contract back into ourselves and exist in our more normal state of isolation and separateness.

This is where most of us reside most of the time, alone with our fears, needs, and wants. We each live our life in the cocoon that we have built for ourselves. It need not be this way. Learning to feel more of anything, including physical sensations can expand your feeling nature. Feel more and it will open you up to more feelings and greater connection and happiness.

Soul: Take a break for a minute and enjoy the sunset, it is magnificent.

Personality: I've got to get this work done before tomorrow. I don't have the time.

Soul: It will only take a few minutes and you may feel inspired. You may even be more
    productive afterwards.

Personality: The sun sets every day. I'll see it tomorrow when I have more time.

Soul: You can see tomorrow's sunset tomorrow, but today's sunset will be gone in a few
    minutes and you will miss this opportunity.

Personality: It's only a sunset. What is the big deal about this one compared to all of the
    others that I've seen? Why don't you go and see it for me and then you can tell me
    about it, later.

Soul: I already see it. My telling you about it will not produce the same results.

Personality: Why not? I already know what sunsets look like.

Soul: Yes, you know what they look like, but how well do you feel them?

Personality: Next you're going to tell me that I should be the sunset.

Soul: You are not ready for that. I was simply hoping that you would see the sunset and then sense how it makes you feel.

Personality: All right already, I'll look out the window and see this most wondrous of sights.

Soul: How do you like it?

Personality: Terrific, I don't know how I could have lived another minute without seeing this. Now I'm going back to work.

Soul: Wait a second. Just step outside and look at the sunset. I promise you that it will be well worth your time.

Personality: I didn't know you had such a big thing for sunsets. All right, I'll go outside and look at the sunset.

Soul: Great, now have a seat and relax for a minute, take a look and tell me about it and how it makes you feel.

Personality: Very nice. I see a big orange sun setting behind the hills and there are some wispy clouds that have a nice reddish tinge to them.

Soul: How does that make you feel?

Personality: It doesn't make me feel anything. It's just a scene. Although I think that if I sit here long enough I'll start to feel cold because the sun is setting.

Soul: Maybe you should sit for a while then.

Personality: Why?

Soul: So that at least you will feel something.

Personality: What is it that you are trying to get me to feel?

Soul: Inspired, animated, simply feeling more alive, and connected to something bigger than yourself. I am trying to get you to feel rather than think.

Personality: Why?

Soul: Because you are more than your head. So much of your focus is internal, within your head. You are not using all of your faculties to their fullest potential.

Personality: But my eyes are in my head. I don't feel with my eyes.

Soul: That may not be your primary pathway to feeling more, but you can feel from all of your senses. Your eyes allow the registration of visual imagery on your retina, which is then transmitted, to your brain and as a result, that experience can stimulate all of your body. The imagery that you see can evoke powerful feelings. Your eyes can also be used to focus your conscious awareness allowing your feeling nature to energetically sense additional information. However, you must be receptive to that information, which can be perceived and felt throughout your entire body if your feeling nature is sufficiently engaged.

Personality: Now that I've been sitting here for a while watching the sunset, I can appreciate its beauty to a greater extent, but it doesn't cause me to feel much. The fresh air and the smell of that apple pie I have inside, however, are making me feel hungry. Now, that feeling has captured my imagination.

Soul: Can you see the pie in your mind's eye?

Personality: I not only can see the pie, but I can also visualize sinking my teeth into it. I think I'll be the pie.

Soul: I thought you had work to do.

Personality: I'll do it over a piece of pie and a hot cup of coffee. It's gotten chilly out here.

Soul: Why don't you leave the work behind and just enjoy the pie and coffee?

Personality: Why don't you want me to finish my work?

Soul: I do want you to finish your work, but I would like to see you do one thing at a time and truly focus on it and enjoy it. When you multitask while you are eating you do not pay attention to the sights, smells, and tastes of the food. You are not anchored in the experience. You just swallow your food, mouthful after mouthful, without appreciating it much. As a result, you eat too fast and you eat more than you need to.

Personality: Why is that?

Soul: Your body will tell you when you have had enough, but you are not paying attention to those signals. When you eat too fast or you are busy talking or reading, while eating, those signals go unnoticed.

Personality: Yes, but I do stop eating.

Soul: Typically when there is no more food in front of you. Then you ask yourself whether you should eat more. That is usually the first time you become receptive to those signals. That is why you feel so full after meals. If you ate more slowly and paid attention to how you are feeling you would more easily recognize when you should stop before feeling too full. If you paid more attention to the smells and tastes you would also feel more satisfied.

Personality: All right, I'll leave my work until after I eat this magnificent appearing, mouth watering slice of freshly baked apple pie. Smell the aroma of this piece of pie as it mixes with the rich smell of the freshly brewed coffee. Now I'll add a scoop of creamy cinnamon ice cream so I can feel the sense of hot and cold on my palate simultaneously. Now I'm appreciating my food.

Soul: Why are you picking up the remote control?

Personality: I thought I would catch up on the news, while I was taking this break.

Soul: This is not a break. It is an experience unto itself.

Personality: I'm capable of doing both at the same time.

Soul: You could be, but you have not developed to that point yet.

Personality: I can eat and watch TV.

Soul: You are watching TV and swallowing mouthful after mouthful. You are missing most of the eating experience.

Personality: If I pay attention to eating the way that you describe I wouldn't be able to watch the news.

Soul: How is the news?

Personality: More senseless violence and some scandal that I don't understand very well. Same old stuff.

Soul: How was the pie?

Personality: It was a pretty big piece. I didn't need to add the ice cream. That on top of the dinner that I ate was a bit too much. I'm glad I had a cup of coffee to keep me awake. I don't want to fall asleep feeling this full.

Soul: Was it satisfying?

Personality: Sure, I just told you how full I feel.

Soul: Why do you equate feeling full with satisfaction?

Personality: I don't know.

Soul: You were not even that hungry before you ate. As a matter of fact you rarely experience hunger.

Personality: I was taught to eat three meals a day, so I eat regularly.

Soul: Why?

Personality: I already told you. That's what I was taught to do.

Soul: Do you ever reevaluate what you have been taught to see if it is still applicable?

Personality: I guess I should do that more than I do.

Soul: That is why we are working on greater conscious awareness of your attitudes. This process will give you an opportunity to reevaluate your beliefs, feelings, and behaviors. Maybe you ought to consider eating only when you are hungry or eating a number of smaller meals.

Personality: But I've become used to my routine and I like the break that mealtime provides.

Soul: Maybe it is time to reevaluate your routines and better understand why you do the things that you do. For instance, why do you equate feeling full with feeling satisfied? What happened as a child that caused you to link the two?

Personality: I used to eat this way as a child.

Soul: Who else in your family ate this way?

Personality: My father used to eat big meals. He always finished what was on his plate. He used to tell my mother that she never had to clean his plate after a meal.

Soul: What about your mother? How did she influence your eating habits?

Personality: She would tell me that if I ate well I would be strong and healthy and that not all children had enough food to eat, so I should be grateful and finish mine.

Soul: How did they respond when you did not finish what was on your plate?

Personality: They encouraged me to eat all my food and when I did, I was rewarded with desert. Then I was really full. My father always cleaned his plate. When I didn't, I was criticized.

Soul: Now do you see why you eat in the manner that you do?

Personality: I was trained to be an eating machine.

Soul: Yes, without ever taking the time to enjoy it. You were punished for not eating and rewarded for eating with more food. You associated fullness with a job well done. Taking the time to enjoy the experience was not a factor during the meal. It was simply a task that needed to be completed. You approached viewing the sunset the same way. You generally take a hands off approach to the physical world.

Personality: So what?

Soul: It fosters a greater sense of separateness. You act as though you are disconnected from your surroundings by not engaging your senses. It is even more pronounced regarding your sense of touch. You actively avoid sensuous experiences in that domain. Do you know why?

Personality: I never thought about it.

Personality: I never thought about it.

Soul: When you were a very small child you used to love to play in the sandbox that your father made for you. When you learned to crawl you would leave the sandbox and play in the dirt, which delighted you, but not your mother. She would carry you back to the sandbox and gently tell you not to play in the dirt and not to get too dirty. One day, after it had rained the night before, you left the sandbox to play in the mud. You were having a wonderful time smearing the mud on your body and even tasting it. When your mother realized what had happened she was mortified. She felt very guilty, feeling as though she was a terrible mother for neglecting you and allowing you to eat "all those germs." She was so ashamed that she did not want anyone to know what had happened. She would not call your father or the doctor for advice, but instead forced you to vomit to evacuate any mud that you had swallowed. Can you see how that affected you?

Personality: No wonder I feel a little sick to my stomach whenever I get dirty.

Soul: You never played in the sandbox again. Your father could not understand why you would cry when he would try to play with you in the sand.

Personality: This is an eye opener. It explains a lot, but even so, I'm an adult now and adults don't play in sandboxes or dirt. Those activities aren't very productive. What is the point in doing those things anyway?

Soul: To experience and enjoy sensual activities.

Personality: Why?

Soul: To learn how to feel more deeply and experience your connectedness. Your physical senses are a vehicle for this learning as they are connected to your deeper feeling nature. By deepening your feeling nature you can better experience how you are connected to the physical world and to All That Is. Your upbringing has made this learning difficult for you.

Personality: I was taught to appreciate music.

Soul: That is a reasonable starting point.

Personality: Reasonable for what?

Soul: To understand how your senses cause you to feel.

Personality: The music causes me to feel a certain way depending upon what I listen to.

Soul: Of course. Different music will evoke different feelings if you allow the feelings to be felt.

Personality: The feelings happen because of the music, not because I allow it.

Soul: The music is no different than the sunset or the apple pie, which you did not feel. They are all sensory experiences. The difference is how you have learned to appreciate them and your subsequent willingness to allow the experience to evoke more feeling. Do you remember what your mother used to tell you about music?

Personality: She would tell me to feel the music.

Soul: Do you remember what you did the first time she told you to feel the music?

Personality: No.

Soul: You walked around the room holding your hands in the air. She laughed and took you into her lap and kissed your hands. She asked you if you could feel the kisses. She told you that your hands were meant to touch and feel other things and that if you wanted to feel the music you had to try to feel it in your soul, deep inside of you. As a child you accepted that concept without much difficulty. You allowed yourself to be receptive to feeling music within yourself.

Personality: Do you feel the music?

Soul: I feel it through you and independently of you.

Personality: If you can feel it independently, then why do you want me to feel it?

Soul: Because that is my primary language.

Personality: Music?

Soul: Feelings.

Personality: But you communicate with me through thoughts.

Soul: Because you have not allowed yourself to feel very much. I could communicate with you much better if you allowed yourself to feel more. It would help us to communicate more accurately and swiftly, even while you are in the midst of living your life. You would be able to feel my impressions with greater certainty.

Personality: Provided I trusted you.

Soul: Trust is built on knowing what is true for you. How do you arrive at knowing what is true for you?

Personality: I figure it out.

Soul: Far greater certainty in knowing what is true for you is determined by how your options make you feel, more than what you think about them.

Discuss and/or Journal

Expanding our feeling nature allows us to experience life more fully, physically, emotionally, intuitively, and spiritually. Our soul can communicate with us at many levels, but its primary language is feelings. We can experience our soul through our physical, emotional, and intuitive feelings.

1. How strong is your feeling nature?

2. What can you do to strengthen your feeling nature through sensual activities (touch, sound, sight, smell, and taste)?

3. How do you experience your soul using your feeling nature?

4. Take a moment and try to feel your soul throughout your body. Where do you feel it?

chapter twelve

FEEL FULL RANGE OF EMOTIONAL FEELINGS

No experiences better demonstrate the duality of our human nature more profoundly than feeling the polar opposites of love and fear, our two primary emotional feelings. All other emotions are simply learned extensions of these two. They have been given names, labels such as joy or anger that we have been taught to apply to the variants of our two primary feeling states. Most of us have learned their names and can identify these secondary feelings, but we do not have a clear understanding of how love and fear have evolved into them. The transformation from two primary emotions into many secondary states has been so complete that we almost never encounter love and fear in their pure forms. They rarely are experienced as such and for the most part they have been reduced to just labels in our minds rather than feelings in the core of our beings. We have purposefully created this situation to manage our fears, but in the process we have limited our access to love.

Most of us are well practiced at feeling fear related emotions despite our best efforts to avoid them. We rarely experience fear in its primary form in isolation. What does primal fear feel like? In its most basic state it is an experience that begins with a sudden alerting response to orient us to potential danger followed by a cascade of neurologic and hormonal activity to support whatever life-preserving measures we choose to take. It is experienced as a level of heart pounding, hair-raising excitability that can be extreme, associated with varying degrees of rapid breathing, sweating, and nausea. We may experience a sense of dread as though our life may be extinguished at any moment. This may cause us to become paralyzed with fear or move us to take action.

This is a rare experience for most of us, as our lives tend to be more routine and familiar with few excursions into unknown territory. In our youth when we were exposed to more unfamiliar events, we learned to associate the feeling of primal fear with a precipitating event. We learned through simple cause and effect. When this occurs, then that may follow. As a result, we developed a belief that the precipitating event or any associated happenings were to be feared in their own right, because they could be a prelude to us feeling fear again. The precipitating events have become triggers, creating links between our belief about what may happen with the emotion of fear.

This learning process also incorporated feelings about ourselves and whoever or whatever caused the precipitating event into our newly formed secondary feeling state. Abused individuals feel fear when abused for the first time because they experience the pain of violation and they experience panic during the abuse about the potential outcomes. While the abuse is taking place, the abused do not know if, how, or when it will end, and how they will be left. They learn to fear the abuse, the abuser, and with further violations to hate the abuser and also themselves. In time, a deep-seated hatred with varying degrees of sadness and despair often become the predominant emotional feelings, although the fear still persists, usually in a partially suppressed form. The original feeling of fear has been transformed into a secondary emotional feeling state, a combination of hatred, sadness, despair, and fear.

When we experience lesser degrees of transgression, such as criticism or insult, we often experience some level of fear that becomes transformed into anger towards the transgressor and fear as to how we appear to others. When we do not live up to our own standards of performance we often become frustrated with ourselves, combining anger towards ourselves with fear of failure or inadequacy. Our anger or frustration may shift to shame if our fear that our unworthiness will be exposed to others develops to a still greater degree. Or our feelings of anger may become mixed with feelings of guilt if we believe that we should not become angry with another. We may even feel sadness, having a sense that we have lost our original goodness that would have, if still present, preempted our feelings of anger or guilt. Our emotional creations spiral onward forming a universe of twisted mixtures of fear-related emotional feelings. How would it feel to be rid of these fear-based feelings?

It may feel as though we have died and gone to heaven. Herein lies the challenge. How do we experience primarily love and its related emotions without dying? Or is there a part of us that must die in order for us to be this way? How nice it would be if all we had to do was remove a part of ourselves, like an infected tonsil, to rid ourselves of our fear based emotional feelings. However, we need that part of us. We require it to keep us alive in the physical world and to take action and make progress. It is our partner in life and it too needs and seeks love. How then do we find love?

The path to love is not found by avoiding fear. On the contrary, feeling fear in all its variations informs us that we are able to feel love. We cannot feel love unless we are willing to feel fear just as deeply. The two emotional feeling states cannot be separated any more than our personality can be separated from our spiritual essence. We either must choose to feel both or neither. Our feeling nature is the gateway to both. We can decide to expand the gateway or close it off. It is our willingness to feel that controls our gateway. If we reduce our willingness to feel fear then we equally suppress our ability to experience love. The path is clear. Open your gateway, experience both, and learn how to deal with your fears in the presence of love.

Soul: At the end of the day, what is important is how you feel.

Personality: At the end of the day I don't want to feel. I want to go to sleep and not be bothered by anything. All too often my feelings keep me awake so I turn them off.

Soul: You numb yourself.

Personality: You could say that.

Soul: You numb yourself during the day as well. Have you noticed?

Personality: I maintain an even keel—not too many highs or lows. I'm balanced. That's the way I like it.

Soul: Why?

Personality: So that I won't overreact. If I were to allow myself to get too excited in anticipation of something good happening and it doesn't happen, then I would become very disappointed. This way I can avoid being too disappointed.

Soul: What if it does happen?

Personality: Then I allow myself to get a little excited, but not too excited because it seems childish.

Soul: Is it childish to be joyful?

Personality: That's why they call it youthful exuberance—it's for the young. You get to a point in life when you become more serious minded. With a little maturity you develop cautious restraint because you never know what the future may bring. You have to set modest expectations.

Soul: So that you will not be disappointed?

Personality: Now you're getting the idea.

Soul: So as an adult you are trying to limit how good you might feel. Is that the idea?

Personality: I think you're pulling that out of context.

Soul: How so?

Personality: It's all part of maintaining balance. In order to not feel too bad you limit the highs as well.

Soul: So you numb yourself to a degree in order to maintain balance and avoid the lows. You only allow yourself little highs in the hope that you will only experience little lows. How do you know how much to numb yourself?

Personality: Whatever it takes to not feel too bad.

Soul: But then you are also reducing the highs and limiting how good you might feel.

Personality: It's a compromise. In life you have to make some compromises.

Soul: Why compromise on the depth of your feelings?

Personality: People often make compromises to avoid certain consequences. I limit my good feelings so that I can avoid my bad feelings. Isn't that how it works for you?

Soul: Although I experience the feelings that you feel through you, I do not judge them as good or bad.

Personality: Why not? Some of them feel good and some feel bad.

Soul: Those that you call bad are every bit as meaningful as those that you call good.

Personality: They may be meaningful, but I don't like the way that they make me feel.

Soul: They do not make you feel one way or the other. You choose to feel the way that you do.

Personality: Who are you kidding? Things happen to me that cause me to feel a certain way. I don't have a choice in the matter. If something bad happens to me then I feel bad. I don't choose to feel bad. I just simply feel that way.

Soul: Where do your bad feelings come from?

Personality: It's just the way I feel. They're a part of me. They arise in me when I'm sad, angry, feeling guilty, or whatever.

Soul: What causes them to appear?

Personality: When things happen that I don't like.

Soul: So your bad feelings are associated with the things that you do not like?

Personality: That's right.

Soul: And you decide which things you like or dislike?

Personality: Of course.

Soul: So you choose to feel the way that you do based upon your likes and dislikes. If you decide to change your mind and like rather than dislike what is happening then you would not feel bad anymore. It is your choice based upon your judgement about what is happening. Your feelings follow your thoughts on the matter. Think one way and feel one way, think differently and feel differently. It is you who decides how you think, correct?

Personality: I guess it is.

Soul: Then why do you think in ways that cause you to feel bad?

Personality: That doesn't make any sense.

Soul: You mean you do not like being accountable for your thoughts and feelings.

Personality: Why would I choose to think in ways that would make me feel bad? That makes no sense.

Soul: Then why do you do it?

Personality: I don't believe that I do.

Soul: Do you know why you do not believe it?

Personality: Because it's not true.

Soul: No, because you are not consciously aware enough to know that you believe or think in ways that cause you to feel bad.

Personality: Prove it.

Soul: How often do you criticize yourself?

Personality: I do it a lot, probably every day.

Soul: Why?

Personality: I don't like making mistakes or being wrong.

Soul: How do you feel when you are criticizing yourself?

Personality: I get angry with myself and then I feel sad.

Soul: Why do you feel that way?

Personality: Because I think I'm stupid for making the mistakes that I do and I believe that I will never get it right.

Soul: What was it that your father frequently said to you when he was critical of your efforts?

Personality: "How STUPID can you be? When are you ever going to get it right?"

Soul: Does that thought run through your mind when you make a mistake?

Personality: Too often.

Soul: And then you feel bad, right?

Personality: I get the point. We've been through this before.

Soul: You are just beginning to understand. This issue and others are still playing out in your life on a regular basis. You carry many thoughts and beliefs that influence how you feel. You have heard those thoughts so often that you have decided that they must be true, which has reinforced painful beliefs about yourself that really are not true. Furthermore, the bad feelings that you now experience prevent you from evaluating and changing those beliefs.

Personality: Avoidance, right?

Soul: Avoidance comes in many forms. Look at what you do when you have those bad feelings. You often go and get something good to eat to distract yourself from your bad feelings.

Personality: I like to eat.

Soul: Your father praised you when you ate and eating allows you to distract yourself from your current state. Before you realize it, you move onto something else. You never go back and try to understand why you felt the way that you did. Instead you take action to terminate the bad feelings and avoid revisiting the underlying thought.

Personality: I guess you're right. I never realized what I was doing.

Soul: Practicing avoidance usually happens below your level of awareness. Avoidance is your payoff so that you do not have to deal with your deeper painful beliefs, which you are afraid to confront. When your father criticized you, did you consider whether what he was saying was true or did you feel bad and hope that the criticism would end?

Personality: I couldn't wait for him to stop. I felt awful when he criticized me.

Soul: You learned to associate the bad feelings with his criticism. Turning off those feelings is your way of ending the criticism.

Personality: This makes me feel sad.

Soul: The feeling of sadness will not hurt you.

Personality: I don't like it.

Soul: Why?

Personality: It makes me feel uncomfortable. I don't like feeling that way.

Soul: Why does it make you feel uncomfortable?

Personality: I don't know.

Soul: If you do not know then who does?

Personality: You do, I'm sure.

Soul: I do, but it would be helpful if you did.

Personality: I don't want to know.

Soul: Why not?

Personality: I'm afraid to know.

Soul: What are you fearful of?

Personality: I don't know.

Soul: You do not want to know.

Personality: It's probably something bad.

Soul: You are frightened, like you were when you were a child, frightened of something that is not in your conscious awareness. It is a subconscious thought or belief.

Personality: Are you going to tell me?

Soul: We have already been through this. Can you remember?

Personality: It's a little hazy. Remind me.

Soul: It is a false perception that you generated at a very young age. It is a deeper painful belief that you developed before your father ever criticized you, but you are reminded of it subconsciously when you are criticized. It is the belief that you hold that causes his criticisms of you and your self-criticisms to be experienced more painfully.

Personality: What could be more painful than being disapproved of?

Soul: Being unloved or undeserving of love. It is a common belief that people hold deep in their subconscious.

Personality: Why do I have this belief?

Soul: When you were very young you were helpless. Not all of your needs were met in the way that you would have liked. You were too young to think and reason effectively so you concluded that you were being ignored, nobody was there for you, your needs would not be met, and so on. Eventually those feelings and thoughts were translated into a sense that you were undeserving of attention, acceptance, and love. With this deep-seated bias in place it was easy for you to think and react negatively. That made the criticisms from your father and every other type of rejection even more potent.

Personality: No wonder I feel sad.

Soul: Experience that feeling and you will better understand what is behind it. Understand the prior violations of your Rights.

Personality: What violation?

Soul: From your perspective as a very young child, you would have perceived that you were not being cared for or accepted as a person with needs. These are some of the deeper roots of your issues around safety and security and self-acceptance.

Personality: This kind of thing happens to everyone. These violations seem so petty and ordinary.

Soul: They seem that way to you now, but they did not when you were crying in your crib. You had real feelings of need from time to time. Later violations such as the repeated criticism from your father reinforced those beliefs. If you were treated differently during childhood the earlier painful beliefs about yourself would have weakened to a large extent because they were not being reinforced, but they still would be with you to some degree until you addressed them. Until you address those painful beliefs you will continue to feel the associated bad feelings whenever they are triggered, which usually occurs subconsciously, below your level of conscious awareness.

Personality: Are you suggesting that most of my bad feelings are remnants of my past?

Soul: That is exactly what they are and you use those feelings to avoid revisiting your painful beliefs. The discomfort that you experience when you feel those bad feelings motivates you to discharge those feelings, typically through avoidance tactics, by turning your attention elsewhere. In doing so, the underlying memory, which in part led to the formation of the painful thoughts and beliefs remains in your subconscious lending support to your false perceptions about yourself. This is why you criticize yourself so often. You do not believe that you are worthy of better treatment. That is what you have learned. Do you treat others in this way?

Personality: If I talked to others the way that I talk to myself, nobody would speak to me again.

Soul: So why are you so hard on yourself?

Personality: Because I was raised that way.

Soul: You believe that you should be treated in this manner and so in the absence of your father's criticism you criticize yourself. How does that make you feel?

Personality: Stupid.

Soul: That is an improvement over STUPID.

Personality: Actually I feel a little better. Understanding myself in this way is helpful.

Soul: Helpful enough to encourage you to feel more and numb yourself less?

Personality: What guarantee would I have that I wouldn't feel too bad?

Soul: None.

Personality: Then why would I want to do it?

Soul: To better understand yourself. In doing so your bad feelings would lessen. In addition you would feel the good feelings more intensely and more frequently.

Personality: It sounds to me as if I would feel worse before I felt better.

Soul: It is all in your attitude about your feelings. If you fear your bad emotional feelings then you will interpret the experience negatively. If you lose your fear of them then you will see them for what they are.

Personality: What are they?

Soul: They are mainly reenactments of your past. Subconsciously you are always scanning your environment for anything that you believe could cause you harm or discomfort. When your scanning mechanism is triggered you experience the same emotional feelings that you experienced in your past when the earlier fear-generating situation occurred. These bad feelings are messengers reminding you of your past. They are links to those earlier memories. Your bad feelings can help you to remember why you have decided to feel the way that you do when similar situations arise in your life today.

Personality: I would be better off if I stayed focused on the present moment and left my memories alone. Then I wouldn't experience those feelings.

Soul: You would be practicing avoidance.

Personality: But it's good to experience life in the present.

Soul: As long as you remain unaware of your subconscious fears and painful beliefs you will be triggered. Your concept of remaining present-centered is to try to quickly ignore or distract yourself every time that you are triggered and then refocus temporarily on something that does not trigger you. That is simply another avoidance tactic that constrains your awareness. It is beneficial to remain present-centered and to fully feel your feelings to help you understand why you feel that way. When you recall a memory in order to compare it to the events that are presently occurring you are still anchored in the present. Creating a coping strategy of distraction once reenacted causes you not to be present-centered. In that situation you are simply carrying out a programmed set of instructions. It becomes a subconscious act intended to avoid your present situation. You would be better off facing your fears and reexamining your old beliefs so that you would not need to distract yourself. Then you could remain present-centered and not constrain your awareness. In that way you would become more aware of your surroundings.

Personality: I am aware of my surroundings. I can see and hear what is happening around me and reach out and touch what is there. What are you talking about?

Soul: Because you limit what you feel on the inside you limit what you feel all around you. You do not feel connected to all of life. When you constrain any aspect of your feeling nature you reduce your ability to feel everything. Becoming less receptive, as you have, causes you to think of yourself as separate, which isolates you. Feeling disconnected in this way even predisposes you to feelings of sadness because subconsciously you are experiencing the loss of that connection to all life. Perpetuating your belief in balancing your emotions through suppression limits your ability to feel, which causes these broader ramifications.

Personality: This is a strange concept to me. I don't ever remember being able to feel in the way that you are describing. This may be something that you can feel, but I don't think this is in the realm of my possibility.

Soul: Because you feel so little of all that there is to feel, it is hard for you to appreciate that you and I are one. We are connected, but the limitations you have placed on your feelings keep you from feeling that connection. Although you are receiving my thoughts you are only appreciating them with your intellect. You could derive much more meaning from them and understand them more quickly if you were more receptive and your feeling nature was more engaged.

Personality: I think I understand what you have been saying.

Soul: There is a difference between understanding something with your mind and feeling it more fully throughout all of you. You tend to understand something intellectually first, but you do not fully appreciate it and know it until you feel it.

Personality: What do you mean?

Soul: You partially understood the idea of grounding to the Earth's energy, but you better appreciated it once you could feel that energy in your feet and legs. It became more real to you after you could feel it. Your sense of reality is impacted more significantly when what you are learning is based on your experience. In general you only consider what you experience to be real. Experiencing more will change your reality.

Personality: How much can my reality change as a result of being able to feel more?

Soul: If you substantially reduce your subconscious fears and increase your ability to feel then your ability to experience love and your surroundings would better approximate my abilities because we are one. This is how you can learn to identify with me to a greater extent. To do so, however, requires that you experience more of what I experience and that is done primarily with your ability to feel.

Personality: How much do you feel?

Soul: All that I can, all that there is for me to feel through you and others.

Personality: Do you mean that you feel others that are close to me?

Soul: And far.

Personality: How do you do that?

Soul: I am connected to All That Is. If I focus my awareness on a person then I can feel what they feel. You are connected to All That Is through your connection to me.

Personality: Why don't I feel others?

Soul: You would feel more if you allowed yourself to do so and you do to a limited extent.

Personality: I don't feel others.

Soul: When your children are suffering you feel some of their pain in addition to feeling bad for them.

Personality: I guess I do. Should I feel more of their pain?

Soul: If you choose to.

Personality: I think that might be a good thing to do. Then I could better understand what they are going through.

Soul: You would have greater empathy for them if you did so.

Personality: Then I would be a better parent if I felt the way that they did, wouldn't I? I could better identify with them and they could better identify with me.

Soul: There is a difference between feeling their feelings and adopting their feelings. When you feel their feelings you still have your own feelings and you can distinguish between the two, but when you adopt their feelings you begin to live through your children. Is that what you want?

Personality: I would like to be closer to them.

Soul: Having greater empathy for your children by knowing how they feel would bring you closer. Knowing how you feel in response to them and their feelings will still allow you to better understand them and also advise them. Adopting their feelings as your own will cause you to lose touch with yourself. If you do so, you may even attempt to manage their feelings for them.

Personality: Why would I do that?

Soul: You could easily confuse their needs with your own. That could cause you to take action on their behalf or project your needs onto them. Over time, acting in this manner could shift your awareness and sense of well being by focusing too much on them. As a result, you may try to live your life through your children because you would not be meeting your own needs more directly.

Personality: I wouldn't do that.

Soul: You do it now on occasion.

Personality: What do you mean?

Soul: There are certain things that you have not accomplished in your life that you had wanted to. On occasion you push your children to move in those directions hoping that they will accomplish what you have not.

Personality: I want to see them have the opportunities that I didn't.

Soul: You also want to vicariously feel their pride in accomplishing what you chose not to. Appreciate their feelings, but separate theirs from your own.

Personality: How is that done?

Soul: By being aware of your own feelings. You can always check in on another, but return your attention to yourself and your own needs. That will keep you more receptive to what you need to be aware of and they can do the same. At the end of the day, it is all about how you feel. It is up to you to determine how you wish to utilize your feeling nature in order to experience your emotions and everything else for that matter, as completely as you desire. Feel and enjoy what you will because you can.

Discuss and/or Journal

Most people suppress what they feel to avoid feeling deeper pain or discomfort. They are unwilling to experience the depth of their negative feelings. As a result, they feel less love than they could otherwise feel. This predisposition limits our ability to receive love from our soul and limits the affect that our soul can have in our life.

1. What does fear, anger, shame, and sadness feel like to you? How deeply do you experience them?

   _____

   _____

   _____

   _____

2. What do you do when feelings of fear-based emotions arise?

   _____

   _____

   _____

   _____

3. What does love feel like to you? How fully do you feel it?

   _____

   _____

   _____

   _____

4. What steps can you take to allow yourself to feel more?

   _____

   _____

   _____

   _____

---

chapter thirteen

EXPRESS EMOTIONAL FEELINGS
FULLY AND HONESTLY

EXPRESSING OUR EMOTIONAL FEELINGS fully and honestly is a rarity in human relations. It is a path for the courageous few that dare to be emotionally honest and withstand insult and retaliation from the rest of us. It is the path traveled by true leaders who are adept at creating change because emotional honesty facilitates understanding and thus transformation faster than any other human trait. Observing how we conduct ourselves emotionally is an unsurpassed window into our own developmental process.

The emotions that we feel and express are mirrored by the rhythm of our breath whether we are honest with our emotions or not. When we inhale deeply and take in breath we can better feel our emotions because a deep breath helps us to be grounded in the physical. When we take in a big abdominal breath we are not afraid to feel, as compared to taking rapid, shallow breaths when we are frightened. When we exhale we communicate and express ourselves. We may exhale in a long sigh, allowing others to witness our emotional release. Or we may hold our breath, releasing it only when we feel safe enough. Our feelings, just like our breath, cannot be fully expressed if they are not taken in. Is the reverse true, that we cannot fully feel if we do not express our feelings?

When we diminish the expression of our feelings we ultimately reduce what we feel. This occurs because we are not fully processing the feelings we are holding and our system backs up reducing what we can take in. The fluidity of our emotions is thus restricted when we suppress their expression. Over time we create a network of constrictions and dams in the main river of our emotional flow and it stagnates. We are less able to experience more feelings. Nevertheless, life goes on and events in our lives trigger our beliefs. As a result, we experience more feelings. We can only suppress their expression for a while before they build up and erupt or we are forced to create other less explosive outlets for them. These other outlets are the tributaries in our emotional river, which travel away from the intended flow. As such, they are less direct, less true to the intended path. They are less honest expressions of our emotions.

Why do we distort the expression of our emotional feelings? At times we find ourselves in situations where we have the potential of violating another's Basic Rights, particularly when we are angry. More often we are involved in situations where we do not want to be perceived as violating another's Rights or we wish to derive benefit through manipulation. In these circumstances we feel pressured and we tend to express our emotions dishonestly. We may suppress their expression or we may displace one emotion and replace it with another. Regardless of how we distort our emotional expressiveness, we are not being truthful in the process. We are operating from the confines of our coping strategies, in a more subconscious, reactive manner. We do this because we have not yet learned how to feel our love-based emotions and express our fear-based emotions simultaneously.

This is a transitional phase in our emotional evolution as we move towards feeling and expressing love without fear. When we are able to infuse love for ourselves into a fear-provoking situation we develop greater understanding. How is this accomplished? Many of us remain silent when we are fearful. We do not express our fears. We sit with them and allow them to dominate our lives. However, some of us express them. Why? Although at times it is done to foster worry in others or to manipulate, it can also be done to receive help from others. When done for the latter purpose self-love is demonstrated, as we are making a conscious effort to reduce our fearful state. Receiving help to overcome our fears facilitates our understanding and thus our ability to change. It is a loving act that with practice enables us to feel love. In time, as our fears dissipate, we learn to express and share the love that we are feeling.

Soul: I feel your anger radiating all over the place. Are you aware how you are affecting others?

Personality: I didn't realize that anyone could see that I'm angry.

Soul: Others can sense it even when you do your best to hide it. Often it may only affect them on a subconscious level, but that is enough for them to alter their behavior towards you. That is why some of your co-workers have avoided you today.

Personality: I wish it affected my boss that way. It seems to make my difficulties with him even worse.

Soul: His subconscious response to your angry state is different from those of your peers. It causes him to want to push you harder because your anger triggers his anger causing him to become even more aggressive.

Personality: I'll say.

Soul: Why not deal with your anger rather than prolonging this situation?

Personality: I don't want anyone to know that I'm angry.

Soul: Why not?

Personality: It's not professional to be this way in the workplace.

Soul: By not dealing with it you will only prolong the feeling, as it is or it may even build in intensity as you stew over what precipitated it. All the while you will remain ignorant of its cause.

Personality: Can I deal with it quietly so that I can keep it to myself?

Soul: Sure. I am not suggesting that you have a temper tantrum. You can do this at your desk. Allow yourself to feel the emotions throughout your body as fully as you are able to. Start by taking a deep abdominal breath with the intent of feeling your emotions fully. As your feelings emerge, ask yourself why you feel this way. In the process allow yourself to remember when in your childhood you felt similarly. That will help you understand why you feel this way now. Sit down at your desk and try it.

Personality: Okay.

Soul: Re-create the feeling to its full extent and allow the thoughts and memories to come to you.

Personality: That's it! During our meeting this morning my boss unjustly criticized me in front of the whole team. It wasn't fair. It reminded me of all those times that my father criticized me and told me I was STUPID.

Soul: What did you do?

Personality: I just let it happen. I didn't respond. I immediately felt paralyzed like I did when I was a child.

Soul: Who are you angry with?

Personality: My boss, he shouldn't have done that.

Soul: Who else?

Personality: No one else was criticizing me.

Soul: How do you feel now?

Personality: I feel a little better, but I'm still angry. Why did he have to do that in front of the whole team?

Soul: Now that you have had a chance to review the episode, what was he criticizing you about?

Personality: I didn't summarize all the expenses in the manner that had been specified in our plan and so, it was hard to compare our results with our planned expenditures.

Soul: It would seem that the substance of his criticism was valid.

Personality: Yes, but his delivery seemed a bit harsh.

Soul: Why did you take it so personally?

Personality: Probably because I felt as stupid as I did when my father used to criticize me.

Soul: How do you feel now?

Personality: I'm a lot less angry. I don't know why I just didn't own up to my mistake and offer to correct the reports.

Soul: You frequently use one of your coping strategies in which you displace your anger. In this case you blamed your boss rather than being accountable for the mistake. Now that you are taking responsibility for your part in the creation of the episode you have less need to feel angry. However, you are still feeling more anger than you are willing to admit to. Why?

Personality: It's a lot better than it was. I can forget about it now.

Soul: You have become quite accomplished at suppressing your anger.

Personality: I do it by simply forgetting about it, then it doesn't bother me anymore.

Soul: That may be how you experience it, but as long as you do not fully understand and release those angry feelings there will be persistent consequences that are detrimental.

Personality: What do you mean?

Soul: Where do you think the anger goes when you forget about it?

Personality: After I forget about it, the anger no longer exists.

Soul: Do you remember all of those unpleasant memories that you have conveniently forgotten about and placed in your subconscious mind?

Personality: Not exactly, but you keep telling me that they are still there.

Soul: They are. Just because you are no longer consciously aware of them, does not mean that they do not exist. They exist and they continue to affect how you feel and behave. Similarly, the forgotten, suppressed anger still influences your mood and behavior and it will continue to do so until you are able to fully release it from your system.

Personality: How do I know it's there if I no longer experience it?

Soul: Allow it to come back. If it is really gone then you will not become angry. On the other hand, if you have only suppressed it, then you will reexperience it.

Personality: How do I do that?

Soul: Take a deep breath and re-create the experience in your mind once again. If you have truly released all of the anger then after you reexperience the episode in your mind you will not be angry. However, if you are still angry then again, ask yourself why you are feeling this way and what does it remind you of from your childhood.

Personality: I don't think it's going to work this time because I'm feeling pretty good.

Soul: You are simply feeling the way that you normally do. In your normal state, you hold a fair bit of anger and as a result, you are accustomed to it. Believe me, your baseline level of anger is a disturbance that I have to deal with all the time while I am working with you.

Personality: You make it sound like a disease.

Soul: It is, but from your perspective the disease has not yet manifested. From my perspective the disease exists. Unresolved fear-based emotions twist your energy system in ways that impede the flow of your emotional and spiritual energy. Your spiritual energy is just as vital to your health and well being as the flow of blood. Without it, the deprived organ or structure will not function normally and in time the dysfunction will manifest physically in ways that reflect your predispositions. That is one reason why it is important to resolve this type of emotional state.

Personality: I'll give it a try.

Soul: Do it just as before.

Personality: I was right. I'm no longer angry with my boss.

Soul: Explore what you are feeling. Try not to analyze it prematurely. Feel the anger and let the thoughts appear without filtering them so quickly.

Personality: Oh, it's not about my boss anymore. I'm angry with myself for feeling so fearful and not standing up for myself when my father criticized me. I should have told him that he shouldn't treat me so badly. I didn't need him yelling at me so much.

Soul: Don't be too hard on yourself. He was and still is your father. It is hard to treat your parents as though they are equals when you are their child. Unfortunately however, this pattern that you have adopted of suppressing your anger over fear of reprisal has persisted and you replay it in a number of your relationships.

Personality: It happens so fast that I don't even know that I'm doing it.

Soul: That is how subconscious coping strategies work. As your awareness of them grows and you understand what is happening as it is happening, you can take action to abort the old patterns. In this instance, if your conscious awareness was greater, you may have recognized that your boss' behavior was triggering an old response that you had as a result of your father's criticism. If you had recognized that this was happening with your boss this morning, what could you have done differently?

Personality: I could have admitted my mistake and told him that I would redo the reports.

Soul: What if his anger persisted and you felt paralyzed with fear as you did when you were a child?

Personality: I could tell him that I don't appreciate his abusive behavior.

Soul: Maybe his behavior was not as abusive as you think it was. That was your interpretation. You take things personally when some of your painful memories are triggered. Rather than relying on your interpretation of someone else's behavior why not consider disclosing how you feel during the episode?

Personality: You want me to express my feelings to my boss? I work in a professional office. We don't talk about feelings here. We talk about plans and results. Feelings are irrelevant.

Soul: Your feelings certainly reduced your productivity today. You have spent much time preoccupied by this morning's incident. You have revisited it in your mind many times in order to justify displacing your anger by blaming your boss for his behavior. As a result, you have been distracted and you may want to check some of your work because you inadvertently made a few more mistakes. Some of your co-workers also needed some advice from you, but they were afraid to consult you because of your moodiness, further reducing the productivity in your workplace. All in all I would suggest to you that your feelings are very relevant even in your professional office.

Personality: What good would come of it if I discussed my feelings about this morning with my boss?

Soul: It might clear the air between the two of you. You could better understand his side of the issue and he could better understand you. If you understood one another better your working relationship might improve. If it does not after several honest attempts on your part, then maybe you should seek employment elsewhere.

Personality: Maybe I'll take your advice, but not today. I'm still a little raw from this morning. I think I'll wait until I'm in a better state. Speaking to him at this time can easily cause me to overreact.

Soul: Waiting will also allow you time to collect your thoughts and review the episode again with your new insights.

Personality: I'll bet this will significantly reduce the level of anger that I normally experience.

Soul: It will to some degree, but you use anger for a number of purposes.

Personality: I get angry, I don't use anger.

Soul: Do you remember when you became angry with your subordinate when he suggested a change in the format of one of your reports?

Personality: He has no knowledge concerning the information within that report. His suggestion was stupid.

Soul: Why did it bother you so? Was he challenging your authority?

Personality: I have significant seniority over him. He's no threat and his suggestion was plain dumb.

Soul: So you decided to treat him the same way that your father treated you. You thought that if you started to show him your anger he would retreat, as you did when you were a child. You learned that tactic from your father. You used your anger as a form of manipulation to intimidate him.

Personality: Well maybe a little.

Soul: Maybe a lot. Were you really angry with him for making the suggestion?

Personality: Not really. It was nothing more than an annoyance now that I think about it.

Soul: It was an opportunity for you to be dominant. He was simply an innocent bystander in your attempt to balance your life's ledger between being dominant and subordinate.

Personality: I never looked at it that way.

Soul: You also use anger to bolster your sense of courage. When you feel that you have been treated unfairly you sometimes wait until you are angry enough before you confront the offender. Remember the last time you confronted your boss. You did so after stewing about an issue for days and when you felt strong enough you confronted him. You did get some satisfaction engaging him in that way, but it had the effect of reinforcing a pattern of interaction between the two of you that is nonproductive. At times you like the feeling of anger because it is a powerful emotional feeling that makes you feel strong.

Personality: Feeling that way does help me to stand up for myself.

Soul: You can stand up for your Rights honestly without trying to manipulate others or giving yourself a sense of false courage. Anger used in these circumstances exposes your underlying sense of fear. You put anger in play in an attempt to obtain the outcome that you desire. You can speak from your heart and even be passionate about what you believe without being angry. You will find that speaking in this manner would allow others to hear you better. Speaking out of anger generally begets anger or causes others to become less receptive. In either case they will not hear you as well.

Personality: You make it sound so simple, as if I have control over my emotions. Events happen so fast that I get swept away and only when it's over can I sort out what has happened and as I have just seen even my own understanding after the fact is limited.

Soul: Remember that how you think creates how you feel and you decide how you think. You have the ability to slow down the process and work through it. By understanding yourself more thoroughly you will come to understand your coping strategies and pay-offs and then you can decide to think differently. It is not a process that is learned overnight, but the effort will produce noticeable results. If you do not come to understand your underlying painful beliefs, your feelings and behaviors will continue to be triggered subconsciously. Life would make more sense to you if you would be more honest with your feelings.

Personality: I don't want to be exposed in that way. It would be too embarrassing. I would feel ashamed.

Soul: You are fairly transparent. Most people already know when you are feeling guilty or ashamed. Others can recognize how you are feeling quite easily.

Personality: No. How could they? I hide it and I don't discuss it.

Soul: You walk around slumped over with rounded shoulders. Your eyes are glued to the floor and your face looks solemn. You appear as though you are going to implode. When you do talk, you do so quietly and at times you even mumble. You create this drama to avoid dealing with your belief that you are unworthy and undeserving.

Personality: It's that obvious?

Soul: I try to reach you before you get too mired in that state, but you are usually unwilling to receive me or anyone else for that matter. After your self-imposed exile, you use another of your coping strategies to emerge.

Personality: Are you trying to make me feel more guilty?

Soul: Not at all. Your coping strategies are simply the beliefs, feelings, and behaviors that you subconsciously choose to employ in different situations. These are old patterns that you have created mainly in your childhood in your attempt to meet your needs and gain approval, love, etc. You created these strategies to help yourself, but many of them are outdated. You always have the choice to create alternative beliefs and feel and act differently. I recognize that you are doing the best that you can. If you accepted yourself to a greater extent, you would not feel guilty about employing your coping strategies.

Personality: You're kidding?

Soul: Not at all. You would see your coping strategies for what they are—a means of escaping your present situation, which conjures up memories that you would rather avoid. You may judge these actions as bad or wrong, but you are doing nothing more than learning your lessons in the order of your choosing.

Personality: How does practicing avoidance lead to learning my lessons?

Soul: You have a considerable portfolio of coping strategies. They in turn protect you from experiencing your deeper painful beliefs. When you do attempt to understand yourself you generally select one area to focus on that has arisen in your conscious awareness. By doing so, you leave the remaining coping strategies in place. You have been working on some of your coping strategies related to anger and criticism. That is why you are becoming more aware of the episodes that have been occurring with your boss. These episodes are designed to show you the relationship between your attitudes concerning the criticism received from your father and your current perceptions. As difficult as it may be, consider your boss as a teacher in this regard, but recognize that he also has his lessons to learn. You are actually helping each other and from that perspective you are also his teacher. While you have been working on coping strategies related to anger you remain largely unaware of your other coping strategies, like those that help you deal with shame and guilt.

Personality: Maybe I shouldn't know about these other coping strategies.

Soul: Becoming aware of them is nothing more than recognizing that you have needs and wants and understanding that you attempt to fill them in a manner that is convoluted. Simply acknowledge that the coping strategy exists. The events that occur in your life will remind you when it is time to actively work on them.

Personality: How does that occur?

Soul: I am aware of your needs.

Personality: When do I get to shame and guilt?

Soul: For you it will not be long after you better understand anger, but if you would like to get a jump on the process you can begin to understand why you use sadness to replace shame and guilt.

Personality: I don't use sadness. I become sad when I feel ashamed or guilty.

Soul: Why?

Personality: Because I think of myself as inadequate or I feel bad for having done something wrong.

Soul: Why do you feel the need to complicate your feelings of shame and guilt with another feeling? If you have judged yourself or your actions to be bad then why must you feel and express sadness?

Personality: Because you're supposed to be sad if you've been bad.

Soul: Who taught you that? Why not simply make amends when required and move on? Or is something else motivating you?

Personality: I'm not aware of what that would be.

Soul: You will learn that you have adopted that strategy as a way of seeking support and forgiveness. You use sadness as a self-imposed punishment in the hope that it will engender pity and diminish angry reprisals from others.

Personality: And you're going to teach me to not do that?

Soul: You will learn as a matter of course. It is all part of life's lessons.

Personality: Is there an easier way?

Soul: It is as easy as you make it. How quickly you learn these lessons is entirely up to you.

Personality: I choose to understand them quickly.

Soul: I have seen no evidence of that.

Personality: Well that's the way I would like it to be. What do I have to do to have it that way?

Soul: Become less fearful.

Personality: Less fearful of what?

Soul: Of uncovering your painful beliefs.

Personality: But they are painful. Everyone fears pain.

Soul: They need not be painful. You generated most of these beliefs as a very young child and therefore they are childish. Many of them are unreasonable and unnecessary now and you will be able to perceive that. Be willing to reevaluate them.

Personality: If I adopt this attitude, how will that allow me to learn my lessons faster?

Soul: You will have less need to use your coping strategies. You will be able to more easily let go of them because you will have less fear of breaching the barrier that they create. By having less fear of inspecting your underlying painful beliefs you will be able to perceive yourself more easily with less pain. This will allow you to accept yourself for what you are.

Personality: What about my feelings and expressions of anger, shame, sadness, and so on? They will still be with me.

Soul: They are a part of your coping strategies. When you have no need for your coping strategies, you will have no need to experience them. They are nothing more than manifestations of fear. Anger is the fear of violation, shame is the fear of being seen as unworthy, and sadness is the fear of having to be without. Recognize these fears as tools that you have created and as such you can discard them.

Personality: Life with less fear, what would I be like?

Soul: You would be more like me.

Personality: I don't know what that would be like.

Soul: You will when you have less fear.

Personality: Then as long as I hold onto my fear I will maintain my identity just the way it is.

Soul: Yes that is in part why you do so. Fear is an impediment to change. It is your way of maintaining the status quo. As long as you fear change you will remain as you are.

Personality: Fearful.

Discuss and/or Journal

Expressing our emotions allows others to see how we feel. That inhibits many of us, causing us to suppress the expression of our feelings. Displacing what we feel is another strategy many of us use to discharge our feelings. We learn to feel less, so that we have less emotion to suppress or displace. This outcome satisfies our personality, not our soul.

1. Are you honest with your emotions? Do you express what you feel?

_____

_____

_____

_____

2. How do you appear to others when you are angry, sad, or feeling ashamed?

_____

_____

_____

_____

3. Why do you become angry?

_____

_____

_____

_____

4. How do you use anger?

_____

_____

_____

_____

_____

chapter fourteen

CREATE HEALTHY SEXUAL RELATIONS

Oᴜʀ ᴜʀɢᴇ ꜰᴏʀ sᴇxᴜᴀʟ activity is the culmination of a number of our needs. We have a need to participate in physical activities, utilizing all of our physicality and a need to experience sensual activities that give us pleasure. We have a need to be grounded in the physical that can be fostered through sexual relations. We have a need to feel and express our emotional feelings, which can also be realized through this activity. Healthy sexual relations can fulfill many of our needs and even create a vehicle to fulfill some of our deeper desires.

As human beings we have the potential to operate at many levels, but we often are not consciously aware of them. The behaviors, feelings, and beliefs that we do experience often have deeper correlations that are obscured by our more superficial needs and wants. There is a spectrum of sexual relations that in its most primal form results in physical orgasm that provides for a release of sexual tension. In its most profound form, sexual relations bridge form and spirit and can become a spiritual act providing a gateway to a higher union. We cannot choose to experience what we are not aware of, therefore we also have a need to understand.

We are aware of and understand the myriad of abuses surrounding sexual relations. Despite the fact that many of us remain ignorant of its vast potential, we instinctively recognize the sanctity of this activity. As a result, we are sickened when the virtuousness of lovemaking is replaced by violation, such as child molestation or rape. We are disturbed by other violations, as when sexual activities are used to coerce, or for some other gain or to prevent loss. These Basic Right violations stem from our coping strategies. They distort the meaning of sexual union and result in unhealthy consequences because the fulfillment of these wants is based in fear not love.

When does sexual activity become lovemaking? When only love is involved. In its simplest form this occurs when the needs of all participants are met without any Basic Right violations including ones that are self-inflicted. The transition from sex to love, like all change, is sparked by our personalities needs and our soul's desire and fueled by our free will. It is a choice that we make to open our hearts, despite our heightened sense of vulnerability when we are intimate with another. How often do we make this choice only to retreat and close ourselves off from love once again? It is a common path that we tend to traverse many times before yielding to love that is less tentative and conditional. It is a choice we hope to make because we sense the promise of what it will bring.

Lovemaking has cosmic correlations and consequences. Making love with an open heart and an intention to feel fully, emotionally and with all of our physical and energetic senses, creates an expansiveness in our being. The space that is created is filled with the love energy that is associated with our state of increased arousal, expectation, and consciousness. Lovemaking creates a union with another and a merging, physically, energetically, and spiritually. By remaining firmly grounded in our own physicality we can cause our expanded state to become focused within the core of our being. This sets the stage for love to explode throughout our being just as love infused us with consciousness in the beginning. Lovemaking in this way is healing, cleansing, and thus transformative.

Many of us tend to participate in only a small segment of the spectrum of sexual relations. We can partake in more if we choose to explore.

Soul: Now you are having some other feelings.

Personality: What are you talking about?

Soul: You are experiencing your sexual needs.

Personality: It's been a little while.

Soul: That should result in a nice evening. Enjoy.

Personality: I didn't expect that response from you.

Soul: Why not?

Personality: I keep equating you with my religious teachings. I'm uncomfortable discussing sexual matters with you.

Soul: Why?

Personality: These are very private, sensitive issues. I don't like discussing them with you or anyone else for that matter.

Soul: Do you know why?

Personality: Because these matters are personal, they aren't supposed to be discussed.

Soul: Where did that rule come from?

Personality: It's just how it is.

Soul: How does this topic make you feel?

Personality: It's embarrassing.

Soul: What is embarrassing about it?

Personality: I was always taught to avoid the subject.

Soul: Why?

Personality: Sex was never discussed when I was a child. Whenever it came up on TV and we were all watching there was silence. I could sense everyone's discomfort. I was left with the sense that sex shouldn't be discussed.

Soul: There are many reasons why you feel guilt and shame in regard to sex. It may be helpful for you to understand some of your beliefs that are triggered concerning this activity. When you have sex now, how does it feel?

Personality: It feels good.

Soul: It could feel even better.

Personality: Now you're going to give me lessons on sexuality?

Soul: If you would like, but you may want to consider simply talking with your partner about your respective needs and wants.

Personality: What do you mean our needs and wants?

Soul: There is no reason why the two of you cannot communicate more directly so that both of you can maximize the pleasurable experience. The two of you have learned to help one another bring greater enjoyment to other activities in your lives. Consider greater communication in this area.

Personality: We're too busy to stop and talk.

Soul: You need not stop.

Personality: Talking would break the mood.

Soul: It may enhance the mood.

Personality: What are you actually suggesting?

Soul: That you make your needs and wants known and that you determine your partner's needs and wants. You can even do this at a time when you are not having sex or making love. Why not try it? It may alleviate much of your shame once you move beyond your fears.

Personality: Well maybe I should do that.

Soul: When you use the word should, it suggests that you are still somewhat resistant. Do you understand the source of your resistance?

Personality: Yes I do. This is an embarrassing topic. I told you that it wasn't a topic that was discussed much.

Soul: You have already developed a level of intimacy with your partner. I am only suggesting that you share your thoughts on the topic. Why would that cause you embarrassment?

Personality: It just does.

Soul: Why?

Personality: I fear being embarrassed.

Soul: You fear being criticized, rejected, and not being good enough. That is what underlies your fear of embarrassment.

Personality: I do not.

Soul: That is why you avoid the topic.

Personality: Why would I fear being rejected?

Soul: Your society glamorizes sexuality and places a high standard on sexual performance for both men and women. The lack of openness about sex creates a situation that allows for much distortion and manipulation from many sources.

Personality: Religion makes me feel guilty and ashamed about sex and advertisers prey upon my lack of self-confidence, and make me question whether or not I have sex appeal, or if I'm performing well enough. Is it any wonder why I don't want to discuss sex?

Soul: Between your parental influences and those of society it is understandable why you feel the way that you do.

Personality: Good, so we don't have to discuss it any more?

Soul: Keeping it buried only keeps you from perceiving the truth. However, if you wish, we can discuss it when you are ready.

Personality: What truths are you referring to?

Soul: Truths about your fears concerning sex.

Personality: You're not going to expose me to anyone, are you?

Soul: We will keep this between us.

Personality: Okay.

Soul: How do you feel emotionally when you are having sex?

Personality: I enjoy it, but I also feel like I'm doing something that I'm not supposed to be doing.

Soul: What does that feel like?

Personality: It feels like I'm being disobedient.

Soul: Does that make you feel guilty or ashamed?

Personality: A little of both.

Soul: How does it make you feel during sex?

Personality: I give in to the pleasurable feelings that I'm having at the time. If I'm going to be judged as being bad afterwards, then I might as well really enjoy it and so I do.

Soul: Then do you feel guilty for having felt so good during sex?

Personality: Not too much anymore.

Soul: Was anyone hurt in the process?

Personality: Nobody was hurt. What are you referring to?

Soul: Having sex. Did you take advantage of another? Did you violate anyone's Basic Rights or yours in the process?

Personality: No. I guess I feel guilty because I believe that I'm not supposed to want sex too often or maybe I shouldn't want it at all.

Soul: When you were younger, having sex made you feel as though you were being bad. In part, you believed that the act of sex was an act of rebellion against those that treated sex as a forbidden act.

Personality: What are you talking about?

Soul: Your parents were very strict in their considerations about sex and promiscuity.

Personality: I remember when my father caught my older sister Abby and her boyfriend kissing downstairs. I thought my father was going to shoot her boyfriend.

Soul: What do you remember?

Personality: My father was pacing in the living room and scolding my mother for allowing them to be downstairs unsupervised. He was thinking of an excuse to go downstairs.

Soul: What were you doing?

Personality: Nobody noticed me. They were too fixated on the situation at hand. I just sat quietly and watched.

Soul: What else did your parents have to say?

Personality: My father was saying that it isn't right for a sixteen year-old girl to be unsupervised when she is with a boy because boys that age only have one thing on their minds. It wasn't something he approved of for his daughter.

Soul: What happened?

Personality: He finally decided to go downstairs after it had become quiet for too long. My sister had been playing music, but it had stopped. My father was convinced they were too preoccupied with each other to realize so he went downstairs without any excuse. I could hear my father in his angriest voice tell the boy to leave immediately and never come back and for my sister to go to her room. She was punished for a month.

Soul: What did Abby do?

Personality: She rushed upstairs. She looked embarrassed. She wouldn't look at me or my mother. I didn't see her again until the next day.

Soul: Did you ever discuss the matter with your sister?

Personality: The next day she told me that it was worth it and that she would do it again, as soon as she could, but not where she could be caught.

Soul: What did you think about the whole occurrence?

Personality: I didn't understand everything that happened and it was never brought up again, at least in front of me. I believed that whatever she was doing must have felt very good even though she wasn't supposed to be doing it.

Soul: That mindset heightens your sexual experience by creating a greater sense of adventure. This payoff is another one of the reasons that you would rather not discuss sexual matters or take any time to reexamine your beliefs. You have used your feelings of guilt to your own advantage.

Personality: Why would I feel guilty about being disobedient if no one is going to find out about it anyway?

Soul: It assists you in enjoying sex more. As long as you feel guilty after it is over you believe that you are punishing yourself. You have deemed that this punishment is sufficient so that you can absolve yourself of the act of sex and enjoying it. It is just another example of how you use guilt.

Personality: If what you're saying is true, then I've already worked through it with good results.

Soul: You have not worked through it. You have subconsciously rationalized your position in order to fulfill some of your needs. You are just playing out another coping strategy, but again, the impact of your parental influences has waned over time. There are more significant issues that you do not want to confront.

Personality: Whatever reasons or issues there may be doesn't much matter to me. I am able to make love and that is what I need.

Soul: Mainly it has allowed you to have sex, not make love.

Personality: What are you talking about?

Soul: Your sexual activities have as much to do with fear, as they do love.

Personality: How can that be?

Soul: Some of your motivation for participating in sexual activities is fear-based. You still have a number of issues to work through that come to light in regard to sexual activity and intimacy. Sex becomes a temporary fix to quell some of those uncomfortable feelings that develop more often than you are willing to become consciously aware of. That is why you prefer to call it lovemaking because that term fits better with your idea about how to create a closer bond.

Personality: It is lovemaking.

Soul: It is to some extent, but you make love in part, as a result of your fear of potential loss. You often initiate sexual relations when you are feeling less accepted or when you feel that your partner is more distant. It is not as truthful a state as you are capable of achieving. These factors contribute to your resistance to discussing sexual matters.

Personality: Is there more?

Soul: Developing greater sexual intimacy creates a heightened sense of vulnerability. Your fears of rejection and criticism cause you to avoid communicating with your partner, before, during, and after this activity. This fear is magnified when you are feeling less accepted or more distant from your partner. As a result, you avoid developing what you seek, greater intimacy.

Personality: It's a vicious circle. If I bring up the subject and mention my needs and wants then I could be made to feel ashamed, as if I'm fixated on some sexual need or fantasy especially if my partner feels threatened by the conversation.

Soul: You would not feel that way if you believe that your sexual needs and wants are reasonable.

Personality: Maybe so, but my partner may feel that I'm not being satisfied when we make love and that I'm being critical.

Soul: The discussion can center around mutual needs and wants, not yours alone.

Personality: Yes, but if I'm bringing it up then it means that I'm the one that is less satisfied.

Soul: Or the one that is most interested in developing greater intimacy.

Personality: And that would imply that my partner is less interested in developing greater intimacy.

Soul: Are your fears about acceptance and abandonment emerging?

Personality: To some extent, but really, what if it's true that my partner isn't interested in developing greater intimacy?

Soul: Then that is what you may discover if it is true, but what if your partner is simply as embarrassed as you are?

Personality: Then the conversation won't go very far.

Soul: Then you can have another conversation at a later date after you have broken the ice. Until the two of you make a change in how you approach sex your fears and those of your partner's will continue to limit your ability to make love.

Personality: I still believe that we are making love.

Soul: You could participate in lovemaking to a greater degree. Accept where you are at in this area of your life and make changes if you choose.

Personality: What do you mean by degree of lovemaking.

Soul: The manner in which you communicate with your partner is only one way that demonstrates the degree to which you make love. The degree to which you make love also depends upon your intent, the other actions that you take, and my involvement.

Personality: How so?

Soul: There are many ways in which lovemaking occurs based upon how your attitudes impact the situation, physically, emotionally, mentally, and spiritually. For instance, when your intent is to bring another life into the world it becomes a spiritual event in addition to a physical event because you are making way for a soul to enter. This can create a feeling of love that transcends that of the physical act of having sex.

Personality: So sex becomes lovemaking when someone conceives.

Soul: Often not. Most people are not aware enough to perceive and experience conception. Oftentimes there is not an intent to have children, even when there is conception. Therefore, the act associated with conception often resembles sex as far as many participants recognize.

Personality: So lovemaking rarely happens in your way of thinking.

Soul: It certainly does happen even outside of conception.

Personality: When does it happen?

Soul: It happens in degrees, when you allow deeper feelings to emerge. A deeper feeling state can develop during lovemaking when you become more grounded in the physical and pay closer attention to all of your bodily sensations with a desire to feel more. Lovemaking is further advanced when you communicate more of your needs to your partner, desire to know and meet your partner's needs, and when you allow my involvement with less filtering. When your intention is to merge with your partner physically, emotionally, mentally, and spiritually, the physical act of sex is transformed into more. The act of sexual union is one path that can allow us to experience All That Is. It is one way that we search for wholeness.

Personality: Is that why you hang around?

Soul: I am always around and within you to the extent that you permit. However my intent is to participate more fully.

Personality: How can that help me?

Soul: I allow you to feel your partner and All That Is more completely. My feeling sense far exceeds your own. When you appreciate what I can feel to a greater extent you have a better sense of what your partner is feeling. It works the same way for you. I can allow you to feel more of yourself beyond the physical. By feeling more of yourself, All That Is, and more of what your partner is feeling your experience can become much more expansive and more fulfilling. I am your conduit to feeling more love.

Personality: You always keep coming back to feelings. Why don't you just enjoy the sex? You don't seem to suffer from any guilt.

Soul: I do experience the feelings associated with sex, but the physical act of sex itself lacks the intensity of lovemaking. My presence can help you experience more.

Personality: You use every chance you get, don't you? Is there nothing sacred?

Soul: Making love is and I can help you experience it.

Discuss and/or Journal

Sexual activity and lovemaking are part of a wide spectrum of activities. Some of those activities include behaviors that violate our Basic Rights.

1. Do you violate another's Basic Rights when you are having sex? If so, which ones?

_____

_____

_____

2. Do you violate your own Basic Rights when you are having sex? If so, which ones?

_____

_____

_____

3. What coping strategies do you use when you are having sex?

_____

_____

_____

4. Do you practice lovemaking? How so?

_____

_____

_____

5. Do you intend that your soul be a part of your lovemaking?

_____

_____

_____

_____

chapter fifteen

TRUST INNER GUIDANCE FROM AN
INTUITIVE FEELING SENSE

Intuition is a gut level feeling sense. It is not a mental process, but what we feel at this level can make its way into our conscious awareness, which enables us to think about it. Where does the feeling sense of intuition come from? How does this sense register upon our bodies? How can we trust something that we understand so poorly and that for so many of us seems so random an occurrence? Is this why so many of us resist or dismiss this sense?

Our bodies receive many sensory inputs. We are all aware of our five physical senses of sight, hearing, touch, smell, and taste. If we choose we can limit our points of contact with the world around us to these five senses. Alternatively we can choose to sense what is happening in our environment by utilizing our energy fields, which also confer a feeling sense. They funnel energetic information into us at the level of our abdomen. Unfortunately, that information remains subconscious to most of us. Therefore, these fields and the information they transmit are easy to dismiss because the vast majority of us are not consciously aware of them. Relatively few of us perceive these fields or what they transmit with sufficient clarity or reliability to learn to depend upon them.

Most of us have gotten this far in life without any practical knowledge of or reliance upon these fields. We have had no reason to pursue an understanding of them. Others have a tremendous reliance upon the information they derive from them. These individuals may have been endowed with a feeling nature strong enough for this faculty to be present from birth or to emerge naturally in early childhood or they have developed it out of need. Why would a person need to develop such a sense? If we fear for our safety and security we rely upon whatever means we can to determine our current level of risk. We become wary and watchful relying upon more than sight and sound. Our feelers are extended in an effort to sense danger before it is upon us and when we do sense it we may feel our gut tighten or a prickly sensation on our skin. This is one way that our intuitive sense communicates with us. It acts as a sentinel and the better we are grounded in the physical, the better it serves us.

Just as visual or auditory cues can trigger a belief that we are in danger so can these intuitive sensations. Intuition is not an emotional feeling, but it can cause them to emerge when certain of our beliefs are triggered. In addition, the more we have learned to rely upon intuition the more we have learned to expand our feeling nature in general and thus feel more of everything, including our emotions. This is why feeling individuals tend to be more intuitive and individuals that prefer to think rather than feel are less so. In societies where rational thought is more valued than feelings, it is no surprise that intuitive feelings are easily dismissed. Fortunately, even in a society that does not value this sense for what it has to offer, some people have learned to enhance and use their intuitive sense to the practical benefit of themselves and others.

We all are capable of developing this faculty provided we wish to utilize our feeling nature in this way. Why would we want to? Our intuitive sense can do more than signal danger. Using our minds we can check our intuitive sense to inform us if a choice we are about to make feels right for us. Our soul can provide inner guidance by communicating with us through our basic intuitive sense. The response may be a sense of calm or peace or a feeling of electricity. We each can learn the language of this form of communication for it has individual variations. We each can derive the benefits conferred by this sense.

For many of us in our present state, our intuitive feeling sense is too subtle for us to perceive and we do not know how to strengthen it. We may believe that it is a gift for some rather than a Right for all. We deny ourselves the possibility of possessing it and never dream that it can become a reliable sense for us to use as a practical tool in life. This line of reasoning is part of a coping strategy, born of fear. In part, it is the fear of becoming more grounded in the physical and feeling more. Becoming more grounded in the physical and learning to feel more coupled with a desire to use our feeling nature for this purpose is the surest path to becoming more intuitive. Who would not want the peace of mind that can be derived by trusting our decisions and managing our lives? Unless of course we would rather live in fear.

Soul: Are you having trouble with your boss again?

Personality: He's crazy. He makes no sense.

Soul: What are you referring to?

Personality: His decisions are illogical and inconsistent. I can't figure him out. How am I supposed to do things right if there are no rules to follow?

Soul: What rules would you like?

Personality: Rules that will help me to determine, which of these candidates are right for the jobs that we have to fill. He is constantly overriding my decisions even though I've picked the best people after reviewing their credentials.

Soul: How have you arrived at your decision?

Personality: I made a list of all of the job requirements. Then I reviewed their applications and put checks next to the requirements that they had accomplished in their past jobs. Then I interviewed them to make sure that what I checked was correct. I determined if they had some experience regarding the unchecked requirements in some other way, then I added up all of the checks to see who the best candidates were.

Soul: What did your boss do?

Personality: He looked at my reports and then interviewed the candidates. After he finished he told me which of the candidates he would hire.

Soul: What is the problem?

Personality: He often chooses people that don't have the most checks. Some people that he chooses have very few checks.

Soul: What are his reasons?

Personality: He says that he has a good feeling about those people and that I should sometimes go with my gut.

Soul: Maybe you should.

Personality: That's illogical.

Soul: Why?

Personality: It isn't a rational approach.

Soul: No it is not.

Personality: See I told you so.

Soul: Just because his approach is not rational does not mean that it is incorrect or not effective.

Personality: What if he's wrong?

Soul: What if he is right?

Personality: He better be.

Soul: Why?

Personality: If he isn't right, then how will he justify his decision?

Soul: How would you justify your decision if your choice did not work out well?

Personality: I would be armed with factual information that any rational person could evaluate. Even if I'm wrong, I have at least followed a logical process.

Soul: Why would that matter? Your methodology would have produced an undesirable outcome.

Personality: But at least it was rational.

Soul: It may make you less confidant in your future decisions if you based your hiring on the same methodology.

Personality: Nothing works a hundred percent.

Soul: Then why criticize the approach your boss uses? Is it ineffective?

Personality: His choices seem to work out fairly well.

Soul: Even the ones that had fewer checks?

Personality: Some of them have worked out the best, but he's not a hundred percent either.

Soul: Few things are when you are dealing with people. So what is it that really bothers you about his methodology?

Personality: I don't understand how he does it. How am I supposed to choose the same candidates that my boss does, if his methodology is incomprehensible to me?

Soul: What you do may be necessary so that the correct candidates are chosen. Your boss first reviews your reports. After all someone needs to verify that the information is correct.

Personality: But even when the information is correct, it doesn't carry that much weight in his decision.

Soul: Does your boss simply dismiss your report.

Personality: No, he considers it.

Soul: Even so, you do not like the fact that he uses other factors in addition to your report to make his decisions.

Personality: That's true, but I want to be able to do what he does and I don't understand how he does it.

Soul: What is it that you do not understand?

Personality: I don't understand what he is feeling that allows him to override the facts. I interview the candidates too, but I don't get any feelings about them.

Soul: What do you get?

Personality: I get the facts. I check the details of their history and I try to see if their experience and skill match the requirements.

Soul: Then your focus is mainly fact based. Why would you expect to derive feelings about the candidates if your exploration is only factual in nature? Do you ever ask yourself during one of your interviews how you feel about the person?

Personality: No, I'm too busy collecting my data.

Soul: Maybe you should take some time in the interview to determine how you feel about the candidate.

Personality: What if I don't get any feelings?

Soul: You may not.

Personality: Why?

Soul: Even if you did get a feeling one way or the other would you trust it if it was in conflict with your data?

Personality: That would be hard for me to do.

Soul: Your boss does.

Personality: He didn't collect the data or develop this methodology. It is easy for him to dismiss my data.

Soul: Maybe you should view your data the way that your boss does, as one aspect of the evaluation. If you do you may be more open to receive feelings about the candidates.

Personality: Why?

Soul: You are so invested in your way of working through this process that you are resistant to other approaches. You are also blocked by your fear.

Personality: Fear of what?

Soul: You fear being criticized for making the wrong choice without having what you believe is adequate documentation. You fear trusting your feelings and possibly having to make a choice between the data and your feelings, which you cannot support rationally. As a result, you short-circuit the process.

Personality: How do I do that?

Soul: You limit your feeling nature by escaping into the safe confines of your head and you rely solely on analyzing and processing information. That is your comfort zone. In so doing you cut off your feelings to avoid potential conflict.

Personality: I'm not aware that I do that.

Soul: Just like your other coping strategies, it is your preprogrammed, automatic, subconscious response.

Personality: Why do I do it?

Soul: Fear of criticism. This is just another manifestation. Can you see your payoff?

Personality: I don't trust my feelings so I avoid having them and potentially being wrong. If I choose incorrectly using my approach, I believe my methodology is correct and that is my defense.

Soul: Precisely. If you would like to select the same candidates that your boss does, then you must operate differently. How does that make you feel?

Personality: It's frightening. I could make mistakes and be criticized for it without being able to adequately defend myself.

Soul: What do you think your defense accomplishes? Your boss views it as an indication that you are rigid and set in your ways. Your peers see you as stubborn because your boss has given you the latitude to use your intuition to override the data, but you persist in your single-minded approach. You are maintaining a defensive posture when it is unnecessary. You have been given the opportunity to do things differently. Your boss is supporting you. No one is attacking you.

Personality: They will if I'm wrong and I recommend hiring the wrong person.

Soul: Your boss presently overrides your recommendations regularly and no one is berating you.

Personality: You're right, it isn't so bad. Maybe I should just continue as I am. I am receiving a reasonable paycheck.

Soul: You are being presented with a risk-free opportunity to try a new way and learn in the process. Would you rather be forced to do things differently?

Personality: That sounds like a threat.

Soul: It is just the way of life, actions and reactions. You are being encouraged to move forward with your life.

Personality: Is this your doing?

Soul: You said that you wanted to be able to do what your boss does. I am working on your behalf to assist you in accomplishing what you desire.

Personality: You've picked a fine way to play genie.

Soul: That was my choice. I have free will too, but on a different level. However, my choice was in response to your desire.

Personality: Thanks a lot.

Soul: You are welcome.

Personality: I meant that sarcastically.

Soul: I know.

Personality: How do I work out of this jam?

Soul: This is not an obstacle. You are being presented with an opportunity to learn how to exercise your feeling nature in another way.

Personality: But I don't know how to.

Soul: The payoffs are considerable. Are you willing to learn?

Personality: I guess I have no choice in the matter.

Soul: You are really finding this difficult. It was not hard for you to do as a small child.

Personality: So what happened to me.

Soul: Your parents wanted you to justify your actions logically, mentally. That process was reinforced in school, with friends, your closer relationships, and in the workplace. You learned to rely on thinking rather than feeling in your attempts to justify yourself. You and many others in your life preferred that approach because actions could be articulated and judged as being right or wrong. It was harder to assign tangible value or correctness to feelings. Your new boss is different in this way. He understands the value of using feelings in addition to rational processes in making decisions. He has had success relying more on his hunches than on the facts at times, particularly when his decisions are about people, where there are so many intangibles.

Personality: But he can't justify his decisions.

Soul: Sure he can. He can simply say that he felt this way or that way about it and offer reasons for why he felt the way that he did. His approach is different, but his feelings are just as valid as your data. In fact his feelings about the candidates often lead him to discover other facts, which may lend support to his feelings, facts that your methodology would not have uncovered. These factors may be more important in discerning the likelihood for success.

Personality: His process seems so random. There is not enough structure to it. I don't know how to implement it in any systematic manner.

Soul: The approach is more fluid, just like feelings. Your boss pays attention to the changing pace of the dialogue and how the candidate accelerates and decelerates with the different topics and their relevance to the job.

Personality: That's it?

Soul: No there is much more. He develops a feel for what motivates the candidate by sensing their enthusiasm. He is accomplished at connecting at an emotional level. The feelings that are then generated within him cause him to decide one way or the other about the candidates. He does this with the job requirements in mind and senses how well the person will do in the job by understanding how well they will enjoy it.

Personality: That's why he sometimes leaves the interview so excited.

Soul: Yes, he is excited because he has sensed the excitement in the individual and how well their aptitudes fit with the demands of the job. When there is a strong match he is able to easily detect it. Because he develops an emotional rapport with the person he is interviewing he feels their excitement. He does that outside of work as well, which helps him make decisions that are right for him. This capability would also help you determine which decisions feel right for you.

Personality: It feels like I need to give this method a try.

Discuss and/or Journal

Our gut-level, intuitive sense can be an invaluable tool that aids us in our ability to reason. For many people, however, this sense seems too mysterious a phenomenon to learn to use, improve upon, and trust.

1. Are you more of a feeling or thinking person?

_____

_____

_____

2. How much do you rely on intuition in making decisions?

_____

_____

_____

3. When you receive an intuitive feeling, do you act on it?

_____

_____

_____

4. Have you ever received a strong intuitive feeling and decided not to follow it? If so, did you later wish that you had?

_____

_____

_____

5. What is the source of your intuitive feelings?

_____

_____

_____

_____

Part IV

Basic Right III

I. The right to exist as a human being in the physical world.

| Accept and Respect Yourself | Be Grounded in the Physical | Feel Safe and Secure | Meet Your Material Needs in a Reasonable Manner | Operate with Healthy Boundaries | Feel Vital, Participate in Physical Activities, and Nurture Yourself |

II. The right to experience physical sensations and to feel and express emotional and intuitive feelings.

| Experience and Enjoy Sensual Activities | Feel Full Range of Emotional Feelings | Express Emotional Feelings Fully and Honestly | Create Healthy Sexual Relations | Trust Inner Guidance from an Intuitive Feeling Sense |

III. The right to think, choose, and create beliefs about yourself and the world around you.

| Form Personal Beliefs and Be Accountable for Your Attitudes | Create and Easily Accept Change | Think Clearly, Reason Effectively, and Make Decisions | Act with Confidence, a Sense of Purpose, and without Fear of Taking Risks |

IV. The right to bring love into the world, to accept it for yourself, and to give it to others.

V. The right to have personal truths and to test those truths for Truth.

VI. The right to envision the purpose of your love in the world.

VII. The right to know and manifest your soul's wisdom.

VIII. The right to accept yourself beyond space and time.

IX. The right to accept yourself as part of an evolving greater whole.

X. The right to spiritualize matter and manifest the higher purpose of humanity.

chapter sixteen

FORM PERSONAL BELIEFS AND BE ACCOUNTABLE FOR YOUR ATTITUDES

WE BEGIN TO FORM our beliefs with the dawn of our awareness in the womb and we continue to do so over time as we experience life. We witness cause and effect: if this happens then that may follow. If that happens then I will feel this way. From these experiences we create beliefs. Imagine that the beliefs that we form are arranged in concentric circles, like the rings of a tree that are laid down year after year. Our early beliefs exist at our core, while our later beliefs surround and encompass our earlier beliefs, as our experiences in life become broader.

During infancy and early childhood our experiences are centered mainly around ourselves and our caregivers. This is when we form our core beliefs about ourselves, our needs, our relationships to those closest to us, and the world in which we live. As we move into later childhood and adolescence our interactions as well as the variety of our experiences grows considerably. The modifications of our beliefs about ourselves and our world become the outer rings of the trunk of our tree. Our interests and the diversity and depth of our experiences in life determine its branches and the leaves, flowers, and fruit that are produced.

By the time we reach adulthood the vast majority of our beliefs, particularly those about ourselves, have been formed and reinforced hundreds or even thousands of times. The more an experience is repeated or the more traumatic an experience is the more fixed our beliefs become. When we are grown we have solidified a base of beliefs from which to operate. We have created the trunk of our tree, which is firmly rooted in the ground. Unwittingly however, as a byproduct of this process, we have also learned to perceive the world in a manner consistent with our beliefs, just as a tree can only view the world from its fixed location.

Our beliefs define a reality that we have come to know and expect. This is the reality that we have become comfortable with and therefore, we have developed a vested interest in perceiving experiences in a manner consistent with our beliefs. This is not only how we have defined our reality, but it is also the process that we have used to define ourselves. Our beliefs about ourselves and our world have become more than simple understandings about cause and effect. They have become the manner in which we identify ourselves. Our beliefs have also become incorporated into the filters through which we perceive the world and our relationship to it, creating our unique perspective.

This process develops slowly over decades. When we take a class in high school or a course in college, we learn a body of information over a term or semester. As we study for the final exam we review all the facts, opinions, and processes that we have learned throughout the course and we consolidate that information. This is not how we approach life's lessons. We rarely take the time to review and reflect upon the chain of experiences that we have used to define an aspect of ourselves or our deeper beliefs about our relationship with other people or the world at large. We do not feel the need to do so because we tend to perceive the world the same way from day to day because our filters allow us to. We have designed them to perform that function.

We perceive ourselves, others, and the world as we think they are. We do not perceive our filters. Therefore, we believe that our perceptions are truthful, but they are not. They are colored by the filters we have created to tailor our new experiences to our expectations. This is how we reinforce our beliefs and how we maintain our reality as we think it should be. We do not feel the need to be accountable for our version of reality because we believe that what we perceive is reality. Yet each of us has created our personal reality through our individual beliefs and filters. Until we become accountable for our individual reality we will never recognize the need to perceive our personal filters. Therefore, many of our beliefs about ourselves and our relationships to others, the world, and All That Is will remain just as we defined them when we were children.

Soul: It would be helpful if you spent some time examining your beliefs, particularly those that you hold about yourself.

Personality: What would you like me to do, sit down and make a list of them. It would go on forever.

Soul: I am not suggesting that you turn this into a pencil and paper exercise. Your everyday life provides you with ample opportunity to see your beliefs in action. Life is your laboratory.

Personality: You mean when someone asks me what I think about something?

Soul: I am referring to situations that challenge your beliefs about yourself. Those are the beliefs, particularly the ones that you keep buried in your subconscious, that tend to limit you the most.

Personality: How do my beliefs about myself limit me?

Soul: Your painful beliefs limit you because they cause you to respond out of fear. When these subconscious beliefs are triggered you engage your coping strategies to avoid remembering them. When your painful beliefs are triggered, you react in a limited, pre-programmed manner, rather than in a manner that would allow you to inspect your old beliefs, challenge them, and change them.

Personality: I don't get triggered all that often.

Soul: It happens regularly. What happened yesterday when your family wanted to go to the park rather than visit your parents?

Personality: We got into an argument.

Soul: Why?

Personality: I thought we should visit my parents. They miss us. We haven't seen them for a while. I was trying to set a good example for my kids.

Soul: How?

Personality: I want them to consider the feelings of others, particularly those who are close to them like their grandparents. Their grandparents have done a lot for them and a visit now and then is not so much to ask.

Soul: What happened?

Personality: Everyone else wanted to go to the park. They didn't want to visit my parents because when we go there we end up staying all day and into the evening.

Soul: Why not strike a compromise and visit your parents for a shorter time and then go to the park?

Personality: We've tried that. My parents would insist that we stay for dinner. We would have never made it to the park.

Soul: Then why not go to the park and then visit your parents?

Personality: Then my parents would complain that we only came to eat and not to visit.

Soul: So what did you do?

Personality: We went to the park.

Soul: How did you feel about that?

Personality: I felt guilty about not having visited my parents. We haven't been there for a while. Thankfully I was smart and I didn't tell them that we might visit. Otherwise I would have really felt bad.

Soul: Why would that have made you feel worse?

Personality: They would have been hurt that we decided to go to the park rather than visit them. They would have been insulted. Why is that hard for you to understand?

Soul: It is not hard to understand, but since my interactions are more direct I do not have feelings based upon presumptions. You create layers of beliefs—some of which even conflict—that often cause you to feel bad. As a result, your choices are narrowed to the point that you feel like you are walking on a tightrope. Understanding your beliefs and how they influence your feelings and behaviors would help you navigate more easily and feel better.

Personality: Heaven must be a nice place.

Soul: Heaven is a state of being. It is what you make it, just like life on Earth. You are making your life more difficult than it needs to be.

Personality: I am not, I'm just trying to keep everyone happy.

Soul: What about you?

Personality: I was fine with the decision.

Soul: I thought you felt guilty.

Personality: It could have been a lot worse. I got over it.

Soul: You suppressed your guilt, but it kept cropping up every so often. You tried to distract yourself with the activities at hand, but it put a damper on your day. You could have felt a lot freer and unburdened if you had been able to release your guilty feelings.

Personality: It wasn't as bad as you describe.

Soul: How was it when your parents called you that evening and asked what you had done that day?

Personality: That was after the fact, but to answer your question, I felt pretty guilty about lying to them.

Soul: Why did you tell them you were running errands rather than the truth?

Personality: I didn't want to hurt them. Is that so bad?

Soul: There is more to it than that. You did not want to tell them that you and your family spent the day at the park. You feared compounding your guilt since you were already feeling guilty because it has been a while since your last visit. You were worried that if you told them the truth they would have asked why you did not visit them. Then what would you have said?

Personality: I would have thought of something.

Soul: Would it have been the truth?

Personality: Probably not.

Soul: Why not clear the air and simply tell them that you went to the park and why?

Personality: If I told them the truth, they might hold it against my family. That would strain everyone's relationships.

Soul: They are strained now. You are unable to be honest with your parents, unable to set boundaries about family time, and unable to make compromises with your family. Most importantly, you are not being honest with yourself because you are unwilling to understand the beliefs that cause you to feel and act in the manner that you do. Whenever you engage your coping strategies you are being untruthful with yourself by avoiding the truth. You are not accepting your own feelings and underlying beliefs and you take actions to keep it that way. You are not being accountable to yourself.

Personality: At least I maintain the peace. Your suggestion would create havoc.

Soul: Temporarily there would be more tension, but everyone would adjust.

Personality: What if they didn't?

Soul: They would in some way. You may not like the short-term results, but at least you would have been honest about your own feelings. In the process you may come to better understand your beliefs. You may become more conscious of the actions you are taking and why you are taking them. The rest of your family can also make more conscious decisions, based upon an understanding of their beliefs and feelings, if they choose to. That is their choice, but you are not responsible for their choices.

Personality: I wouldn't want to be responsible for creating disharmony.

Soul: Why not?

Personality: It would be my fault.

Soul: It is your doing whenever you take action or avoid taking action. Even though the current level of disharmony is not being discussed openly you are still accountable for your part in creating and maintaining it. You may as well be proactive and try to improve the situation, by achieving a greater understanding of how your beliefs are driving your feelings and behaviors.

Personality: What beliefs are you referring to?

Soul: There are a number of them being triggered in this situation. Why did you want to visit your parents in the first place?

Personality: I already told you. It's been a while and they miss us.

Soul: They can visit you if they miss you.

Personality: They typically wait for us to visit them. They expect us to come to them or for us to call them.

Soul: Why is that?

Personality: That's just the way it is. When I haven't called them in a while my father calls and asks me if there is something wrong with my finger.

Soul: What do you say?

Personality: I tell him I'm very busy and I don't always have time to call.

Soul: Are they as busy as you are?

Personality: No.

Soul: Then why not tell them that they can initiate the calls since they have more time than you do.

Personality: That would make it seem like I don't want to take the time to talk to them.

Soul: It is your belief about needing to initiate contact that needs to be reexamined and possibly changed.

Personality: Okay. I guess I could look at that.

Soul: That is not the sole reason for wanting to visit your parents. Are you aware of others?

Personality: I feel guilty when I don't go to see them. After visiting with them I no longer feel bad.

Soul: Do you only visit them to alleviate your feelings of guilt?

Personality: That's a big reason.

Soul: Are you aware of others?

Personality: Like what?

Soul: You had said that you are setting an example for your children. By taking them to visit your parents are you hoping that they will visit you in the future with their children?

Personality: I would like that.

Soul: Would you want them to feel guilty if they did not?

Personality: I don't know, but it would seem unfair to me if my kids wouldn't take the time to visit me since I visited my parents all these years.

Soul: I am sure you can think of other ways to motivate your children to visit you rather than attempting to make them feel guilty. After all, you visit your parents for other reasons too.

Personality: It seems like guilt is the major reason.

Soul: Why is it that you do not mind staying into the evening when you visit them? Everyone else is ready to go. Could it have something to do with the way that your mother dotes on you?

Personality: She often makes my favorite meal, desert and all. I certainly don't mind that and then she insists on cleaning the dishes without our help. It's like going to a great restaurant with no bill after the meal, except the guilt that develops later when I don't call or visit.

Soul: That is your doing. You feel that way based upon your beliefs. If you reevaluated your boundaries you might decide to operate differently. That would reduce your feelings of guilt.

Personality: It's a thought, but I don't want to upset the apple cart too much.

Soul: You seem to have struck a balance between the payoff of the nurturance you receive and the guilt that you experience. Do you know why that is?

Personality: No.

Soul: Your mother senses your guilt and she feels bad for her role in creating it. In essence you retaliate by attempting to cause her to feel guilty through some of the comments you make and with your body language. It often works and she feels bad enough to make you your favorite meal. That is her apology. Subconsciously, you recognize this dynamic and you are satisfied with the outcome. You feel closer to her when she acquiesces to your subconscious demands.

Personality: I don't like it when you analyze me.

Soul: These are my observations.

Personality: It makes me feel uncomfortable.

Soul: As your awareness about yourself grows, there is often some discomfort because in this present moment you have not yet engaged a coping strategy to cut off this dialogue. As a result, you are moving closer to some of your underlying painful beliefs.

Personality: Here we go again.

Soul: Each time you evaluate yourself in this manner observe the fact that your discomfort has lessened. You are realizing that there is less reason to be fearful. When you acknowledge this you will make progress more quickly because you will have less need to engage your coping strategies and greater acceptance of your present situation. You will see yourself with greater clarity more of the time.

Personality: I still don't like it.

Soul: You do not like it because you have moved closer to some of the painful beliefs that you created in childhood. Being with your parents brings some of those closer to the surface. As a result, some of your behaviors change accordingly. That is why your children become uncomfortable and why they want to leave. They do not like seeing you in that way.

Personality: In what way?

Soul: Your children are accustomed to seeing you in the role of an adult. You sometimes fall back into the role of child when you are with your parents.

Personality: But I still am their child.

Soul: You will always be their child, but your response to them more often resembles the response of a child who is still dependent upon their parents for their emotional well being. When you are criticized unnecessarily by your father, you look down at the floor, slump forward, and remain quiet rather than voicing your opinions.

Personality: If I don't engage him any further the episode will pass more quickly. I tell my kids that's why I let him go on like that.

Soul: If you stood your ground you might be able to help your father understand why his criticisms are unjustified.

Personality: He wouldn't change. He's too old for that.

Soul: That is your excuse for avoiding the attempt. As long as he is alive there exists the possibility for change. You give him no reason to change. I thought you wanted to be a role model for your children.

Personality: I do, but not at the expense of alienating my parents.

Soul: Do you know why you are so reluctant to stand up for your Rights?

Personality: Fear.

Soul: Fear of what?

Personality: Of not being approved of.

Soul: That and more.

Personality: What else could it be?

Soul: Your old safety and security concerns are triggered. Whenever there is any tension between you and your parents or even when your parents disagree, as they did when you were a child, you fear separation. You become quiet, hoping it will pass, as it always has.

Personality: I have my own family now. Why would I fear separation from my parents?

Soul: I know it seems strange to you.

Personality: I find it hard to believe.

Soul: Your actions reveal your true beliefs. Why do you act the way that you do? What is your explanation?

Personality: I always have acted that way.

Soul: Since you were a child.

Personality: So what.

Soul: You harbor those old fears, which are the cause of your actions. Many of your actions are nothing more than the subconscious, automatic, preprogrammed behaviors of your coping strategies. Your behaviors have not changed even though you now have a family of your own because you have never addressed your old fears and beliefs. Although they are subconscious they still exist and they continue to influence your present-day feelings and behaviors.

Personality: I'll think about this.

Soul: While you are at it, think about your lack of groundedness the moment you walk through the door of your parent's home.

Personality: Why would that happen?

Soul: You become fearful.

Personality: Of what?

Soul: Of the criticism you are expecting to receive. You begin to move into a coping strategy before you even encounter any difficulty.

Personality: What do you mean?

Soul: You try to flee the situation ahead of time.

Personality: I don't run away.

Soul: You would like to. Your subconscious fears cause your personality to literally want to exit your body. That is what lack of groundedness is all about. It is hard to stay present and focused when part of you wants to escape.

Personality: Of all the things you talk to me about, this is the most confusing.

Soul: Your culture only embraces the concept of groundedness to a limited extent. The interplay between spiritual essence, soul, the energetic fields more closely tied to the personality, and the physical body is poorly understood. As a result, it seems very foreign to you because you have learned so little about it and have experienced it even less. Therefore this concept does not seem real to you.

Personality: That's for sure, but what's the difference anyway?

Soul: When you become less grounded you become more susceptible to your subconscious fears. Therefore, you are more easily triggered.

Personality: I always do have a sense of apprehension when their front door opens. I never know what to expect.

Soul: That is when it starts. Your guilt is replaced by fear. As the time spent there passes you become more apprehensive until what you fear occurs. Your father's criticisms cause you to retreat from yourself. You become so distant that you can hardly hear him. That is when you are the least grounded. Afterward, even though you sulk, there is a sense of relief because it is over. What you might find even harder to believe is that your father subconsciously reacts to your growing apprehension. Those feelings that are triggered in him actually cause him to become more critical of you, which then releases the tension in him and you.

Personality: So, it's all my fault. Is that what you are saying?

Soul: I am not assigning blame. I am just explaining the various actions and reactions. These things happen for a reason. Why do you think they occur?

Personality: They are nothing more than old habits.

Soul: That they are. However, there are mechanisms at work that cause what occurs and the principal mechanism that initiates these processes is your beliefs. You believe that you are bad if you do not visit your parents every so often and that you must initiate the contact. You believe that you should be responsible for how others feel. You believe that it is your job to keep the peace and make others happy and also that it is reasonable for you to manipulate others through guilt because you allow yourself to be manipulated that way. You fear being left by your parents and at times you even fear being present in your body. These beliefs cause you to feel guilty and anxious; to compromise yourself by violating your own boundaries and integrity. You are driven by these beliefs, many of which reside below your conscious awareness. These beliefs are creating your reality. You do not realize this so it is difficult for you to be accountable for creating it or recognizing the need to change.

Personality: I guess my parents don't bring out the best in me.

Soul: That is often the case. Your painful beliefs are easily triggered by your parents because they were present when you formed those beliefs. Visiting your old home brings them closer to the surface. When your parents no longer trigger your old fears and beliefs you will have come far.

Personality: I would call that heaven.

Discuss and/or Journal

Our beliefs lie at the center of our attitudes and cause our feelings, which motivate our behaviors. We define our personality by the beliefs we hold about ourselves. Our personality clings to those beliefs and they become our identity. It also influences our perceptions so we can maintain our reality intact.

1. Do you blame others for your circumstances or how you feel?

    _____

    _____

    _____

2. What are five deep beliefs about yourself that cause you to feel bad?

    _____

    _____

    _____

3. What are five deep beliefs about yourself that cause you to feel good?

    _____

    _____

    _____

4. What do you believe about your soul?

    _____

    _____

    _____

5. Can you see how your beliefs shape your life? Are you accountable for the life you have created?

    _____

    _____

    _____

chapter seventeen

CREATE AND EASILY ACCEPT CHANGE

Does a stable self-image help us navigate through life more easily? We each have a self-defined image of ourselves based upon a set of beliefs. Our beliefs cause us to feel as we do and motivate us to act as we do. Typically this is done to achieve certain outcomes, often in our attempt to create greater consistency in our lives. To make this process less cumbersome we have assigned many of our attitudes to our subconscious mind. As a result, the process happens more automatically. We function in this way to manage our lives with less effort. However, by doing so we maintain fixed attitudes that oppose our more fluid spiritual nature which embraces and creates change.

If we plan to grow, develop, and evolve, then we must change. Holding onto fixed beliefs in an effort to maintain a static self-image is contradictory to this goal. It causes us to maintain our filters, resulting in an unchanging, untruthful reality. Why do we do this? It is our way of defining ourselves and structuring our interactions to maximize our feelings of safety and security. Although many of us believe that growth and development are nice, feeling safe and secure is necessary, and usually far more immediate. Can we have both?

Just as we can learn to transition from experiencing fear-based emotional feelings to love-based feelings, we can also learn to transition from attitudes that preclude change to those that embrace or even create it. When experiencing our fears we can consider a change rather than defaulting to our coping strategies. Each one of us has the ability to pause and alter our behavior. It is a choice we can make. Although we have a Right to feel safe and secure, we also have a Right to create and easily accept change. Why do these two Rights so often create attitudes that appear mutually exclusive? The answer lies in our ability or inability to trust.

Many of us have learned to fear change and not to trust anything that is outside of our own control. When we have been surprised in the past—even when unexpected events worked out well—they were most likely either considered to be an unusual occurrence or we believed we were the beneficiaries of luck. In general we tend to feel safest when we understand and are in control of events and their causality. This is why we trust our coping strategies, because they give us the illusion of control. Nowhere is this more important to us than in regard to our own safety and security concerns.

Learning to trust that all will work out for the best is a tremendous leap of faith for most of us. It implies that there is a vast, unseen intelligence at work in the universe which has our best interests at heart. It signifies that when things do not work out, as we believe they should that we are incorrect in our assumptions and that we do not know what is best for us. Adopting trust in a system that we do not perceive, understand, or readily control in the face of our fears seems too much to ask. This is why we resist change, hold tightly to our existing beliefs, and employ our coping strategies so often.

As long as our self-image is principally identified with our personality—exclusive of our spirituality—we will operate from the confines of fear rather than the freedom of love. Our beliefs, generated by our personality, reflect our understanding of ourselves, our relationship to others, our world, and All That Is. For the most part, they have been formed without significant input from our spiritual nature. For us to change by adopting attitudes that are more spiritually oriented necessitates redefining ourselves by incorporating our soul and spiritual essence in a practical way. This would create a fundamental shift in our self-image. How can this possibly be accomplished in the face of our fears?

Small steps. Any change though, seems contradictory when applied to our beliefs, because we are not accustomed to reviewing and modifying them. We treat our beliefs as though they are rigid structures that serve a permanent function. We can choose to adopt a different attitude toward our beliefs. We can think of them as serving a temporary function so that we can more easily modify them as our understanding about life grows. We may come to understand that we are not our beliefs. Beliefs are simply tools that allow us to temporarily define our reality. We can develop a self-image that is stable in its flexibility and less tied to our beliefs. Greater flexibility would certainly help us create and easily accept change in our lives. Then we would be more aligned with the changing nature of life and our spiritual side.

Soul: Are you surprised? You thought your boss was looking to replace you and you would be out of work. Instead you have been offered a promotion. How do you feel about that?

Personality: It's better than being fired, but I don't like the idea of moving. I've lived here most of my life. We're comfortable here and the kids like their schools. I don't want everyone to be uprooted and have to start over.

Soul: It seems like a nice opportunity. You can manage a new branch office the way that you want to, move into a new neighborhood, and create some new friendships and affiliations. It is an adventure.

Personality: I haven't decided to take the promotion.

Soul: Fear getting the better of you?

Personality: I almost wish that I hadn't been offered this new assignment.

Soul: Then turn it down.

Personality: That would be the smart thing to do.

Soul: Okay.

Personality: Things are okay the way they are. I don't even know why I should consider taking the promotion.

Soul: You were complaining about needing more money. This would give you what you wanted.

Personality: We're getting by as long as we continue to be careful.

Soul: This would give you the opportunity to create your own guidelines at work. You would no longer need to deal with your boss' unpredictability.

Personality: I've gotten used to it. It's not so bad.

Soul: Are you going to play it safe and be happy with what you have?

Personality: That's the reasonable thing to do, isn't it?

Soul: But you are not happy.

Personality: I may not be the happiest person in town, but I'm not the saddest.

Soul: You have been avoiding your feelings. What are you feeling?

Personality: Thinking about this makes me feel nervous.

Soul: Why?

Personality: This is a big step.

Soul: In what way?

Personality: Everything will be different. I don't know that different will be better and it certainly could be worse. I didn't ask for this, you know.

Soul: Yes you did.

Personality: When did I ask for a new job.

Soul: When you voiced dissatisfaction with your present job and a desire for more. An opportunity has been provided for you.

Personality: Thanks a lot.

Soul: Gratitude does not seem to be one of your stronger qualities.

Personality: Well I am grateful that I'm not being fired. Although maybe this is how my boss plans to get rid of me. He'll probably make it tough on me around here, so I'll definitely take the new assignment. He figures I'll fail at it and be fired and he won't even be the one who has to do it.

Soul: Actually, your boss recommended you to his boss for one of several different opportunities, all of which would be promotions. When he had to choose which position was to be offered to you he chose the one where he thought you would be most successful. By the way, your boss is being promoted. You will still be reporting to him if you take this new assignment.

Personality: Really?

Soul: Yes. How does it feel now that your reporting structure may stay the same?

Personality: I'm comfortable with that.

Soul: I thought you wanted to do things your way without his oversight.

Personality: If he remains my boss, then at least one thing will stay the same. Wait a minute. That means that if I don't take the new job then I'll have a new boss.

Soul: That is true.

Personality: So things are going to change no matter what I do.

Soul: Correct.

Personality: I hate it when I have no control over the events in my life.

Soul: That has been your nature.

Personality: It should be any reasonable person's nature. I don't know how things are going to turn out.

Soul: Why are you assuming that things will turn out badly?

Personality: Because they might.

Soul: That depends to a large extent on you.

Personality: Not everything is under my control. Bad things can happen regardless of what I do.

Soul: Good things can happen as well. Do you know why you worry about bad things happening?

Personality: It's probably some strange, insignificant memory filed away in my subconscious mind that you're about to remind me of. Am I right?

Soul: I would not call it strange or insignificant, but it is not something that you choose to think about on a conscious level very often.

Personality: Are you going to tell me or make me guess?

Soul: Do you remember when you started elementary school?

Personality: Yes, it was awful.

Soul: You did not like attending school and spending most of the day away from home. Fortunately, you had a very nurturing teacher, but after two months she had to leave and she was replaced with a teacher who was strict and even harsh at times.

Personality: And then my grandmother died. She lived with us and I was very close to her. My whole world changed for the worse. I couldn't understand why I was being punished.

Soul: That is why you were so easily triggered by any argument that your parents had. You feared that you would be left alone because you had already lost a significant member of your family from whom you had received much love and support. This is one of the reasons why change frightens you.

Personality: Just taking this new job doesn't mean that I would suffer that kind of loss.

Soul: You maintain a subconscious fear of separation. Loss of a loved one is a more extreme form of separation, but if you moved away you would see your parents, other relatives, and your friends and acquaintances less often. The thought of moving away is enough to trigger your fear of separation and loss of loved ones.

Personality: When I think of it that way it does make me feel sad.

Soul: That is only one of the fears that is triggered by your potential promotion. It also calls into question another of your coping beliefs.

Personality: What would that be?

Soul: Your rationalization that you are not smart enough. In your way of thinking it would be more difficult for you to make that claim to those who you would be managing.

Personality: Yes, you're right. I would have to be their leader. I would have to answer their questions. I would need to appear confident and know everything that they need to know. This isn't going to work.

Soul: Why not?

Personality: I just told you. Weren't you listening?

Soul: Actually, when you become fearful in this way I work to perceive what is underlying the fear. I still hear you, but I become more focused on the truth, which often escapes your awareness.

Personality: The truth is that I'm not as good at faking it as I would need to be. I don't have all the answers.

Soul: It is unreasonable to expect anyone to have all the answers. You do not need to fake it and pretend that you do. Does your boss know all the answers?

Personality: He certainly appears to know most of them.

Soul: What does he do when he does not know an answer?

Personality: He asks what others think.

Soul: Then what happens?

Personality: He takes the different opinions and then he chooses.

Soul: You can do the same.

Personality: It's not that easy.

Soul: Why not?

Personality: When he started in his position people challenged his decisions.

Soul: So?

Personality: He had to be right to gain their respect.

Soul: Can you do that?

Personality: What if I'm wrong?

Soul: Then you would be wrong.

Personality: Then it wouldn't work.

Soul: Why not?

Personality: I would need to be right.

Soul: Why?

Personality: Otherwise they wouldn't listen to me.

Soul: Was your boss always right?

Personality: Not really.

Soul: Yet everyone still listened to him when he made his decisions. Why?

Personality: That's a good question. I'll have to think about that. If I do take this new job it sure would be easier if I had people working for me who weren't the type to challenge me.

Soul: What type of person would that be?

Personality: Maybe someone who doesn't have much experience.

Soul: Or?

Personality: Someone who isn't very confident. You know.

Soul: Or?

Personality: Someone who isn't too smart.

Soul: If you surrounded yourself with people like that your job would be more difficult.

Personality: Why? It would be easier for me to be right or at least not be challenged. That way I would be in control. My rules would be followed more easily. If I had to fake it, I could do it more easily.

Soul: Now I think you are not listening to yourself. Your fears are influencing you to such a great extent that the solutions you are proposing only serve the purpose of maintaining control. Do you know why?

Personality: I would need to be in control. I would be the branch manager. It's my job on the line if things don't work properly and that's why I get to call the shots.

Soul: Then why make it harder to do the job well? Why not hire the best people for the job and assist them in doing the best job that they could do?

Personality: People like that are the ones most likely to challenge my authority.

Soul: Do you believe that they may be better at your job than you are now?

Personality: That thought had crossed my mind.

Soul: What if they are better at doing the job that you do now?

Personality: Then I wouldn't be the right person to manage them. I wouldn't have anything to teach them. They wouldn't respect me.

Soul: If you were promoted your job would be different. You would see to it that the branch office is successful. You would no longer be required to do so much of the day-to-day work that gets done.

Personality: That might be harder.

Soul: For you it would be a challenge. You are accustomed to stepping in and doing the work for some of your peers when they do not do what is required of them.

Personality: I wouldn't be able to do that for the entire branch office.

Soul: You would have to operate differently. You would have to hold others accountable for doing their job. That is why it would be helpful for you to hire the best people that you could find.

Personality: But they may not feel accountable to me if they don't respect me.

Soul: Why do you think they should be accountable to you rather than be accountable to themselves?

Personality: Because I'm their boss. They need to keep me happy so that they will still have a job.

Soul: They need to have your approval, is that it?

Personality: Yes that's the way it should be.

Soul: And for them to want your approval it would be helpful if you were perceived as better than they are.

Personality: Now you're getting it.

Soul: Yes it is very clear to me.

Personality: But not to me, right?

Soul: Not consciously.

Personality: What is it now?

Soul: You are looking for absolute control over your employees. You want them to seek approval from you the same way that you look for approval from your boss and your father. You want them to seek your approval rather than have them learn to approve of themselves.

Personality: If I'm their boss then they need my approval.

Soul: If you hired them, then why would you not approve of them from the start?

Personality: I would hire them to give them a chance to prove themselves.

Soul: Is that how you felt about being born?

Personality: What are you talking about?

Soul: Were you born to have a chance to prove yourself worthy to your father?

Personality: It felt that way.

Soul: It felt that way because you were always being judged rather than supported. That is what you learned from your experiences with your father, but is that what you have been learning from your boss?

Personality: My boss gives me more latitude and encourages me to try to do things in different ways.

Soul: He is accepting of you.

Personality: He still criticized me.

Soul: Was he criticizing you or what you had done?

Personality: It felt like he was criticizing me, but I guess he was really critical of some of my work.

Soul: It is easy to personalize criticism when you have learned to be critical of yourself. How would you treat your employees?

Personality: I would try to be supportive, but they have to do a good job.

Soul: Why would they want to do otherwise?

Personality: Some people are just interested in getting by and getting a paycheck.

Soul: There are many people who want to do a good job and that feel accountable to themselves to do a good job. What can you do in your hiring process that could help you identify them?

Personality: People say what they think others want to hear so that they can get hired. You can never know what truly motivates them.

Soul: Can you ask them what motivates them to do a good job and how they plan to accomplish that?

Personality: Sure, but it won't do any good.

Soul: Can you hold them accountable for their answers?

Personality: It's easier to hold them accountable for their results.

Soul: Then some of them can get by the same way that some of your co-workers do now. They get you to do some of their work. Can you have your employees be accountable for how they do their work? After all, it is your branch office and you can set the guidelines. Effective managers manage accountability.

Personality: Yes by firing people that don't do a good job.

Soul: Some managers go further and support their employees in accomplishing their own goals, including doing a good job and being personally accountable for doing so. You can determine what the individual's goals are in the interviewing process and talk to him or her about being accountable for their goals.

Personality: Then I would have to track that to be able to measure their performance.

Soul: Yes. That would be a significant part of your job, but in doing so you could better ensure accountability.

Personality: Why are you so focused on accountability?

Soul: I am trying to help you understand personal accountability.

Personality: I understand it. I usually do a good job.

Soul: Yes you do. Personal accountability also includes the underlying motivation for being accountable. Often you accomplish what you set out to do in order to gain the approval of others rather than doing what seems right for you. Being personally accountable implies doing a good job of one's own accord for reasons other than seeking the approval of others—for reasons of your own.

Personality: What's the difference as long as the job gets done?

Soul: When people learn to be personally accountable they become more accepting of themselves. As a result, they become more accepting of others. Your boss recognizes this and he encourages others to find creative solutions even if they fail from time to time. If his decisions do not work out as well as he would like, others are less likely to be critical. Your boss creates an atmosphere where an occasional failure is acceptable.

Personality: He did earn our respect.

Soul: Not by being right all of the time or knowing all of the answers.

Personality: Now I see how he did it.

Soul: If you were more accepting of yourself you would not fear change and the potential negative outcomes to the extent that you do. Consider that when you make your decision about your new job assignment.

Personality: There's a lot to think about.

Discuss and/or Journal

There are many different reasons why we resist change. They all result from fear—the fear that we will be worse off. This is a characteristic of our personality and not our soul. Our soul creates and embraces change because that is how we learn and evolve.

1. What are the reasons that you fear change?

_____

_____

_____

_____

2. What changes have you experienced that have resulted in a positive outcome?

_____

_____

_____

_____

3. How have those change experiences influenced your attitudes about change?

_____

_____

_____

_____

4. When you are in the midst of a change experience, are you able to perceive the influence of your soul? Would you like to experience it more?

_____

_____

_____

_____

chapter eighteen

THINK CLEARLY, REASON EFFECTIVELY, AND MAKE DECISIONS

Rarely a day passes when we are not challenged by questions, perceived problems, or choices. When we are asked a question we search for an answer. When we are faced with a problem we attempt to find a solution. When we are confronted with a decision we wrestle with choice. In many instances, not knowing the answer, solution, or choice creates fear in us. We all would like to know the correct answer, the most efficient solution, and the best choice with the least amount of effort. How far does thinking take us toward this goal? By only using our mental ability to think, are we likely to find the best answer, solution, or choice? Our selection may be the most logical, rational, and defensible, but how do we know that it is the best?

Does reasoning improve our odds? How does reasoning differ from thinking? Thinking primarily involves the rational processes of our brain and mind, while reasoning utilizes that functionality plus our feeling nature. Reasoning is the search for understanding using more than just our mental abilities. It is our way of uncovering the motivating factors that underlie our beliefs, feelings, and actions. To reason, we must be able to feel, because our feelings create our most powerful motivations.

Reasoning moves us out of the domain of logic alone and personalizes our considerations. Because our feelings are involved, we begin to understand the personal relevance that our answers, solutions, and choices have for each of us. We feel how our selection will impact us. With an ability to reason effectively, it is likely that the selection we have arrived at is the best one for us, but do we know that it is the best for all concerned?

What gives us the ability to know that? We have more tools available to us than our ability to think and reason. We have the ability to perceive what is best for all concerned from our spiritual side because that is our connection to All That Is. Unfortunately, when we attempt to access perceptions from that source we are likely to experience our fears because we are opening our feeling nature to our subconscious. Doing so causes us to feel more vulnerable because we are in a more receptive state with greater exposure to our fears.

When we become fearful, our ability to think and reason deteriorates. Our thought processes become confused and uncertain and our memories become clouded. Fear also limits what we are willing to feel, undermining our ability to reason. We become more likely to resort to reactive patterns of thought and behavior as we operate from the confines of our coping strategies. To maximize our thinking and reasoning abilities we construct a barrier to receiving input from our spiritual side. We simply avoid opening our broader feeling nature for the purpose of consulting the information we seek. The payoff for using this coping strategy is the avoidance of fear. Although we preserve our ability to think and reason we deny ourselves the ability to perceive what is best at a deeper level.

Fear has taken us full circle. We often fear not knowing the best answers, solutions, and choices, yet we fear the process of knowing. Why? There are several reasons. If we did know the best answers, solutions, and choices, then we may feel compelled to act on them. That would result in us being accountable for the outcome of our actions. However, even if we wish to avoid accountability by not taking action, we are still accountable for the outcomes resulting from our lack of actions. There is no escaping the accountability that we each have for our own lives.

In addition, by learning to access perspective from our soul and spiritual essence we seemingly reduce the importance of our personality and its ability to think and reason. In doing so we may also sense that we are less in control of our day to day lives than we would like to be. Fear, in this instance, serves our sense of importance and control by maintaining a greater degree of separation from our spiritual side. We limit our functioning to that of a fear-based personality, which is incapable of receiving a higher perspective. This is our attempt to maintain a greater level of independent control.

This fear is also without merit because there is never any reduction of our free will. The choice is ours to access a higher perspective if we open ourselves to that possibility. By doing so we can choose whether or not to blend our thoughts and feelings with our spiritual perspective. We are always in control of this process. We have the Right to think clearly, reason effectively, and make decisions. By exercising this Right and considering everything that we can perceive we can choose how best to proceed.

Soul: How are you going to approach making your decision?

Personality: I'll think about it tomorrow.

Soul: How will you approach it then?

Personality: I'll figure it out.

Soul: What if you do not?

Personality: Then I'll just make a decision when I have to.

Soul: If you had to make a decision now, what would it be?

Personality: I don't know.

Soul: Do you not want to know?

Personality: Of course I do.

Soul: Why?

Personality: Then I wouldn't have to worry about it anymore.

Soul: What does that tell you?

Personality: I understand that I'm avoiding the issue.

Soul: Why?

Personality: Because it's a hard decision.

Soul: Why?

Personality: Because there is a lot at stake.

Soul: What?

Personality: My career, money, family considerations, friends, and on and on.

Soul: You have a lot to think about.

Personality: That's what I said.

Soul: Why wait any longer? Try to figure it out. It will only prolong your nervousness the longer you wait.

Personality: There are so many issues that it's hard to get started.

Soul: Yes, these issues are significant and when you begin to consider them they create conflicting emotional feelings. As a result, you develop fear, become paralyzed, and resort to avoidance to rid yourself of the uncomfortable feelings. You would do well to ground yourself in the physical to a greater extent before considering these issues.

Personality: Why?

Soul: It would help you to focus and relax. Then you could consider these issues with less fear and greater clarity of thought. Otherwise you are simply sitting in the midst of your coping strategies and practicing avoidance. What are your present thoughts about taking the promotion?

Personality: If I decide to take the job my family may not like my decision. I may not be any good at it. If I decide not to take the promotion then my career would be on hold, I wouldn't make more money and I would have a new boss that may not like me.

Soul: Why is it that you are only able to envision potential difficulties?

Personality: They are all real possibilities. Can't you see that?

Soul: Certainly, but there are other possibilities. Your fearful state is clouding your outlook. Why are you so intent on considering only these possibilities?

Personality: I must prepare myself for when I talk to my family about taking the job or for the conversation that I would have with my boss if I decide not to take the job. I need to manage the situation.

Soul: How does having a dismal outlook help you to prepare for these conversations?

Personality: I want others to see how difficult this is for me.

Soul: Why?

Personality: I want my family to understand how bad it may be if I make the wrong decision. I want my boss to see why I may need to make the wrong decision.

Soul: Why not simply determine what the best decision would be?

Personality: My family would view that as being selfish. I want them to realize what the best decision would be without my telling them.

Soul: So, you want them to arrive at the decision that you want, but you do not want to help them understand why that decision would be the best one for you?

Personality: Sort of.

Soul: In other words, you would rather portray yourself as a victim by leading your family to believe that you might be forced to make a decision that is not in your best interests. You would do that in the hopes that they would rescue you from making the wrong decision. You hope to sway them such that they will arrive at the decision that you favor instead of the decision that they might otherwise prefer. Futhermore, you want to be able to justify your decision to your boss if it does not meet with his approval.

Personality: When you put it that way I feel cowardly.

Soul: You are proceeding this way because you are not willing to be accountable for making your own decision. You would rather place this responsibility on your family. Do you know why you would like to do that?

Personality: So I don't have to decide.

Soul: If you had to make the decision then you believe that you would be responsible for all of the outcomes that resulted from that decision. You believe that others would blame you if things did not work out well for them.

Personality: It would be my fault.

Soul: Why?

Personality: If I took the promotion and we moved and my family wasn't happy, then I would have put them in a situation that caused them to be unhappy.

Soul: So you would rather have them make the decision, is that it?

Personality: Sure.

Soul: Then why not ask them what they would like to do?

Personality: Because they may simply say that they don't want to move and that would be the wrong decision.

Soul: It sounds as though you have made your decision.

Personality: I have not.

Soul: You have implied that the wrong decision would be to not take the promotion. I assume that you believe the best decision is to take the promotion. Is that a correct assessment?

Personality: Absolutely not. That would be the right decision from the perspective of my career and avoiding the difficulty that I would have in telling my boss that I was turning down the promotion. However, it might be the wrong decision from my family's viewpoint. Why is it that you are having difficulty following my thoughts?

Soul: I can understand your thoughts and feel your feelings. It is important for you to understand that you are approaching this decision by only taking into account the consequences that you perceive to be negative and not even considering those that may be positive.

Personality: I'd rather not think about this whole mess. I think I know what will happen anyway.

Soul: Have you reached a decision that you are uncomfortable with or have you not yet reached a decision?

Personality: I'm not sure.

Soul: It does not matter.

Personality: Why not? You've been telling me to make a decision and now you're telling me that it doesn't matter.

Soul: I was asking how you were going to approach making your decision. It does not matter whether you have not yet reached a decision or whether you have reached a decision that you are uncomfortable with. In either case, it would be helpful for you to figure out how best to proceed.

Personality: Proceed where?

Soul: How are you going to proceed in terms of working through your decision-making process?

Personality: I don't approach it that way.

Soul: I know. You do your best to avoid it and then the decision is made by others or by external factors.

Personality: Then that's how I'll proceed.

Soul: You can certainly do that, but in this case, you will have to provide an answer to your boss sooner or later. He will demand one of you.

Personality: It will be easiest if I just maintain things the way they are.

Soul: You will still have a new boss.

Personality: Yes, but that is all that will change.

Soul: I know that you would like to minimize change, but further change is inevitable.

Personality: What else will happen?

Soul: That depends upon your choices.

Personality: Tell me what will happen in either case.

Soul: The future is not set in stone.

Personality: Then how do you know that there will be further changes?

Soul: Growth implies and requires change. We are all on a path of growth, therefore change is ever present. It is your choice whether or not you decide to initiate change and how well you learn to accept the changes that befall you. Either way, change is a part of life.

Personality: So what would you do in my situation?

Soul: I would change the way that I approach making decisions.

Personality: I already know that. I'm asking you what your decision would be about taking the job promotion.

Soul: You will resort to anything to avoid making this decision.

Personality: You're not going to tell me are you?

Soul: I am not inclined to take advantage of your present state of vulnerability.

Personality: I'm asking you of my own free will.

Soul: You are asking me out of desperation. I am here to give you insight, not run your life.

Personality: Please, just this one time.

Soul: It might be easier for you to simply turn down the promotion at this time.

Personality: Really?

Soul: Sure.

Personality: I can't believe you're telling me to do that.

Soul: Why not?

Personality: It makes no sense. It's the safe way out and I would be going nowhere as a result. Where is your sense of adventure? What is wrong with you anyway? I can't believe that you would tell me not to take the promotion.

Soul: All right, maybe you should take the promotion.

Personality: Why are you doing this to me?

Soul: I am just pointing out the obvious. You have two choices to consider. You have strong feelings about them, but you are having difficulty using those feelings to help you understand which way would be best for you to proceed.

Personality: Why is this so hard for me to do?

Soul: The feelings you are having are those of your coping strategies. That is why you persist in viewing your choices as only having negative outcomes and that is why you are avoiding thinking about it. You have been unwilling to consider your deeper desires related to the new opportunity. If you did so you would have some positive feelings and be more willing to consider the issues at hand. What do you desire? When you can answer this simple question you will be able to reason more effectively.

Personality: When I ask what I want I feel selfish because I think that my family won't want what I want. That makes me feel guilty.

Soul: If your emotional feelings are causing this process to grind to a halt, then maybe it would be better for you to first approach it more rationally. Ultimately, however, it would be best for you to consult your feeling nature to determine if the decision feels right for you.

Personality: How can I be rational when I'm so conflicted.

Soul: Ground yourself, relax, and focus your mind on the task at hand. Make a list of pros and cons and if you would like to, do it for all concerned. Think of it from your perspective as well as that of your family's. Be as honest and straightforward as you can.

Personality: Then what?

Soul: Examine each pro and con and determine how each one makes you feel. Determine where the fear is coming from and better understand the underlying beliefs that are driving your feelings. Feel your desires and determine what excites you. Move to the heart of each issue. Feel and think about them until you can clearly articulate the issue so that you can discuss each of them more meaningfully with those that you need to, and also be prepared to discuss your feelings. By determining how each issue causes you to feel, you will be better able to use your ability to reason. You will understand what is underlying your thoughts and fueling your emotions.

Personality: Then I can discuss the issues with my family so that we can make a decision.

Soul: Not so fast.

Personality: What's wrong?

Soul: Before you discuss it with your family make a determination yourself about what you believe is the best choice for you. Then try to identify with me to gain a perspective about what is the best path for all concerned.

Personality: Why shouldn't I consult my family first before arriving at the best choice?

Soul: I am not suggesting that you make the final decision without consulting your family. After all, the decision will impact their lives as well. However, it would be helpful for you to better understand how you feel about the decision before you are strongly influenced by how your family feels. It would also help them to hear from you exactly how you feel. In this way you can be completely honest with them and honest with yourself.

Personality: They already know about the possible promotion and they have voiced their concerns.

Soul: Everyone needs some time to contemplate the issues involved. Tell them to take some time and consider the pros and cons from their perspectives as well as from yours.

Personality: I think we can work through this process.

Discuss and/or Journal

We make better decisions when we gather all of the necessary information. Our decision-making process can benefit from our ability to think, reason, and understand the issues involved from a spiritual perspective. Feeling more completely facilitates the process, even when we experience fear-based emotions, as long as we work to understand their relevance. Opening our feeling nature and seeking guidance from our spiritual side can assist us with this understanding.

1. How do you make decisions?

_____

_____

_____

2. Does fear get the better of you when you are confronted with the need to make decisions?

_____

_____

_____

3. How much do you rely on your ability to think during your decision-making process?

_____

_____

_____

4. How much do you rely on your ability to reason during your decision-making process?

_____

_____

_____

5. How much do you consult your soul or All That Is during your decision-making process?

_____

_____

_____

chapter nineteen

ACT WITH CONFIDENCE, A SENSE OF PURPOSE, AND WITHOUT FEAR OF TAKING RISKS

Our actions and behaviors for the most part reveal our true feelings and beliefs to all that witness them. They are caused by our beliefs and are motivated by our feelings. We can hold our beliefs in silence and mask the way that we truly feel, but we cannot hide our actions. We can temporarily act in a way that is misleading, however, our cumulative actions or lack of them, speak volumes about us. There is much we can learn about ourselves by understanding the motives underlying our actions. There is also much we can learn about ourselves by recognizing the manner in which we behave.

Do we experience an intuitive sense of knowing that allows us to act with confidence or do we struggle trying to predict the outcome before we reluctantly take action? Do our deeper feelings, needs, and desires create our sense of purpose in daily life or do we busy ourselves with more superficial actions in an attempt to derive a sense of purpose? Do we perceive risk as an opportunity to make a choice and a difference or do we perceive risk with fear? How we move in the world and our degree of effectiveness is dictated by our confidence, sense of purpose, and fear of taking risks. Why do few of us glide effortlessly through life, while most of us move with fits and starts or become inactive and inert?

It is mostly a matter of will, fortitude, and persistence. Do we will ourselves to move forward in life honestly or do we avoid facing life head on because we cannot accept what we perceive about ourselves and our circumstances? It is a choice that we make whenever we act or avoid taking action. When we avoid accepting ourselves and our circumstances we are not being honest. Our actions or lack of them become mainly subconscious reactive patterns of activity that constitute our coping strategies. They are habits with a pay-off of avoidance and manipulation. They don't benefit us because they are only lies that we tell ourselves. Coping strategies impede our progress in life because they obscure what we do not wish to perceive. They are motivated and created by our fears.

The vast majority of us conduct our affairs using our coping strategies most of the time. We yield to our fears. We have relegated the majority of our actions primarily to our subconscious although we do retain some conscious awareness of what we are doing. We have done so in order to lessen our negative emotions and to avoid the beliefs about ourselves that creates these feelings. We have constrained ourselves to a small existence within the confines of our personality, like a fearful child hiding in the closet. This is the opposite of how we can live our lives. For the most part we are pretending to be alive, since we are mainly reacting rather than living. Is it in us to change?

Of course it is, but do we really want to? We have created this reality for a reason. Why would we want to dispel it? Maybe we are happy with ourselves and our lot in life or at least satisfied enough to stay as we are. Maybe we are not truly satisfied and we recognize that it is time for a deeper dive into who and what we are and how we can be in life to maximize what it has to offer us. Life is our living laboratory with the ability to explore something new each and every day.

Rather than live in a reactive mode we have the ability to re-create ourselves and our experiences whenever we choose. This transformation is a matter of will. We first need to become our own advocates, accept ourselves and our circumstances in life, and determine for ourselves how we plan to live our lives. From that perspective we can more easily learn to act with confidence, a sense of purpose, and without fear of taking risks. To do otherwise is to live in fear.

Soul: What have you decided?

Personality: I decided that I should take the new job opportunity.

Soul: You seem reluctant.

Personality: I'm moving forward aren't I? What's wrong now?

Soul: It appears as though you are doing so out of obligation and not desire.

Personality: Why do you say that?

Soul: Why do you say that you should do it?

Personality: Because it's the right thing to do.

Soul: Why is it the right thing to do as opposed to being right for you?

Personality: I think it is right for me. I began to realize that many of my peers, even some with less seniority, have already been promoted and that if I don't take this opportunity for a promotion, I may not get another chance. It's now or never.

Soul: You do not know that for sure.

Personality: Although the future's not set in stone my career path is beginning to feel like a boulder positioned on the edge of a cliff.

Soul: How did your family react to your decision?

Personality: When I told them why I thought it was the right thing to do, they were more supportive than I thought they would be. My kids are still a little concerned about new schools and friends, but they're willing to give it a try.

Soul: Yet it does not seem that you are very enthusiastic about the new position. If it is the right step for you why are you not embracing the opportunity with greater excitement? I sense mainly resignation on your part as though you have agreed to do something that you would rather not do. When you talked to your family what did you tell them was the major reason that you wanted to take the promotion?

Personality: I told them that if I didn't do it, I would probably regret it in the future.

Soul: Like you did five years ago when you stayed at your present job and did not take that other opportunity.

Personality: I would have made so much money by now that I wouldn't even have to work. I'm still angry with myself about that decision. That was stupid.

Soul: What caused you to not take that job?

Personality: I took my father's advice. If he wasn't so conservative I would be rich now.

Soul: Why did you listen to him?

Personality: I played it safe, like he suggested. My whole family thought it was better for me to stay put.

Soul: Did your father ever take any risks?

Personality: He was with the same company for most of his career. Times have changed and I should have approached my career differently than my father did.

Soul: Change is ever present.

Personality: I heard you the last time.

Soul: Is that why you are taking this new assignment?

Personality: It reminded me of how much I regretted not taking that other job.

Soul: If your new assignment does not work out the way that you expect it will, then you may regret having taken the promotion.

Personality: Thanks a lot. Are you suggesting that I shouldn't take the promotion?

Soul: Not at all.

Personality: Then why are you telling me that I may regret it?

Soul: You have a tendency to yield to regret rather than accepting what is and learning from your choices that have not worked out as well as you would have liked them to.

Personality: What's wrong with regret?

Soul: It is not right or wrong. It is your way of not accepting your current situation in life. When you regret something you believe that your current situation in life is somehow not right for you. As a result, you feel a sense of loss. You believe that things should be better than they presently are.

Personality: But my life could have been so much different.

Soul: Of course it could have been different, could be different, and will be different because your life was, is, and will continue to be influenced by your choices. You create your life situation by the choices you make. Your opportunities are based upon your life situation. Therefore, even your opportunities are created in part by your choices.

Personality: Fine, I get it, but why can't I regret some of my choices?

Soul: You can, but as long as you remain mired in regret, a coping strategy that causes you to stay focused on the past, you will not fully accept the present. As you play out your regret, you become self-critical as a way of punishing yourself, much like your father punished you. Your self-punishment provides you with the justification to terminate your feelings of regret. By doing that, as opposed to accepting your current situation, you are less likely to examine and learn from the choice you made, including an understanding of the reasons that led you to make your choice. As a result, you are less likely to be accountable for that choice.

Personality: Well, at least regret is leading me to make a change now and I think that is a good thing.

Soul: It would be beneficial for you to understand your judgements regarding the outcomes which resulted from your prior choice. If you could do that, you would be more likely to accept your present situation, be accountable for your choices, and be more consciously aware of your decision-making process.

Personality: The outcome is clear. I stayed in the same job rather than becoming more successful.

Soul: How do you know that you would have flourished in that other job?

Personality: They were ready to hire me. They thought I was qualified to do the job.

Soul: The person that they did hire was fired six months later. The next person lasted only three months. Neither one of them were on the job when the company became successful.

Personality: It may have been different if I took the job.

Soul: It may have been, but then again it may not have been.

Personality: Why?

Soul: The supervisor for that position was threatened by successful subordinates. If you were successful it would have been likely that you would have been fired by that supervisor. All this time you have believed that you would have been very successful, but it may not have worked out that way.

Personality: That means my ability to be successful there may have had nothing to do with me.

Soul: Correct. Furthermore, much of what you have learned during the past five years in your present job has positioned you for a successful career and the type of responsibility that better suits your abilities. It is difficult to make judgements about your situation when you only have some of the information.

Personality: If you help create my opportunities, then why was that one created if it wasn't going to work out well for me.

Soul: So that we could be having this conversation to assist you in your development.

Personality: You mean that you knew I wouldn't take that job.

Soul: It would have been highly unlikely.

Personality: Why?

Soul: You had very little self-confidence. It would have been difficult for you to make a decision based upon your own feelings because you were more reliant upon other's opinions regarding the potential outcome. You were unable to make a decision that others close to you opposed.

Personality: So it was you that caused me to feel so much regret during these past five years.

Soul: Again, your thoughts and assumptions caused you to feel the way that you did. It was your choice to think as you did. I do not control your thoughts. Insight and opportunity, remember?

Personality: So it was a good thing that I didn't take that job.

Soul: It would have worked out.

Personality: You mean I would have been successful.

Soul: It is unlikely that you would have stayed at that company, but other opportunities would have become available.

Personality: With so little self-confidence, what makes you think that I would have taken one of those jobs?

Soul: You would have been unemployed. What do you think you would have decided to do?

Personality: I would have had little choice. I don't like the idea that I am being manipulated in this way.

Soul: You are the one who makes the decisions. Your opportunities are dependent upon your circumstances, which are also based upon your decisions. It is you who creates your life whether or not you choose to be accountable for doing so. It is my hope that you become more comfortable with this process.

Personality: Why?

Soul: If you better understood this process you would become more consciously aware of how your decisions create your life. That knowledge would encourage you to become more engaged in the process. You would be more inclined to search within yourself and understand your needs and desires. As a result, you would be more likely to approach your life with a greater sense of purpose.

Personality: I do have a sense of purpose.

Soul: By taking the job to avoid regret?

Personality: Somewhat.

Soul: By having your family make the decision for you?

Personality: It wasn't entirely that way.

Soul: By having others agree with what you want out of pity rather than stating what you truly need?

Personality: Well.

Soul: By choosing this job out of obligation rather than desire?

Personality: All right, I haven't been acting with as strong a sense of purpose as I thought I was.

Soul: By not doing so you are choosing not to be accountable for your life. You would rather have others make your decisions for you. Do you know why?

Personality: I don't want to be wrong and be criticized.

Soul: It is deeper.

Personality: I don't want to be responsible for their lives.

Soul: You believe that you are responsible for your family's lives and well being, but you are not. Are you violating anyone's Basic Rights by making a decision that benefits you?

Personality: But if I take this new job, then I'm changing their lives.

Soul: Change is inevitable. Sometimes change happens to you and other times you create change. It is up to your family members how they choose to react to change. They have agreed to move of their own free will. They are accepting of this and they will have the chance to make decisions based upon the opportunities that are presented to them. Then they can consider the outcome in the manner of their choosing.

Personality: I hope they won't regret it.

Soul: That will be their choice.

Personality: It probably doesn't help that I have shown them how importantly regret has played into my decision.

Soul: Do you regret that?

Personality: Sure I do.

Soul: So what are you going to do about it?

Personality: What's done is done.

Soul: But not forgiven?

Personality: Are they not going to forgive me?

Soul: Are you not going to forgive yourself?

Personality: Not if I don't take some steps to remedy the situation.

Soul: Such as?

Personality: I'm going to let them know that there are other reasons that have more significantly influenced my decision.

Soul: What are they?

Personality: I'll be making more money. We can loosen the purse strings a little and maybe even take a vacation. It's long overdue. I think that they will really appreciate that.

Soul: I do not think that money was a big reason that your family decided to support your decision.

Personality: Moving to a larger city will provide them with opportunities that they don't have now.

Soul: That was not a big factor either.

Personality: They will benefit as much as I will.

Soul: Certainly, but again you are focusing on examples that allow you to justify making the decision based upon the perceived benefits that others may get rather than fulfilling your own needs.

Personality: Focusing on my needs is selfish.

Soul: Fulfilling your needs is essential.

Personality: Essential to what?

Soul: To your growth.

Personality: What about the growth of my family?

Soul: What about it?

Personality: Shouldn't I be focused on their growth?

Soul: What causes you to believe that you are not?

Personality: You would have me focus on only what is good for my growth.

Soul: How do you know that making choices that benefit you will not also benefit them?

Personality: I don't, but how do I know that it will?

Soul: You do not.

Personality: That is my point.

Soul: What point is that?

Personality: If I don't know which decision is best, then why make one?

Soul: You do believe you know which one is best for you. Is that so?

Personality: Well, yes.

Soul: Then if it feels right to you, choose it.

Personality: But it may not be right for my family.

Soul: It may be just what your family needs. Your decision to take the promotion and move may provide opportunities for your family that are right for them.

Personality: But I don't know that.

Soul: It is their job to know that and they have already consented.

Personality: They're doing it for me.

Soul: Did you make it easy for them to voice their concerns?

Personality: Yes and they did.

Soul: Although they chose to support you, if they had significant fear about the decision, they would have voiced it. I believe that they are looking forward to certain aspects of the move.

Personality: They didn't voice any.

Soul: Why would you expect them to?

Personality: If they were excited about it, then why wouldn't they talk about it?

Soul: Like you did?

Personality: I haven't been the best role model in that regard, but it would have helped me if they had voiced some positive feelings about the move.

Soul: Maybe they did not want to influence you by doing so.

Personality: Why not?

Soul: Because you made it sound as though you were not sure that you wanted to take the job. They did not want to say anything that would have caused you to make a decision that you did not want to make. That is why it was important for you to tell them why you wanted the job.

Personality: Instead, I mainly talked about regret.

Soul: If you had mentioned some of your desires, they would have felt free to discuss theirs.

Personality: I can fix that by having another discussion.

Soul: About money and big city opportunity?

Personality: There's nothing wrong with that.

Soul: What other reasons are there, particularly those that are more personal?

Personality: I get to maintain a relationship with my boss. He has taught me a lot and there is still more to learn from him. I don't want to lose that relationship.

Soul: What else?

Personality: I get to be the boss.

Soul: I thought you were anxious about that.

Personality: I am, but I'm also excited. It will be a great opportunity for me to try some of the things I've learned and to add some twists of my own.

Soul: What if you fail?

Personality: I suppose I will at times, but my boss is only a phone call away. I'll get through if everyone understands that I don't have all the answers.

Soul: What caused the change in your attitude?

Personality: I decided that I could only succeed if I try. Not trying is the same as failing. Even if I do fail, I'm no worse off and if I succeed then I'll be better off.

Soul: The no-lose scenario.

Personality: Exactly.

Soul: Do you realize that every opportunity that you are presented with fits that description?

Personality: That's not true. If I had made a different decision five years ago I would have been worse off.

Soul: You do not know what the following opportunity would have been.

Personality: Are you saying it would have been better?

Soul: Maybe.

Personality: Then it could have been worse.

Soul: Different options present you with different growth opportunities. Some of the best opportunities for growth are those that you would judge as bad outcomes. However, the growth you achieve in the process may position you for opportunities that you presently would consider to be unattainable. In the end it is all about your growth and experience.

Personality: Are you suggesting that I should take any opportunity that you present me with?

Soul: I suggest that you evaluate each opportunity in the manner that we have discussed and make your decisions accordingly. You get to choose your path so that you can accomplish your goals in life.

Personality: Why don't you just tell me what you think my purpose is and I'll just plot my own course?

Soul: What you call your purpose is actually the attainment of certain experiences. At this time in your life, if I told you your purpose in life, you would probably reject it because you would not understand its relevance. Even if you did come to know more about your purpose and adopted it, you would attempt to plot a straight-line path to accomplish that goal.

Personality: What's wrong with that? The shortest path between two points is a straight line.

Soul: Accomplishing your goals requires many small steps in order to acquire the knowledge and wisdom that is your purpose. The path has many twists and turns that are difficult to perceive. That is why it is easiest to stay focused on the present; so that you can be receptive to the next step along your path and not be concerned about arriving at some future destination that is really only the sum of the preceding steps.

Personality: But isn't achieving my purpose accomplished by arriving at my destination?

Soul: Achieving your goals is accomplished by taking all of the small steps along your path because that is how experience is gained. It is the experience gained on the path, not the destination that is your purpose. That is why it is important for you to understand yourself and learn how to make decisions by feeling what is right for you each step of the way. When you do, you can take those steps with greater confidence and trust that the decisions that you make will also be best for all concerned.

Personality: How can I be sure which decisions will be right for me?

Soul: Determine which decisions feel right for you. If your feeling nature is engaged, you can operate with a greater sense of purpose and direct your actions accordingly.

Personality: That sounds too simple.

Soul: Life is as simple as you make it.

Personality: Or as hard as you make it.

Soul: Yes, life is simple, unless you make it hard. The attitudes that you choose in life will determine your perceptions. Choose wisely.

Discuss and/or Journal

The motives that underlie our actions and the manner in which we behave relate to our level of confidence, sense of purpose, and fear of taking risks. It is a balancing act. On the one hand we are compelled to satisfy our wants, needs, and desires. On the other hand, there is fear. Having confidence and a strong sense of purpose combats our fears.

The personality typically gains confidence by taking actions that result in outcomes that are positively perceived. A real sense of purpose is generally obtained by knowing our true needs and desires. The personality often has difficulty acquiring that knowledge. The soul is confident in the knowledge that its purpose will be served through experience. It does not fear risk. To act with confidence, a sense of purpose, and without fear of taking risks is natural for our soul.

1. Are the motives that typically underlie your actions more reflective of your personality or soul?

   _____

   _____

2. Is the manner in which you behave more typically reflective of your personality or soul?

   _____

   _____

3. How much of your level of confidence is due to past successes and failures versus the knowledge that you are on your path?

   _____

   _____

4. What are your true needs and desires?

   _____

   _____

5. How much do you fear risk?

   _____

   _____

   _____

Part V

Tools

Observe

Forgiveness

Compassion

Hope

Relaxation

The Feel, Deal, and Let Go Process

Meditation

Love, Truth, and Will

May these tools assist you in claiming your Basic Rights.

---
chapter twenty

OBSERVE

LEARNING TO OBSERVE OURSELVES is a skill that requires practice, patience, and a close working relationship with our souls. On the other hand, observing others is something that we do quite easily. Our observations of others, all too often migrate to judgements about others or their actions. Why? We have a need to be judgmental, to reinforce in our own minds that we are right. We do this in our attempt to achieve greater self-acceptance. Our personalities believe that self-acceptance is earned in this way.

Self-acceptance is a Right and need not be earned. The soul knows this, but the personality does not accept it due to its intrinsic lack of self-worth. The personality does not wish to consider its worthiness, because of the haunting fear that persists within—am I good enough? So it attempts to show that it is good enough by making judgments about who or what is right or wrong to demonstrate its superiority and prove that it is worthy of acceptance.

If we accepted ourselves more we would have less need to prove ourselves right and be judgmental. Our judgmentalism demonstrates our lack of self-acceptance, which we project on others. Our negative judgments of others principally occur for two reasons.

Sometimes we judge others negatively for being or doing something that we ourselves do and don't like. This reminds us that we continue to be or act in ways that we disapprove of. It irritates us and we pass judgment. Yet we continue to behave in this way. Why? What is our payoff? If there isn't some want or need that we are trying to fulfill, we wouldn't continue to act this way.

More often, we observe someone acting in a way that we won't allow ourselves to act. This also irritates us. It reminds us at a subconscious level that we can't behave that way because it is in conflict with the way that we believe we should behave. We are annoyed that others can act in ways that we cannot. If we did that we would violate our own coping strategies and so we don't. Instead we judge that others are wrong for behaving that way and we want them to stop.

Learning to observe ourselves when we are judgmental can help us better understand ourselves. We can learn what we don't like about ourselves and what we won't allow ourselves to do. Then we can probe deeper and try to understand why. Our spiritual side can help our personalities as we better learn to observe.

Soul: You were surprised when you ran into your old friends, John and Mary, last weekend. When are you getting back together with them?

Personality: Oh, we plan to some time. It's nice to know that they're here in town, but we had closer friends back home.

Soul: I detect that you are not telling me everything that is on your mind.

Personality: Well, as a matter of fact, we can only take so much of them. They're fine for an evening, now and then, but that's about it.

Soul: You seemed so happy to have reconnected with them.

Personality: It was such a surprise! We do like seeing them from time to time, but they're not the kind of friends we want to see too often.

Soul: Why not?

Personality: For one thing, once John gets going about his business, all the deals he's doing and the money he's making you might as well forget about discussing anything else. Unless, of course, the topic changes to sports. He's so competitive that everything turns into a challenge or a bet to see who is smarter or who is right. He always thinks he's right. It gets tiring.

Soul: What about Mary?

Personality: She acts like his biggest fan, but I think she does it to stay on his good side. She likes his income and the fact that she can shop endlessly. She is always talking about what she has that we don't have, their latest trip to wherever or the last fancy party thrown by some notable that they attended. They're fun to be with and very smart, well read and up on the latest trends, but I don't think that they really take anything to heart.

Soul: Why not?

Personality: They're just very superficial. They don't have any kids, always on the run, and trying to climb the social ladder. Their lives seem pretty meaningless.

Soul: Maybe they are doing just what they need to be doing at this time in their lives.

Personality: I don't think so.

Soul: Why not?

Personality: I think they're just wasting their lives on meaningless things.

Soul: Why is it meaningless?

Personality: They aren't accomplishing anything of substance. They're not raising children or doing anything else that would make a positive difference in the world. I think it's wrong to live like that.

Soul: Yet you had fun reuniting with them.

Personality: I don't mind hearing how the other side lives. Meeting them for an evening now and then, if we're doing something like seeing a movie or getting something to eat is fine, but I'm not looking for a closer relationship with them. I always get the feeling that they're judging us and that we don't really measure up to their standards. I think the only reason they want to go out with us is so that they can feel better about themselves because of what they have that we don't.

Soul: It sounds like you are judging them.

Personality: I'm sure that they judge us when they drive home after being with us.

Soul: They may, but why do you judge them or anyone?

Personality: Isn't it normal to judge others? Everyone does it. Isn't that how we know how we are alike and different from one another?

Soul: Understanding how you are alike and different only requires observations, not judgements.

Personality: That's all I'm doing is observing our differences.

Soul: You observed your differences, but then you added a value judgement—it's wrong to live that way. Why do you make judgements about what is right and wrong for someone other than yourself?

Personality: Because I feel it is wrong for them to live their lives the way that they do.

Soul: How can you make that determination?

Personality: It just seems wrong to me.

Soul: Do you mean that it would be wrong for you to act as they do?

Personality: Of course it would be.

Soul: Is that why you believe that it is wrong for them?

Personality: I guess so.

Soul: They are not you. Why are you imposing your value judgements on them?

Personality: Because I think that there is a right way and a wrong way to act and live.

Soul: There is a right way for you and a right way for them, but it does not have to be the same way. Why do you have a need to judge them?

Personality: I don't know that I have a need to judge them.

Soul: Then why do you do it?

Personality: I'm not sure. Why do you think I do it?

Soul: Because you only accept yourself to a limited extent. If you accepted yourself and your situation in life more you would have no need to judge others.

Personality: Why do you always turn it back on me?

Soul: Because your beliefs, feelings, and actions all concern you. Your behaviors stem from your beliefs and feelings. That is why you act as you do.

Personality: How does not accepting myself translate into being judgmental about others?

Soul: How do you feel when you judge others negatively?

Personality: I usually feel anger towards them.

Soul: Even when what they are doing does not have a direct affect on you?

Personality: I guess so, even then.

Soul: Why?

Personality: Because what they're doing is wrong.

Soul: Even if what they are doing does not violate anyone's Basic Rights?

Personality: What do you mean?

Soul: Your friends are not violating anyone's Basic Rights by living their lives the way that they choose and yet you are angry about it.

Personality: So what is your point?

Soul: If you accepted them as they are, would you feel angry?

Personality: I doubt it, but what does that have to do with not accepting myself?

Soul: You are not accepting of them because you are not accepting of yourself.

Personality: That's ridiculous, you're just repeating yourself.

Soul: They are not doing anything that violates anyone's Rights and yet you are angry. When you understand why you are feeling angry, then you will see that you are not very accepting of yourself.

Personality: Are you saying it's right for them to be the way they are? I don't think so. I believe that most people would agree with me too. I think I'm right.

Soul: You often do.

Personality: What do you mean by that?

Soul: You like to be right, just like your friend John. You do not like to admit this to yourself, but you know it is true.

Personality: I admit that I don't like to be wrong, so I argue too much, sometimes even when I know that I'm wrong. It's a bad habit of mine. I don't like myself when I'm that way.

Soul: You were critical of John's need to be right.

Personality: When I see someone else doing something that I do and don't like about myself, I do get angry.

Soul: Why?

Personality: It makes me feel very frustrated.

Soul: Yes, it is a reminder to you that you still act in a way that you would rather not. To avoid dealing with yourself, you displace your anger towards others—in this case, your friend. If you no longer had the same issue with yourself, do you think that you would feel so angry?

Personality: It wouldn't be such a source of irritation, that's for sure, but I still wouldn't like it even if I no longer did it.

Soul: With the passage of time it would bother you less and less as long as you no longer acted in that way.

Personality: Maybe so, but that doesn't explain away the rest of what they do that I don't like. I'm not that way and it still bothers me. I don't see how that results from my lack of self-acceptance.

Soul: I am not surprised. Because of your coping strategies, it is easier to perceive some of what you actually do as opposed to those things that you do not allow yourself to do.

Personality: What are you referring to?

Soul: You were raised in an environment that placed a premium on humility and sacrifice. Boastfulness and arrogance were strongly discouraged. Being a show off was also considered a sin. As a result, the approval you received from your parents depended on your not acting that way. You developed beliefs that acting in those ways was unacceptable or wrong. These were some of the rules that you followed in order to receive love and acceptance from your parents. In order to accept yourself, which was based on how well your parents accepted you, you chose to act in this manner. All of these beliefs are still with you. They represent some of your most ingrained coping strategies.

Personality: I admit that I was raised that way and that I believe these things, but how does disliking these behaviors in others indicate that I don't accept myself?

Soul: How do you truly feel about the fact that your friends have so many things, travel, and do so much more than you do? Are you somewhat jealous?

Personality: Maybe a little.

Soul: Maybe more than a little. There were times when you were growing up when you wanted things that you could not have. You became angry about not getting them and sad about not having them. Later on, you deprived yourself of certain things that you wanted, like taking vacations, because you felt that it was the right thing to do. Even though it was you who made these decisions, it still caused you to subconsciously recall how you felt when you were deprived of what you wanted as a child. That is why, when you see what your friends have that you do not, you become angry and sad. You experience jealousy, which is a blend of these emotional feelings.

Personality: Maybe I am a little jealous. I put aside some of my own wants and make sacrifices for my children. I accept that and so I accept myself.

Soul: If you fully accepted this situation you would not feel angry or sad. You would be at peace with it. It is because you do not fully accept your situation that you feel the way that you do.

Personality: Even if I have a little problem accepting this situation I still accept myself overall. I can live with the choices I've made.

Soul: This situation is simply an example of the compromises you make in order to accept yourself through the eyes of your parents. In your mind, your continued sacrifices justify your acting in a way that is consistent with your old beliefs, allowing you to feel a false sense of acceptance. This is your version of self-acceptance. Do you think that you can simply accept yourself more completely for the person that you are right now rather than trying to justify that you are right?

Personality: I am trying to accept myself by proving that I am right. How can I accept myself if I am wrong?

Soul: You do not need to be right in order to accept yourself. You needed to be right in order for you to be accepted and loved by your parents because they did not differentiate between you and your behaviors. They demonstrated affection and acceptance of you when you acted in a manner that pleased them and they withheld affection and acceptance when you displeased them. That is how you were trained to accept yourself. In the process you adopted their standard. You gave up the ability to deem yourself as acceptable.

Personality: This is how I've chosen to be.

Soul: Precisely. You made these choices when you were a child and you have never changed your beliefs.

Personality: Even now though, when I evaluate my beliefs I would still choose to be this way. I believe that the way that I am is the way others should be.

Soul: Would it surprise you to learn that when others evaluate their beliefs they often come to the same conclusion?

Personality: No. That's why people are different and why we each believe that we are right by being the way that we are. This is why we have to look around to find others who are like-minded to be friends with.

Soul: This is how you perpetuate your dislikes, which often includes the dislikes and prejudices of your parents. This is how you and others create exclusionary behaviors. Carry it a step further and you develop hatred and war, rather than acceptance, tolerance, and an appreciation of diversity.

Personality: Are you saying that all of these problems stem from our coping strategies?

Soul: Coping strategies are developed in response to people having their Basic Rights violated. It is their attempt to meet their needs. Judgments follow as a result of how the behaviors of their coping strategies are perceived as right and wrong. By passing judgment one attempts to exert control.

Personality: For what purpose?

Soul: Because deep inside, the child in them who created the coping strategy says, "how can they do what I cannot?" The child who adopted the coping strategy is saying, "make them stop doing that because it is wrong." That child is still alive in you because you continue to hold those beliefs and play out those coping strategies.

Personality: What do you mean?

Soul: When people develop their coping strategies they deny themselves some behaviors in order to receive some payoff. In your case you have denied yourself much in order to feel deserving of your parent's approval. When you see others doing what you have denied yourself, it causes you to remember those feelings of anger and sadness. Your jealousy results from seeing your friends doing things that you have deemed as wrong because if you did them you would be doing the opposite of what your coping strategy demands of you. That is why you believe that what they are doing is wrong.

Personality: So my friends don't think that what they are doing is wrong because they don't have the same coping strategies.

Soul: Your friends may have overcome those early coping strategies or they simply may have learned to respond with different behaviors. Both you and they are still driven to action and judgment by your beliefs and how those beliefs make you feel.

Personality: I'm beginning to understand how what you are saying applies to some behaviors, but there still is a right and a wrong when it comes to many things, like stealing or killing.

Soul: How would you judge a child with no parental support who is hungry and steals food for survival?

Personality: That's different.

Soul: It is still stealing. How would you judge a woman in her own home who is threatened by a rapist at knifepoint if she kills in self-defense?

Personality: You're just choosing examples that are on the far end of the spectrum. There are many more examples of these acts that are simply wrong. We have laws that define acceptable behavior. Stealing and killing are violations of the law. Sure, there may be mitigating circumstances, but in general these acts are considered wrong. The structure of our society would break down without holding people accountable to these laws.

Soul: Stealing and killing are also violations of a person's Basic Rights although it is important to understand all of the circumstances involved. There is a need for laws at this time.

Personality: Then why did you bring up the examples that you did?

Soul: Simply to demonstrate that most rules have exceptions, particularly those that are imposed on people, those rules that are of external origin.

Personality: Rules that we have to follow are always external, aren't they?

Soul: That is why they are often not followed.

Personality: Why is that?

Soul: Because people do not internalize them. If the rules come from inside of us, we are more likely to feel them and consider them in our actions.

Personality: You're not very practical. How are you going to internalize an entire system of law in each person?

Soul: When people understand love to a greater extent, it becomes an easy feat.

Personality: How would you implement a set of laws using love?

Soul: In every action, simply ask yourself, "what would love do?"

Personality: Like I said, you aren't very practical.

Soul: I recognize the lack of love that exists in society today and the improbable use of a love consideration. The point remains that until a more personal code is instituted into the minds and hearts of individuals there will be less caring and tolerance for one another and greater disregard for laws.

Personality: You may be correct, but I don't see how we are going to get to the point where we can adopt a personal love consideration.

Soul: Understanding your Basic Rights can move you to that point. These Rights are for everyone. Uphold your own Basic Rights and do not violate other's. In time, you will arrive at a love consideration.

Personality: You are simply replacing one set of rules with another.

Soul: I am suggesting that you internalize your Rights by coming to know them through your feeling nature, as opposed to adopting a set of external rules. These Rights do not tell you what you cannot do. They will lead you to greater awareness, fulfillment, connectedness, and a consideration of love for yourself and others.

Personality: The likelihood that these Rights will be adopted and followed in our society is virtually nonexistent.

Soul: One day, in one form or another, they will be adopted.

Personality: What makes you so sure.

Soul: Society cannot progress without them. These Rights are the path that allow every member of society to evolve and leave no one behind because they too can choose this path.

Personality: It all sounds very nice. Let me know when it starts to happen and I'll do my part.

Soul: You may begin now.

Personality: Why would I want to, when nobody else seems to be?

Soul: Why wait?

Personality: I feel as though you are being somewhat judgmental of me by suggesting that I do this now.

Soul: It is not my nature to be judgmental. I am simply asking you why you feel the need to wait.

Personality: Adopting these Rights makes me feel as though I shouldn't be judgmental towards others because I would need to respect their choices for themselves.

Soul: Why does that bother you?

Personality: It makes me feel less secure. All this time I've operated from a set of beliefs about what is right and wrong. I would have to disregard my sense of rightness, which to a significant degree defines who I am. It makes me feel as though I would be losing my sense of identity and my sense of security.

Soul: Maintain your sense of what is right for you rather than imposing your sense of what is right on others. You are not aware of the path that they have chosen. To achieve their purpose they may have to do things that many would consider wrong, but that are necessary for their understanding or the understanding of those around them who are affected by their actions.

Personality: This would be a hard habit to break.

Soul: Allow yourself to observe what others are doing. Even allow yourself to identify whether or not those actions would be right for you. There is no need to limit the free will of others, unless you are trying to control them for your own purposes or unless they are violating your Rights or those of another.

Personality: I guess under those circumstances, giving others the free will that they already have is somewhat liberating. I almost feel that I've lost some responsibility that I wasn't even aware I had taken on.

Soul: That responsibility you are feeling is the weight of maintaining your coping strategies. Removing that weight allows you to more easily change your own beliefs and as a result, not be so tightly bound by them.

Personality: Then I wouldn't be as certain about myself and what I stand for.

Soul: You would reach a point of conscious self-determination. Presently much of what you stand for is what your parents wanted you to stand for. Now it is time to choose for yourself.

Personality: It's exciting and frightening. I don't even know how to go about doing it.

Soul: Observe others without judging them and determine if what they are doing would be right for you. If it seems like it would be, then give it a try and see how it feels.

These actions will allow you to form new beliefs. Use all of your relationships for this purpose. Learn from everyone around you. This is how you can redefine yourself. By accepting others in this way and not judging them, you will learn to more fully accept yourself. It makes the process more enjoyable.

Personality: I'll judge for myself.

Discuss and/or Journal

You can learn much about your payoffs and subconscious coping strategies by observing your likes and dislikes. You can also learn much about how you could be or act by observing others and their behaviors and determining if you would like to be or act that way.

1. What negative judgments have you made about others recently?

_____

_____

_____

2. Are you that way or do you act that way? What are your payoffs?

_____

_____

_____

3. Do you not allow yourself to be or act that way? Why?

_____

_____

_____

4. What traits or actions have you observed in others that you would like to emulate?

_____

_____

_____

5. Can you use your soul to help you be more observant?

_____

_____

_____

chapter twenty-one

FORGIVENESS

Bᴇɪɴɢ ᴊᴜᴅɢᴍᴇɴᴛᴀʟ ɪs ᴀ coping strategy that the personality uses in its attempt to become more self-accepting. Being unforgiving justifies our judgmental attitude and fortifies our belief that we are right in remaining judgmental. Being unforgiving is a harsh and critical attitude that develops when we don't practice forgiveness. When we choose to maintain this attitude we become more isolated from others. Our lack of forgiveness is a self-inflicted punishment that results in a self-imposed exile for as long as we maintain this attitude.

Being unforgiving affects all of our relationships, including our relationship with our spiritual side. Conversely, practicing forgiveness closes the gap between our personality and soul. It allows us to better accept ourselves for who we are and others for who they are. If forgiveness truly helps us become more self-accepting, while judgmentalism doesn't, then why don't we practice forgiveness more often? Is it because we don't really understand who we are forgiving? We don't realize that we ourselves are the ones that benefit from this practice.

Soul: In the process of judging for yourself, try not to be so hard on yourself.

Personality: By being critical of myself I can identify my faults and improve.

Soul: You have a tendency to be tough on yourself out of habit. You treat yourself like your father used to treat you when you were a child. You do not have to be this way. You can observe in yourself those things that you would like to be different and then make the desired changes, if you choose. There is no need to be self-critical in the process.

Personality: Why not? Being critical of myself will motivate me to change faster.

Soul: Being critical of yourself will make you either angry, sad or both.

Personality: Yes and that will motivate me to change.

Soul: Why?

Personality: Because I won't want to feel bad.

Soul: Sounds like a coping strategy.

Personality: Oh, I get it. I'm being critical of myself to motivate myself to change so that others won't be critical of me. My payoff is avoiding being criticized by others.

Soul: You have been listening, but there is more.

Personality: By being critical of myself in the ways that my father used to be critical of me, I would be more like my father and be more worthy of his acceptance and love.

Soul: You are getting the hang of coping strategies and their payoffs.

Personality: So that's it.

Soul: There is more.

Personality: I guess that if I believe that he accepts me then I will accept myself.

Soul: That has been your belief.

Personality: But I don't accept myself very well. I realize that self-acceptance must come from within, otherwise I'm only accepting myself through the eyes of others.

Soul: What stops you from accepting yourself more?

Personality: I do not feel good enough about myself. If I change, and I consider myself good, then it would be easier for me to accept myself more using my own standards. All I need to do is to change and become what I would judge as good.

Soul: How will you do that?

Personality: I need to determine what is good by determining what is right for me. That means I should also determine what is wrong for me. If I want to accept myself more then I must be accountable to myself and be willing to judge myself as being either right or wrong and then doing what is right.

Soul: Using what criteria?

Personality: My own.

Soul: Are you going to separate judging your actions from judging yourself?

Personality: There is no difference when it comes to myself. You even said that my actions result from my beliefs and feelings.

Soul: That they do, but your actions are not you just as your beliefs and feelings are not you.

Personality: But that's how I identify myself.

Soul: Yes, I know.

Personality: What are you not saying?

Soul: Changing your attitudes—actions, feelings, and beliefs—will not allow you to truly accept yourself to a greater extent as long as you judge yourself. Judging others or yourself does not lead to acceptance.

Personality: Then what does?

Soul: Acceptance. Understand that acceptance does not result from a judgment about oneself. Acceptance comes from embracing who you are and your circumstances in this moment and then being open to discover more about yourself and your life. It is also not about being a victim of what is and surrendering to your circumstances. With an attitude of openness you will come to understand the value in what you would call the negative aspects of yourself.

Personality: I'm lost. If I can at least make a judgement about myself that is more positive, then I should be able to accept myself more.

Soul: You will come to understand that judging anything, including yourself, is simply a coping strategy. Many of your coping strategies exist because you do not accept yourself. If you accepted yourself more, you would judge less.

Personality: I'm beginning to understand that judging is a coping strategy. I understand that I do it to avoid dealing with my own stuff in one way or another.

Soul: Do you understand how you maintain your judgmental attitude and your payoff for doing so?

Personality: How?

Soul: By being unforgiving.

Personality: What payoff would I get from that?

Soul: In your mind, maintaining an unforgiving attitude justifies your being judgmental of others. It allows you to believe that you are right in being judgmental because you do not forgive others who are wrong in your view. This mentality provides you a false sense of superiority, which is your attempt to counteract your lack of self-acceptance. If you practiced forgiveness you would lose your justification to be this way. By practicing forgiveness it would also be more difficult for you to play the role of a victim, which is another payoff for you.

Personality: Why should I forgive someone when I've been wronged?

Soul: Forgiveness leads to acceptance. It is all about you.

Personality: This sounds like I would be compromising myself in order to achieve greater acceptance. Sounds like a coping strategy to me, like I'm pleasing others so that they will accept me.

Soul: That is because you do not understand forgiveness.

Personality: Sure I do. When someone does something to me that violates my Basic Rights, I tell them that they are forgiven.

Soul: That is appeasement, not forgiveness. You are doing nothing more than accommodating or pacifying someone by simply stating that you forgive them. Forgiveness is not a meaningless reflex, it is a process that enables you to transform yourself.

Personality: Really?

Soul: Yes, really. Not forgiving is simply a way of maintaining your coping strategies to justify being as you are. Because of the way that you think, maintaining an unforgiving attitude vindicates your judgmentalism, which leads to a sense of superiority and righteousness and at times also allows you to feel victimized. Furthermore, it not only affects your relationships with the people whom you believe have wronged you, it affects all of your relationships because in general you come to expect that others intend to take advantage of you. Your unforgiving attitude biases your perceptions and causes these expectations to be fulfilled, which serves to reinforce this attitude.

Personality: This whole forgiveness issue seems really important to you. I don't ever recall you becoming so intense about anything.

Soul: The passion that you are feeling is a reflection of the truth within me and the need within yourself. The issue of forgiveness is just as important to you. Many people imprison themselves behind a defensive wall created by an unforgiving attitude. The longer they stay there, the harder it is to reverse the process. Utilizing this set of coping strategies widens the gap between us.

Personality: I still don't understand why I should forgive someone who has wronged me.

Soul: Do you wish to accept yourself more completely?

Personality: Sure.

Soul: Then learn to forgive.

Personality: According to you I don't know how.

Soul: It is not hard to learn. Look at the situation that you are having with the contractor you hired to fix your garage door opener.

Personality: What about it?

Soul: Why are you angry with him?

Personality: He was hired to fix the garage door opener. In the process he claimed that he had to reset the tracks that keep the door in alignment when it moves up and down because that caused the motor in the garage door opener to burn out. He said the garage door was never installed properly in the first place.

Soul: So?

Personality: I wanted the garage door opener to be fixed or even replaced if necessary. I didn't want to pay to fix the whole structure. He's overcharging me.

Soul: What did you agree to in the beginning when you hired him?

Personality: He says that I told him to fix the problem with the garage door opener, but I told him to fix the garage door opener.

Soul: Did you understand that there was a more primary problem that caused the garage door opener to fail?

Personality: That's not the point. He did more than I asked him to do and I don't want to pay for it.

Soul: Not according to his recollection of what he was asked to do. Was your initial request of him put down in writing?

Personality: No.

Soul: Do you understand why he did what he did?

Personality: Sort of, but I would have liked to know about it before he did the work.

Soul: How are you planning to resolve the situation?

Personality: I don't know. He just gave me the bill yesterday.

Soul: Did he violate any of your Basic Rights?

Personality: He must have, otherwise I wouldn't be so angry.

Soul: I think your anger relates to you violating your own Rights now as in the past.

Personality: How so?

Soul: You do not like dealing with garage door openers or other appliances because you believe that you have difficulty with mechanical devices. You wanted to avoid dealing with this issue as quickly as you could. As a result, when you met with the contractor you were not fully present. You were quick to rid yourself of this problem, which led to the misunderstanding that developed. You are angry with yourself because of how you dealt with this issue.

Personality: In addition I'm angry with the prior owner for not having installed the garage door properly in the first place. I'm also angry with my realtor who should have recognized this problem before we bought this house.

Soul: You are simply blaming the prior owner and your realtor in an attempt to displace some of your own feelings of self-criticism. You are really angry with yourself for avoiding the problem before you purchased the house. When you opened the garage door before you bought the house you noticed how noisy it was, but you chose not to pursue it because you simply did not want to deal with it. All of your feelings of self-blame are being brought to the surface at this time because you are now being confronted with the consequences of your past actions and you are being forced to deal with them.

Personality: I suppose you would just go ahead and forgive him and pay the bill.

Soul: The process of forgiveness is a little more involved.

Personality: I don't see why I have to waste more time on this than I already have.

Soul: Do you know why that is?

Personality: I'm too busy to deal with this nonsense.

Soul: Becoming a little angry? This is about the time when you move into your avoidance tactic.

Personality: What would that be?

Soul: You either suppress your feelings and thoughts about the matter or you displace your anger towards another and blame them for what is happening.

Personality: Then it would be over.

Soul: Not so. You would simply continue to ignore the real issue.

Personality: I can feel it happening again. You're about to tell me that it's all my fault, aren't you?

Soul: This is not about fault or blame. This is about actions and reactions or consequences of your actions. Avoidance of this situation will only lead to continued ignorance. Remain consciously aware. Accept that the situation you are in is part of the life that you are creating. This will allow you to understand why things are happening the way that they are. It will also allow you to change how you operate so that these events will no longer repeat themselves.

Personality: How long is this going to take?

Soul: It all depends on how long you continue to resist accepting your part in the creation of this event.

Personality: Fine, my life is all about me. Go ahead and tell me how I could have done things differently.

Soul: I think you already know that.

Personality: I could have paid more attention in the first place. I suspected something was wrong with the garage door before we bought the house, but it was working then and I figured it would just keep working even if it continued to be noisy.

Soul: What about your dealings with the contractor?

Personality: I can see his point of view. I don't really remember how specific I was. What does this have to do with forgiveness?

Soul: The process of forgiveness begins with assessing what has happened. What damage has been done and who was responsible for what actions?

Personality: The damage amounts to about $100. That's what he says it cost him to reset the tracks. He should have let me know that before he did the work.

Soul: That certainly would have corrected any misunderstanding between you.

Personality: And I could've done a better job from the start by telling him to figure out what was actually wrong rather than telling him to just fix it.

Soul: How would you prevent this from happening again?

Personality: I need to catch myself when I start to feel impatient with the situation or myself and slow down and figure out how I want to proceed.

Soul: How are you going to proceed in this situation?

Personality: I'm going to pay the bill because if I had asked him to determine exactly what the problem was and he had told me in advance, I would have told him to proceed as he ultimately did.

Soul: Anything else?

Personality: That should do it.

Soul: What if he had fixed $500 worth of problems without telling you in advance?

Personality: I guess I should let him know that in the future he needs to give me an estimate before he actually does the work.

Soul: That would work.

Personality: I still don't see why I should forgive him.

Soul: Nor do I.

Personality: Then why are we talking about forgiveness?

Soul: So that you can consider forgiving yourself.

Personality: For what?

Soul: For your self-critical attitude.

Personality: I wasn't that hard on myself.

Soul: You were tough enough on yourself to push yourself into a repeat performance of your coping strategies related to self-criticism. If this is an example of how you plan to motivate yourself to change then please tell me what you plan to do next.

Personality: I always thought that the way to become less self-critical was to do what was considered right.

Soul: That is because in the past, when you were wrong, you were taught to feel guilty about what you had done or to be ashamed of yourself and then apologize, but never to forgive yourself and move on. You learned that you need not feel guilty or ashamed if you were not wrong. You have developed a strong need to be right and not suffer ill feelings or feel required to apologize.

Personality: I learned that when you did something wrong you did have to go and apologize and then it was appropriate for the person receiving the apology to forgive you.

Soul: That ritual does not move you closer to acceptance.

Personality: What would?

Soul: Accountability. Your life is all about you. How are you going to act and how are you going to deal with the consequences of your actions and the actions of others?

Personality: Accountability. How dare you bring up accountability, apologies, forgiveness, and the consequences of actions and imply that I haven't been doing it right. Look at what happened to my son three years ago. Talk to me about accountability when someone does something about that stupid kid who ran into us with his car and hurt my son. Matt is going to spend the rest of his life in a wheelchair. The stupid kid who ran into us got a traffic ticket and another new car.

Soul: Did he apologize?

Personality: Yes, but so what?

Soul: Did you forgive him?

Personality: I said I did.

Soul: But you did not.

Personality: Of course not. Where's the justice in what happened? Where's the accountability?

Soul: What would you have wanted to happen?

Personality: I don't know exactly, but I would like to see him pay for what he did.

Soul: What he did was to not notice a stop sign. He did not purposefully attack your child.

Personality: He may as well have. The results speak for themselves.

Soul: He made several attempts to contact your family to try to make amends.

Personality: He can't fix my son's spinal cord.

Soul: No he cannot, but maybe some other good could have come from his interaction with your son and your family.

Personality: Maybe not. He was a reckless kid driving through that intersection at 40 miles per hour.

Soul: You seem to forget your role in the collision. If you had looked more carefully you would have seen him coming.

Personality: I'm sorry, but not everything results solely from my actions.

Soul: No, but it is still your life.

Personality: You think that I should forgive him.

Soul: You would be the beneficiary.

Personality: How so?

Soul: It would allow you to shift your attitude. You have held onto this unforgiving attitude for the past three years and it has tainted all of your relationships including your relationship with yourself.

Personality: How can that be?

Soul: Maintaining an unforgiving attitude has kept you from forgiving yourself for not seeing the car approaching the intersection. Your anger towards the other driver is to a large extent a symptom of your inability to forgive yourself. Being unable to forgive yourself has intensified your inability to forgive others. That is also why you have become more critical of everyone during the past three years. It is time to learn how to forgive and move on.

Personality: Do you think I've punished myself enough?

Soul: There was never a need to punish yourself.

Personality: But I could've prevented the accident if I had noticed.

Soul: As you have said, it did not result solely from your actions.

Personality: Yes, if that kid wasn't speeding and if he had stopped when he should have, then it wouldn't have happened. Either one of us could have avoided the tragedy, but it is my son who was injured and is now disabled. I'm supposed to protect him and keep him safe. I failed. I let him down and now he's going to suffer for it for the rest of his life.

Soul: So it is only right that you suffer too, is that it?

Personality: Yes.

Soul: Did you ever realize that your suffering is affecting the way that Matt perceives his circumstances?

Personality: What do you mean?

Soul: When you are angry you refer to your son as being disabled and you talk about how his life has been ruined. You are teaching him to be less than he could otherwise aspire to be. Despite your inadvertent lack of support, he is still doing well and even now he serves as an inspiration to others.

Personality: I did not realize what I was doing.

Soul: You have been too self-absorbed. You have never allowed yourself to go through the grieving process about this episode. As a result, your suppressed grief manifests as pity and hopelessness at times, and as anger and critical behavior at other times.

Personality: Forgiving myself seems meaningless in the context of how I feel.

Soul: Forgiveness is more than assessing the damage, being accountable for your role in the event, taking steps to prevent a reoccurrence, and making reparations. It also includes grieving the loss and then pardoning all concerned, including yourself. Forgiveness is not a simple meaningless ritual. It is a thorough accounting of what has transpired physically, emotionally, mentally, and spiritually—although the spiritual side of the equation is beyond your perceptual capabilities at this time.

Personality: There is much to think about.

Soul: There is more to it than thought. If you do not deal with your feelings regarding this matter, you will remain in your present state.

Personality: When you described how people imprison themselves behind a defensive wall by having an unforgiving attitude, I didn't realize that you were referring to me.

Soul: I was referring to almost everyone. It is done to a variable degree, but it is done by almost all. If it were not, then there would be widespread acceptance, tolerance, and love and that is not the case. I am here for you and I am ready to do my part.

Personality: I thought this was something that I had to do.

Soul: It is something that you must initiate and direct and then we do it together. This is one of the ways that we close the gap between us.

Personality: You mean that you are the one that forgives me.

Soul: Only you can determine that. I already accept you unconditionally.

Personality: Then what is your role in this process?

Soul: Both you and I do the giving, but you determine who it is for.

Discuss and/or Journal

Practicing forgiveness is a process. It consists of assessing what has happened by determining what damage has been done and who was responsible for what actions. It involves taking steps to prevent a reoccurrence and making reparations. It also includes grieving the loss and then pardoning all concerned, including yourself.

1. Outline your practice of forgiveness?

_____

_____

_____

2. When was the last time you forgave another?

_____

_____

_____

3. When was the last time you practiced self-forgiveness?

_____

_____

_____

4. What do you think your soul was doing when you practiced forgiveness?

_____

_____

_____

5. Are there people in your life at present that you would like to forgive? Would you like to forgive yourself?

_____

_____

_____

---
chapter twenty-two

COMPASSION

Typically, when we see another in pain or in need we feel bad. Why? Some people worry that they could find themselves in similar circumstances and would want others to feel bad for them. Some people connect with those suffering and feel their pain as if it were their own, while others connect, identify the pain, and don't adopt it as their own. How we feel in these circumstances is a reflection of our beliefs. If our beliefs direct us to feel bad when we witness another in pain or need, we will.

If some people witness another in pain or in need and don't feel bad, are they less likely to be compassionate than those who feel bad? Does how we feel in such a situation determine whether or not we are compassionate? Our feelings motivate us to take action. It stands to reason then, that feeling bad for another will likely cause us to be more compassionate. Or does it? We can exhibit the same behavior regardless of how we feel. What is it that determines whether or not we are being compassionate? Is it how we feel or what we do?

We practice compassion by engaging another to determine their needs and then by acting towards them in a way that we believe will result in the most benefit. How do we engage them? We can do it with our mind, our feeling nature, or both. However, if we wish to identify their true needs, then feeling what they feel will facilitate the process. In determining what actions to take it is often helpful to consult our minds, but not to limit ourselves to only that capability. We are more likely to determine the best course of action when we synthesize all of the available information. This includes not only what we feel and think, but also the input we receive from our soul.

Our strongest connection with our soul resides within our heart. That is why compassion is best practiced with heart. It is the place where the information from our mind and feeling nature meet the influences from our soul. It is where we bring to bear all of our human nature. Is there a better place to relate to others from? No. Practicing compassion is an excellent way to learn how to blend the influences of our personality with those of our soul.

Personality: Can this giving you refer to be done for any purpose and not just for forgiveness.

Soul: Certainly.

Personality: If I direct the giving, then I would like it sent to my son. He is the one who was wronged.

Soul: What would you be giving?

Personality: Whatever it is that you give. You said I got to determine who it is for. So go ahead and give it to him.

Soul: I said that we do the giving together. You must also be engaged in the process.

Personality: Fine, let's get started. What do we do?

Soul: We do what love would do.

Personality: That's it! We send him love?

Soul: We treat your son with compassion. That is what love would do towards your son.

Personality: I already do that. I feel very sorry for him. I am sympathetic for the difficulties he's facing now and will face in the future.

Soul: Yes, you pity him. That conveys your judgement concerning his situation, but how is that compassionate?

Personality: What are you talking about? That is what being compassionate is all about. Go look it up.

Soul: Many of your words have little or distorted meaning to you because your society has been neglectful of the deeper emotional feelings associated with these words. Your understanding of forgiveness is an example and compassion is another. When you say these words you do not feel their truest meaning. They are just words to you.

Personality: That is how we communicate.

Soul: Yes, you communicate primarily on an intellectual level.

Personality: What is wrong with that?

Soul: It is not wrong. It is simply limited because it does not engage your feeling nature all that deeply. As a result, the meaning that you derive from interpreting what you hear relates mainly to intellectual concepts with little in the way of associated feelings.

Personality: It's too hard to feel words when I'm busy trying to interpret what they mean.

Soul: If you could impart more feeling into your words your communications would have more meaning.

Personality: You said that people don't feel much from words anyway.

Soul: At this time most do not feel much from the words themselves, but they do feel something from how words are spoken. Your tone of speaking carries meaning. In time, when you allow me to speak through you, more meaningful words will be chosen that carry an even greater resonance.

Personality: What does all of this have to do with compassion?

Soul: Often it is not what you say, but how you say it.

Personality: How I say what?

Soul: Whatever it is that you say.

Personality: In general?

Soul: Of course.

Personality: I should talk to everyone as though I feel sorry for them?

Soul: I do not communicate to anyone in that way.

Personality: But that is what being compassionate is all about. It's about sympathizing with their plight, their hardship in life, or their misfortune.

Soul: How does feeling sorry for them or pitying them help their situation?

Personality: It lets them know that others feel bad for them.

Soul: How does that help?

Personality: It acknowledges their pain and suffering.

Soul: You can do that without feeling sorry for them.

Personality: How?

Soul: By simply letting them know that you acknowledge their plight.

Personality: But then I may not appear compassionate to them.

Soul: How does one appear compassionate by appearing to pity another? Is that how you would like to appear to your son?

Personality: Yes, I want him to know how much I care about him and his difficulties.

Soul: Does it help your son to know that you feel sorry for him?

Personality: Sure, he knows that I'll always be there for him.

Soul: Can you be there for him without feeling sorry for him?

Personality: Yes, but I want him to know that I feel his pain.

Soul: Why?

Personality: So that he knows that I can identify with it.

Soul: That creates a strong bond between you two.

Personality: Yes it does.

Soul: I think there may be other reasons that you choose to feel his pain.

Personality: What reasons?

Soul: For starters, to avoid feeling your own guilt. Focusing on your son's pain allows you to avoid dealing with your guilt.

Personality: Maybe it does, but I must deal with his pain first and try to make him feel better.

Soul: Then what will happen when he is no longer in pain?

Personality: I will feel better.

Soul: What of your guilt?

Personality: I will no longer need to feel it because he will feel better.

Soul: In your words, however, your son will still be disabled. How will you not feel guilty about that? After all, you have not forgiven yourself for the collision.

Personality: I'll cross that bridge when I come to it.

Soul: You may avoid coming to that bridge.

Personality: What do you mean by that?

Soul: You may choose to continue focusing on your son's pain and suffering.

Personality: But at some point he may feel better.

Soul: He may not feel better until you do.

Personality: That's backwards. How do my feelings influence his?

Soul: You have bound them together. Your feelings are dependent upon your son's. His feelings, whether you know it or not, are dependent upon yours.

Personality: How are his feelings dependent upon mine?

Soul: You have been teaching him how to perceive his limitations.

Personality: How?

Soul: By labeling him as disabled or challenged and by maintaining your unforgiving attitude.

Personality: Life is a challenge for him.

Soul: Life is a challenge for everyone. His challenges are simply more easily seen because they are physical in nature. Challenges present opportunities for development. If you continue to portray sorrow, then it will be difficult for him to perceive his challenges as opportunities. If you wish him to develop then help him to see his opportunities. That would be compassionate. That would help him move along his path.

Personality: How do I do that, when I don't see his opportunities?

Soul: Learn what they may be. He has primarily been affected physically, although if you persist with your unforgiving attitude, you will burden him with additional emotional and mental challenges beyond what is necessary for what he had intended to learn and do.

Personality: How does it affect him if I remain unforgiving?

Soul: He senses your anger towards the other driver and he is aware of how close you two have become. As a result, he chooses to be in agreement with your position on this matter, which causes him to adopt the role of a victim. Your son has begun to incorporate your unforgiving attitude into his nature.

Personality: But I am also to blame.

Soul: He has not allowed himself to see that possibility because it is in conflict with his need to remain close to you.

Personality: When he does become aware of that he will hate me.

Soul: He certainly will have mixed emotions towards you if he accepts that you are to blame for his disability. His anger could be transformed if he were to learn how to forgive.

Personality: You want me to learn how to forgive so now you're using my son's emotions to force me into learning forgiveness.

Soul: You are doing that all by yourself. At some point in time you will face the consequences of your actions. You are creating your life through your own decisions. I provide insight and assist with opportunities. If you teach your son forgiveness sooner rather than later the adjustments in your relationship will be less tumultuous.

Personality: Did you arrange the car accident?

Soul: I was a willing bystander.

Personality: Why didn't you prevent it?

Soul: It was in the best interests of all concerned.

Personality: Then who arranged it?

Soul: Your son arranged it and you and the other driver accommodated.

Personality: They didn't know this at a conscious level, did they?

Soul: Not then, but your son has developed some awareness that this is his path. That is why acceptance is less difficult for him than it is for you.

Personality: But you said that I make it more difficult for him.

Soul: Yes, you do by virtue of your unforgiving attitude, your guilt, and your sorrow.

Personality: If the accident was planned to occur then it really isn't my fault is it?

Soul: It is not a matter of fault.

Personality: But you said that I wasn't being accountable for my role in the accident.

Soul: Accountability is accepting responsibility for your role in the event, not assigning blame. That is a judgement.

Personality: How responsible was I if it was all planned to happen anyway?

Soul: You were the driver of the car, were you not?

Personality: So you are blaming me.

Soul: I am simply reminding you of the fact that you were driving the car and you did not perceive the oncoming driver. In this situation, being accountable means nothing more than acknowledging that you were driving the car and you were not aware of the other driver.

Personality: If I look at it that way, then it would be easier for me to forgive myself.

Soul: Yes, because you would no longer be judging yourself as wrong.

Personality: Being judgmental limits my ability to forgive.

Soul: Which limits your ability to accept yourself, all because of your need to be right, which in your way of thinking leads to greater self-acceptance. You have not been very compassionate towards yourself.

Personality: I am feeling a bit overwhelmed by all of this.

Soul: It is a lot to consider when for so long you have been held hostage by your old beliefs and fears.

Personality: I am beginning to feel that my life is not my own. There are so many forces at work that are beyond my awareness and comprehension.

Soul: That is why it would be helpful if you were more compassionate towards yourself and others.

Personality: I'm starting to feel sorry for myself, but I'm beginning to understand that in your view that has nothing to do with compassion.

Soul: The present-day view of compassion is often twisted. The way compassion is generally practiced today, it enables others to accept themselves as victims and to maintain that status.

Personality: But when we are compassionate toward others we often help them by being charitable.

Soul: Being compassionate will help you in your charitable efforts by allowing you to understand how to best offer your assistance. By learning how to become compassionate you can avoid enabling others to stay as they are, particularly if they view themselves as victims.

Personality: How do I learn to be compassionate?

Soul: With heart. All of the influences in your realm that pertain to any situation you will encounter register on the human heart. Let your feelings, in addition to your thoughts, guide your actions.

Personality: What would love do?

Soul: Yes. Your heart provides a strong connection to me and through me to All That Is. Open your heart and feel all of the influences that bear upon it and you will know how to act with compassion.

Personality: How would it change my relationship with my son?

Soul: It would cause you to be more truthful with one another.

Personality: Then he would know that I am to blame and that would cause a problem between us.

Soul: He does not wish to condemn you. Matt is more forgiving than you give him credit for. He understands that you did not intend for the collision to occur and it is unlikely that he would hold you responsible.

Personality: But I was to some extent responsible.

Soul: You did have a role to play. You were driving at that time and in that way you were a part of the event. He already believes that you did the best that you could to avoid the collision. However, he has come to realize that your feelings of guilt allow him to manipulate you into doing more for him than you need to.

Personality: I have begun to see that attitude in him. He triggers my guilt by appearing to be sad or too tired to pick up his clothes and clean up after himself.

Soul: It is time for you to reevaluate your boundaries. Your feelings and actions enable your son to do less than he can.

Personality: I will make him do his chores regularly and even add a few. I've been a little too easy on him. I've heard that from others, but I've made excuses for him.

Soul: It is also time to reevaluate your emotional boundaries. Much of what you allow yourself to feel is felt through your son. You lose yourself in his feelings and you have had increasing difficulties identifying your own emotional feelings. Of late you have been avoiding your own fear by focusing on your son. As a result, you have done things that retard your son's progress.

Personality: Why, because I won't let him be reckless?

Soul: Participating in physical activities would allow him to feel more connected to other children. It would also help him to feel that he has more power over his situation.

Personality: He may be injured.

Soul: Playing basketball in a wheelchair is unlikely to produce a significant injury. The benefits far outweigh the risks. You do not fear physical injury as much as you fear his reduced dependence on you.

Personality: Why would I fear that? I want to see him have friends and enjoy himself.

Soul: You like the fact that he is heavily dependent upon you. His physical limitations have given you a distorted sense of purpose. Before the collision you felt as though you were drifting through life without much purpose.

Personality: It is my job to take care of my son. I don't see why doing my job, which is my purpose, is distorted.

Soul: It would be helpful for you to evaluate which of your actions stem from compassion and which do not. Then you would better understand your true purpose as it relates to your son.

Personality: How could my purpose where my son is involved be anything different from taking care of him and protecting him so that he can grow up as normally as possible.

Soul: Every relationship is a two-way street. Of course you are providing for some of his needs, but he can also provide for some of yours.

Personality: Naturally I want to receive my son's love and I wish to participate and enjoy his successes in life.

Soul: There is more for you to learn from your son. You are resisting perceiving what that may be just as you are attempting to prevent its emergence in him.

Personality: How can that be? I only want the best for my son.

Soul: Then allow him to develop as fully as he can. Encourage him and do not impose the limitations on him that you have been.

Personality: I am only trying to keep him safe.

Soul: In part you are, but that is not your only motivation. Allow him to take prudent risks and grow. He may surprise you.

Personality: How so?

Soul: In time you will come to know provided that you develop further yourself.

Personality: Is it going to happen or not?

Soul: That depends upon the choices that both of you make. Consult your heart. That will give you the direction that you need.

Discuss and/or Journal

People typically wish to appear compassionate. They may express strong feelings when sympathizing with others in pain or need. When they also adopt the feelings of others, as their own, they often take steps to reduce the pain, or satisfy the need, without helping others understand why they are experiencing it. As a result, those people suffering don't learn how to cure or fix it themselves. This scenario often creates a dependency, when the people in need are enabled by having their needs met, without learning why they have them, or how to meet those needs themselves.

A co-dependency can develop when people's actions, intended to remedy a situation, are motivated in part by their own perceived needs. Dependencies and co-dependencies develop because of the needs and wants of the personality and not the soul. They arise from our coping strategies.

1. When was the last time you enabled another?

   _____

   _____

   _____

   _____

2. What did you feel and think?

   _____

   _____

   _____

   _____

3. When was the last time you were enabled by another?

   _____

   _____

   _____

   _____

4. What did you feel and think?

   _____

   _____

   _____

   _____

5. Which of your relationships are in part dependent or co-dependent?

_____

_____

_____

_____

6. Which of your relationships encourage you to be independent?

_____

_____

_____

_____

7. When was the last time you practiced compassion?

_____

_____

_____

_____

8. What did you feel and think?

_____

_____

_____

_____

9. What were the influences from your soul?

_____

_____

_____

_____

_____

_____

_____

chapter twenty-three

HOPE

Being hopeful is an attitude, just like being compassionate, forgiving, and non-judgmental. These attitudes are biases that alter our lives—they have a real affect in our practical world. How can that be? How can being hopeful really matter? It is an attitude and our attitudes shape our lives and define our reality.

Let's dissect the attitude of hope. What is the belief underlying hope? It is an optimistic belief that things will work out for the best. How does this belief cause us to feel? Hopeful. What does hopefulness feel like? It is a feeling of openness—a sense of welcoming and excitement felt in our hearts and throughout the core of our being. How does this feeling affect our actions? Feeling hopeful causes us to be receptive and proactive. We are less fearful in venturing outside our comfort level.

Contrast hopefulness with hopelessness. When we are hopeless we believe that things will not work out well. We feel deflated, hopeless, or despair. As a result, we do not take action and we practice avoidance. Our hearts and minds are closed to the influences around us.

The difference between the attitudes of hopefulness and hopelessness is dramatic. They represent two ends of the spectrum of hope. Most people have an attitude that lies somewhere between hopefulness and hopelessness. Why are they not hopeful? They have experienced disappointment and as a result, they have become less hopeful to reduce potential feelings of disappointed in the future. That fear limits their belief and feeling of optimism, receptivity, and their ability to be proactive.

So how does that affects their lives?

Personality: It sounds like my son will develop nicely. I hope it happens.

Soul: That is unusual for you.

Personality: What is?

Soul: Admitting that you have hope.

Personality: Did I say that?

Soul: You said, "I hope that it happens."

Personality: I guess I did. So what?

Soul: You are rarely openly hopeful. Generally you frown upon those who are hopeful.

Personality: There's little advantage in being hopeful. What does it get you, but disappointment?

Soul: That attitude stems from your need to remain emotionally balanced. Avoid the highs and you will not have to suffer through the lows, is that it?

Personality: Something like that.

Soul: Some people use hope very effectively.

Personality: They are deluding themselves.

Soul: They would disagree.

Personality: What does it get them?

Soul: It keeps them moving forward on their path. It enables them to envision their destiny.

Personality: What you're describing sounds like blind optimism.

Soul: On the contrary, it is what allows them to see.

Personality: How so?

Soul: When you hope I am drawn to you and through you into the physical realm.

Personality: How can that be?

Soul: Try it.

Personality: Try what?

Soul: What would you hope for? Choose something that you want for yourself.

Personality: How about something for my son?

Soul: Consider something for yourself.

Personality: It's difficult for me to want something for myself even when I know that it's the right thing for me to do.

Soul: Then why not hope for the strength to do what is right for you?

Personality: That's something that I would like.

Soul: Then go ahead and hope for it.

Personality: What exactly do I do to hope for it? Do I just say it to myself?

Soul: If you do that I will hear you and try to accommodate you, but the experience could be greater if you would be willing to feel more.

Personality: Feel what?

Soul: Me and All That Is.

Personality: Is this necessary?

Soul: The experience may instill in you more of a reason to believe in me, which may give you greater hope.

Personality: It can't hurt to try. What do I do?

Soul: Feel your whole body all at once and imagine that you are opening yourself to me. Allow the warmth and love of my presence to fill you and surround you. Now feel your heart as you repeat to yourself what you are hoping for.

Personality: I do feel something. What is it?

Soul: I have strengthened you.

Personality: Why?

Soul: That is what you hoped for.

Personality: How long will this last?

Soul: As long as it is what you hope for.

Personality: Can I hope for anything?

Soul: Certainly.

Personality: And you will participate in the same way?

Soul: That depends on whether your will and my will are aligned.

Personality: Of course, I should have known. You're not my genie.

Soul: Correct.

Personality: I'm sorry, but this whole thing seems a little silly. How do I know that it is real?

Soul: You can observe yourself and determine whether or not it is easier for you to do what you would consider to be right for you.

Personality: Even if it is, it could simply be easier because I expect that it will be easier. So nothing has happened to me that wasn't of my own doing. This same thing could result from my own shift in attitude.

Soul: Precisely.

Personality: So you admit that you have done nothing.

Soul: In both cases your attitude would shift. If you practice hope in the manner that I suggest, you would also become more receptive to me. That would allow me greater access to assist you, but you must initiate this process.

Personality: Why do you need greater access to assist me?

Soul: When we coexist in greater alignment you have greater access to all that I am and through me to All That Is. You are closer to the knowledge that you seek and the feelings that you desire. You become more connected to all of life because I am connected. Your life becomes richer and more fulfilling.

Personality: All this from hope?

Soul: Hope opens the door.

Personality: I learned that prayer does what you are describing.

Soul: What is prayer, but hope?

Personality: Prayer is not directed to a person's soul. Prayer is directed to a higher authority.

Soul: If your prayer is directed to a higher authority, then I am involved. As I said, I am connected. The message will be received by all if I receive it.

Personality: This is still not very real to me. I guess I'm hopeless.

Soul: Not really. You have more hope than you are willing to admit to.

Personality: You mean that I do have some hope.

Soul: Of course you do. You are simply not openly hopeful because you do not like to view yourself or have others view you as an optimist or as unrealistic. As a result, you are less willing to allow others to see your hopeful aspirations. Do you know why?

Personality: I don't want to be disappointed.

Soul: There is more.

Personality: Like you said, I don't want to appear optimistic.

Soul: Why is that?

Personality: Optimists are usually unrealistic. Things never seem to work out the way that they would like them to.

Soul: What do they do then?

Personality: They remain optimistic anyway.

Soul: Do you know why?

Personality: No.

Soul: Because they still have hope.

Personality: That's my point. They continue to hope when it is in vain. That is foolishness.

Soul: Why?

Personality: Because they have already been proven wrong.

Soul: That is what you fear.

Personality: What?

Soul: That by openly demonstrating hope you will be proven wrong and others will notice. That is why you attempt to hide your hope, but it does not work.

Personality: Why not?

Soul: Because you are disappointed anyway.

Personality: So.

Soul: You would not become disappointed if you were not hopeful.

Personality: At times I hope for things to work out one way or another, but mostly I'm pessimistic. I don't believe that things will work out well.

Soul: That is how you mask your optimism.

Personality: I do not.

Soul: You do not mind being wrong when things work out well because you are not disappointed. For you this resembles balance. On the other hand, if things do not work out well then at least you were right and again you have achieved balance.

Personality: I guess I do that more than I realize.

Soul: But you are not hopeless.

Personality: Do you have hope?

Soul: I have no need of it.

Personality: Why not?

Soul: I know that everything will work out for the best.

Personality: Maybe that is what I should hope for.

Soul: By all means, do so.

Personality: I don't feel any different.

Soul: I did not expect that you would at this time, but you will in the future if this hope remains.

Personality: Why in the future?

Soul: It will happen as you abandon your short-term fears. Knowing and trusting that things will work out tends to be associated with perceiving a longer time horizon than you presently attend to. Your focus is typically short term, as in days and weeks. You rarely extend your thoughts to months or years.

Personality: My life is practical, remember. I have to deal with the here and now each and every day.

Soul: And that is why your focus tends to be short term, but you can always take a precious moment and envision your future with a broader time frame. It would also help you understand that the problems that overwhelm you are not as large as you believe them to be at that moment. When you examine them within the scope of a greater time horizon, their significance is diminished. Remember what it was like right after your son's injury?

Personality: Yes I do. Time seemed to stop and all I could focus on was what had happened and how horrible it was. I don't even want to think about that.

Soul: What happened as the days turned into weeks?

Personality: I began to focus on the care that Matt required. I also started to realize the extent of his disability, as he didn't recover as much as we had hoped. When I finally realized that he wasn't going to be able to walk again I was crushed—I felt utterly hopeless.

Soul: But then there was hope.

Personality: I thought he was asleep as I sat on the bottom of his bed. I started to cry. My sobbing awakened him and he wiped my tears away. He said it would be all right.

Soul: How did that affect you?

Personality: My perspective began to shift. He was way ahead of me and moving forward with life. I decided that I needed to catch up. His attitude restarted my life.

Soul: He gave you hope.

Personality: I guess he did, but I was still hoping for a better recovery for him.

Soul: You remained disappointed.

Personality: Yes and I continue to feel that way. I feel let down.

Soul: By whom?

Personality: Why do you have to ask?

Soul: So that the answer can fully materialize.

Personality: What good will that do?

Soul: So that for once and for all you could proclaim your anger.

Personality: Why did God let this happen to my child? Matt never did anything to deserve this.

Soul: And.

Personality: Am I being punished? Why couldn't I have been hurt instead? Was I so bad that this horrible thing had to happen to my son?

Soul: Go on.

Personality: Why couldn't he get better? Why weren't my prayers answered? What kind of God are you?

Soul: You have had these thoughts bottled up for some time.

Personality: I want answers not another lesson.

Soul: You have already been given the answers, but you choose to not accept them.

Personality: You can't honestly believe that I'm going to accept free will as an answer. My son would not willingly bring this upon himself.

Soul: Why not?

Personality: He doesn't want to be disabled.

Soul: At times he becomes frustrated, but oftentimes to manipulate you. He accepts his condition much more than you do. Why is that?

Personality: I probably don't accept it because I still feel guilty about my part in it. Anyway, what choice does he have?

Soul: He has the same ability to choose as you have. You find his situation difficult to accept because it is not your path. You are projecting what is right for you onto him, but his path is different. You are once again judging what is right or wrong from a limited viewpoint.

Personality: I hate it when you tell me that. I'm not a child.

Soul: Why does it make you angry?

Personality: You make me feel as though I'm operating in the dark with limited awareness.

Soul: You are.

Personality: Why does it have to be this way?

Soul: It does not.

Personality: Then why is it this way?

Soul: Because you choose to operate using your coping strategies, which limit your awareness to only that which you allow yourself to perceive.

Personality: I want to perceive more.

Soul: Then you must change.

Personality: Why?

Soul: Like perceives like. To perceive more within my realm you must become more like me.

Personality: Why can't I simply operate through you as you operate through me?

Soul: Your coping strategies are not compatible with love and truth. That is why you must change in order to become more like me. Then you would understand more of what I understand.

Personality: That seems impossible for me at this time.

Soul: There is hope.

Personality: I think I'm going to need more than that.

Soul: You have been given much. Hope, compassion, forgiveness, and being non-judgmental can take you far. It is now time for you to put these tools to use, but you can begin with hope.

Personality: Why start with hope.

Soul: It is the foundation of your reality.

Personality: You've got to be kidding.

Soul: Not at all.

Personality: How can that be?

Soul: It is the spark that begins the process. Hope triggers your dreams and aspirations. Hope can bring your intent to life and rally the unseen forces to your side.

Personality: Why?

Soul: Because without hope there is only despair. You cease to be a force in life. There is no progress or movement and in time there is nothing to be supported or to rally around.

Personality: Sounds pretty hopeless.

Soul: But then there is hope, dreams, aspiration, creativity, and finally manifestation. That is why it is the basis of your reality. It all begins with hope.

Personality: I guess the only disadvantage is disappointment, as long as I don't let others see that I'm too hopeful.

Soul: Even disappointment has its advantages.

Personality: How can that be?

Soul: It can give you insight about your path.

Personality: If that is true then being disappointed is like hearing no from heaven.

Soul: No is an echo from your past, but even then you had hope.

Personality: I have not lost those hopes. You have reawakened them in me.

Soul: That is the nature of hope.

Discuss and/or Journal

We each have the ability to be hopeful. Although past disappointments have reduced our optimism, we can at any time become more hopeful. Your soul can help you understand the nature of those disappointments and assist you in gaining a different perspective. As you learn from and realize the importance of those disappointments, you will have less fear of the future and more reason to be hopeful.

1. Take a moment and identify and then reflect on some of your past disappointments. From your present-day perspective, with the assistance of your soul, can you identify any benefit that you derived from those events?

    _____

    _____

    _____

    _____

2. Adopt a hopeless attitude and feel what hopelessness feels like to you. What does it feel like?

    _____

    _____

    _____

    _____

3. Adopt a hopeful attitude and feel what hopefulness feels like to you. What does it feel like?

    _____

    _____

    _____

    _____

4. How do you wish to feel?

    _____

chapter twenty-four

RELAXATION

W<small>E TYPICALLY RESPOND TO</small> the stresses in our daily lives in a reactive, unconscious manner. Our coping strategies are triggered and we become tense. Our physiologic, emotional, and mental states change and we experience the affect that stress has on us. It takes a toll on our health and well being physically, emotionally, mentally, and spiritually. Why does this happen? Because we allow it to happen.

We blame our circumstances or events in our lives, but we determine how we react to them. Our beliefs are triggered, but we determine what we believe. If we were more accountable for the reality that we create for ourselves, we could more easily change it. How? We don't have to respond to the stresses in our lives in the manner that we do. How can we learn to be different? Relax. Being more relaxed is physically, emotionally, mentally, and spiritually beneficial.

This is common knowledge, but not commonly practiced. Only a small minority of individuals practice relaxation. Those people recognize that learning how to deepen their state of relaxation has considerable benefits. They enjoy the relaxation sessions themselves, but it is the affect of being more relaxed more of the time that confers the greatest benefit. Once we learn what it feels like to be more relaxed we can more quickly recognize when we have become tense. As a result, we can take steps to regain a more relaxed state.

If we are functioning in a more relaxed state we are less likely to have our coping strategies triggered. Even when they are triggered, if we are more relaxed, we stand a better chance of observing ourselves to a greater extent so we can learn more from the experience. Being more relaxed allows us to shift our gears so that we can slow down and better understand how we are responding to the circumstances in our lives. We can better perceive why our lives are the way they are and then make changes in ourselves if we choose to improve our lives.

Becoming consciously aware of how we feel when we are more relaxed is a prescription for greater health and well being. It is pleasant to perform and makes us feel good. Why then do we avoid it?

Personality: You have given me much to consider, but I'm feeling drained. I'm in no state to work on anything at this time.

Soul: Then maybe you should relax.

Personality: That would sure feel good, but I don't have time to relax. Anyway, what does relaxation have to do with any of this?

Soul: Relaxation affects you physically, emotionally, mentally, and spiritually. Being relaxed will help you to absorb what we have been discussing more easily.

Personality: I already know how to relax.

Soul: Please, tell me how you do it.

Personality: I turn on some music, lie down, close my eyes, and drift off to sleep.

Soul: What do you observe?

Personality: I'm asleep. I don't observe anything unless I happen to remember a dream.

Soul: It would be beneficial if in your ordinary daily activities you could feel as relaxed as when you sleep.

Personality: I already told you, I don't know what that feels like.

Soul: Do you know what your body feels like at this moment?

Personality: I really don't pay that much attention to it. I know if I focus on a part of my body I can feel it, but in general I don't walk around sensing what my body feels like.

Soul: How do you know how relaxed you are?

Personality: I never think about how relaxed I'm feeling. I only know if I'm feeling stressed or not.

Soul: When you are not feeling stressed are you relaxed?

Personality: I doubt it. I'm just not feeling stressed.

Soul: You are just feeling neutral, is that it?

Personality: That's me, neutral and balanced.

Soul: How do you feel physically when you are feeling neutral?

Personality: When I'm feeling neutral I don't feel my body. I only feel my body when it doesn't feel right, like when I'm stressed or in pain.

Soul: What do you feel like when you are feeling stressed?

Personality: The muscles in my neck and around my shoulders tighten up and I usually get a headache.

Soul: Anything else?

Personality: I perspire more and I feel a little queasy if it gets worse.

Soul: What is your breathing like at that time?

Personality: I don't know. I must just keep breathing.

Soul: Then what do you do?

Personality: I take some aspirin for my headache and I continue to do what I was doing.

Soul: Why not stop for a moment and relax?

Personality: I don't have the time to simply stop what I'm doing and take a break like that. Anyway it's hard to just switch gears and relax. I have to ease into it when I know that there won't be any demands placed on me.

Soul: Your motor is running a bit too fast.

Personality: I have to run that fast to get everything done on time. You simply don't understand what the real world is like.

Soul: I see how chaotic and disorganized it is and what people's priorities are.

Personality: Are you suggesting that I am not organized or that my priorities need to change?

Soul: You would benefit considerably by slowing down a bit.

Personality: I don't think so. I wouldn't get done what I need to on the job and at home. The complaints would drive me crazy and I would feel miserable.

Soul: I think you would feel better, as would those around you. You would become more efficient with the time you spend doing work and other activities.

Personality: I suspect you're going to tell me to find a guru and take up meditation.

Soul: You do not need a guru to learn how to meditate and you are not ready to learn.

Personality: Why not?

Soul: Why are you interested?

Personality: I have heard that it's good for you, so I have considered learning more about it.

Soul: What has held you back?

Personality: It seems a little too foreign to me. I have this feeling that I would have to switch religions or the way that I think about things.

Soul: Meditation is nothing more that a natural extension of relaxation. First learn to relax physically and emotionally. Then you can learn how to meditate, which can be understood as an extension of relaxation mentally and spiritually.

Personality: I would rather just dive into it and learn how to meditate if I'm going to do anything at all.

Soul: Many people try that approach and fail. I would not recommend it.

Personality: Have some hope, let's give it a try.

Soul: For hopes sake I will accommodate you.

Personality: What do I do?

Soul: Assume a relaxed position, close your eyes, breathe using your abdomen, and surrender yourself to me.

Personality: Wait a minute. Why would I want to do that and what are you going to do if I do surrender to you?

Soul: I thought you wanted to learn how to meditate.

Personality: I do, but you're taking advantage of me.

Soul: How so?

Personality: You're using this as an excuse to take control of me. You want me to surrender to you. What about my free will?

Soul: It is your choice. Surrender or not.

Personality: I choose not.

Soul: Then let us work on relaxation.

Personality: I would rather learn how to meditate.

Soul: You have chosen not to.

Personality: Are you saying that I must surrender myself in order to meditate?

Soul: What do you think meditation is?

Personality: I told you that I didn't want to switch religions.

Soul: I was in existence before mankind created religions. I have no religious affiliation.

Personality: Oh, sorry.

Soul: No need to apologize.

Personality: Religion is a touchy issue.

Soul: Relaxation would help you with that.

Personality: I still would rather learn how to meditate.

Soul: What do you think meditation is?

Personality: I think it's a deeper form of relaxation that is more spiritual.

Soul: Am I not spiritual?

Personality: You're an extension of me. I don't think of you as being spiritual.

Soul: That is because you do not think of yourself as a spiritual being.

Personality: No I think that I'm a human being.

Soul: And a human being in your way of thinking is composed of a physical body and a personality, is that correct?

Personality: That's how I would define it.

Soul: If I am an extension of you, then how do I fit into your definition?

Personality: Oops. I never considered you. I guess you would be an extension of my personality, but I would say that you are my better half.

Soul: Then what do you consider to be of a spiritual nature?

Personality: God or, as you put it, All That Is. I would consider that to be spiritual.

Soul: Am I not a part of All That Is?

Personality: I guess you are.

Soul: And what of you?

Personality: Yes, I guess I am, but then so is a rock.

Soul: Everything is part of All That Is, but you are not aware of the connectedness between what you consider to be yourself and All That Is, which includes everything that is around you. Everything is spiritual because everything contains the spiritual essence of All That Is. It simply manifests in different ways. That which sustains the matter you perceive with your five senses is of a spiritual nature.

Personality: Fine. You've convinced me that everything is equivalent to All That Is, which only reinforces my belief that it means absolutely nothing because it's not specific to anything. Meditation must simply be a deeper form of relaxation.

Soul: Your spiritual beliefs are constrained by a belief in a force that you call God that you have defined as being external to you. That is why you would rather assign everything that is spiritual to a specific external entity. Spirituality involves everything, including you. Through me you can be elevated to perceive spiritual forces, including those of a higher vibrational nature. That is why meditation is a spiritual practice. As you become more adept at it you can become more aware of spiritual forces within and outside your physical realm. However, to do so requires that you surrender yourself to me.

Personality: Will you return control back to me, when it is over?

Soul: You are always present when you surrender control. As such you can resume control whenever you choose. It is your attitude of allowance that creates the meditative state and your attitude of surrender that deepens it.

Personality: As long as I can remain in control, then I'll give it a try.

Soul: Assume a comfortable position, close your eyes, breathe with your abdomen, and surrender yourself to me.

Personality: I'm not very comfortable sitting like this. Do I have to sit with my legs crossed?

Soul: Make yourself comfortable.

Personality: I need to loosen my belt. I can't breathe with my abdomen when my belt is this tight.

Soul: Please do so.

Personality: I can't stop thinking of all the things I should be doing right now.

Soul: Acknowledge the thought and then let it go. Imagine that thought as if it were a cloud and watch it drift away as you exhale and then return your attention to your breath.

Personality: It is simply replaced by another thought.

Soul: Acknowledge the thought and then let it go. Imagine that thought as if it were a cloud and watch it drift away as you exhale.

Personality: And then another.

Soul: Continue the process.

Personality: The muscles in my neck are getting tight.

Soul: Move your head and shoulders. Tighten the muscles and then let them relax.

Personality: That feels a little better.

Soul: Good.

Personality: I'm starting to worry because I haven't heard from the kids yet. I better get up and call them.

Soul: Okay.

Personality: Meditating doesn't seem to do much for me.

Soul: You have not been meditating.

Personality: I did everything you told me to do.

Soul: You have made your first attempt at learning how to meditate although you only attempted to do so for about five minutes.

Personality: How long does it take?

Soul: As long as it takes.

Personality: I don't like your open-ended answer. I need to see some progress. Can't you be more specific as to how long it will take before I can see some results?

Soul: It is entirely dependent upon you. How long do you think it will take?

Personality: I have no idea. This seems confusing to me. I don't understand the end point or the process. I'm feeling more stress than when I started.

Soul: That is why you should first learn to relax.

Personality: How long will that take?

Soul: Relaxation, like meditation, is not an all or none process in terms of reaching an end point because there is no definable end point to which you can easily relate.

Personality: I need to have a more specific goal in mind so that I know what I'm trying to achieve. You must be able to tell me something.

Soul: Remember what it feels like when you are relaxing after vigorous exercise or on some Saturday mornings when you partially awaken and realize that you can stay asleep for a while longer.

Personality: I know what that feels like.

Soul: Put yourself into that state.

Personality: How?

Soul: Re-create that feeling state.

Personality: Just like that.

Soul: Try it.

Personality: I feel a little more relaxed, but I'm not nearly as relaxed as after I've exercised or partially awakened.

Soul: You can achieve that level of relaxation during your normal activities if you practice relaxation.

Personality: I thought that the benefits are derived only during a relaxation session.

Soul: Relaxation is a state of being. The benefits are derived whenever you are relaxed and the greater the level of relaxation, the greater the benefits. More significant benefit is derived by being more relaxed more of the time, not just when you are practicing. The relaxation sessions are practice sessions to learn how to relax more deeply so that you can achieve that state throughout the day. This will enable you to more easily and quickly return to a more relaxed state when your coping strategies are triggered and you become tense during your daily activities. More importantly your baseline state of being will be more relaxed allowing for greater tolerance to the stresses in your life so that you are less easily triggered.

Personality: So the more relaxed I become, the less my coping strategies are triggered.

Soul: And then the more relaxed you can become.

Personality: And then I can learn to meditate.

Soul: At that point meditation will be a natural extension to the state that you have already achieved.

Personality: How do I begin?

Soul: Assume a relaxed position, close your eyes, breathe using your abdomen, and surrender yourself to me.

Personality: Wait a minute. These are the same instructions for learning how to meditate.

Soul: Meditation is an extension of relaxation. At present you need only focus on the physical and emotional aspects. Later you can work on the mental and spiritual dimensions.

Personality: Aren't there any rules I can follow?

Soul: There are many methods that have been created to learn how to relax.

Personality: Which one will work best for me?

Soul: Part of the process is learning how you respond to different techniques.

Personality: I want to know that what I try will work before I invest time into it.

Soul: Most of what you try will work to some extent at this early stage. Remember what it feels like to be relaxed and replicate it.

Personality: I get that, but how do I best do it?

Soul: Turn the practice of relaxation into a habit, as that will reinforce the process. If possible, practice at the same time each day, preferably in the morning to avoid falling asleep. Your body will recognize the new schedule after a few weeks, making it easier to attain a deeper state of relaxation. Set aside a period of time when you can be assured that there will be no interruptions. This is your time. Also, practice in the same place, one that is comfortable. Darken the room if you prefer. Unplug the phone in that room or turn off the ringer to avoid interruption. If you are waiting for the phone to ring, you are maintaining a vigilant state that is in opposition to the state of relaxation that you are attempting to achieve. Position yourself comfortably sitting or reclining. Be as comfortable as possible. Try not to cross your arms over your chest or cross your legs, to avoid reducing the blood flow to your limbs.

Personality: What about my breathing?

Soul: The process of relaxation is greatly assisted by breathing originating in your lower abdomen. To learn to breathe in this way place your left hand on your lower abdomen, well below your navel. Breathe into this area for several breaths. Breathe slowly and deeply. Continue to feel yourself breathing into your lower abdomen with your left hand. Now place your right hand at the level of your diaphragm, midway between your navel and your heart. Your right hand should be at the top of your abdomen, at the bottom of your rib cage. Breathe slowly and deeply into this area for a few breaths, as you continue to breathe into your lower abdomen. Feel that both hands are moving outwards as you breathe in. You should be feeling your left hand moving first. Since you are breathing more deeply you do not need to breathe as often because you are delivering more oxygen to your body. Simply focus on deeper breathing using your entire abdomen and allow your breathing rate to slow down. A few slow, deep abdominal breaths are helpful at the beginning of your relaxation session. Paying attention to your breathing is also another way to become better grounded in the physical and to feel more.

Personality: So I should just focus on my breathing?

Soul: Focus on your breathing and how your entire body feels. Feel your body more completely and instruct it to relax more deeply. If you wish, focus for a while on each group of muscles with the intention of having them relax further. Allow yourself to relax as you do when you sleep.

Personality: What if I fall asleep?

Soul: Then you will sleep.

Personality: But then I'm not learning how to relax.

Soul: That is correct. Your conscious awareness will be lost and you will not appreciate how relaxed your body is.

Personality: Maybe I should also try to retain my awareness at night when I go to sleep.

Soul: That would tend to disrupt your sleep and you would be tired the next day. During your relaxation sessions it is helpful if you can learn to expand your conscious awareness into ever-deepening levels of relaxation. You will notice that at times you fall asleep and at other times you simply lose awareness as you try to expand your conscious awareness. In time, your mind will remain awake, while your body sleeps. Then you will appreciate how deeply relaxed you can be.

Personality: How long will it take me to achieve that level of relaxation?

Soul: How ever long it takes you to allow this state to develop. How quickly will you learn to move into the background and observe?

Personality: I don't know.

Soul: You will have to weigh the payoffs and come to that decision over time. Each day consider allowing the relaxed state to develop to a greater extent.

Personality: Is this all I have to do to learn how to relax?

Soul: Your ability to relax more completely also depends upon your willingness to allow your emotional feelings to flow and emerge. Blocked feelings or stuffed feelings create bottlenecks to that flow and impair your emotional well being, which has a direct impact on the level of relaxation you will allow. Holding your feelings in check will limit your ability to relax more deeply because in the process of controlling your feelings you maintain a higher degree of watchfulness. That is contrary to a relaxed state of being.

Discuss and/or Journal

Imagine that you are home on a Friday evening, reclining in a very comfortable chair. The excitement of the week is behind you. Everything that you had planned worked out well. Life for the moment is worry-free. You are comfortably reclining with your eyes closed, feeling completely relaxed, and at peace.

1. What does this state feel like to you?

   _____

   _____

   _____

   _____

2. Contrast this with how you normally feel.

   _____

   _____

   _____

   _____

You are still in the relaxed state described above. Your dog begins to bark at your children playing outside. The annoying, high-pitched barking continues for a while, but you remain in your relaxed state realizing that your dog is simply being a dog and doing what dogs do. A short while later you can hear your son and his friend outside playing in the driveway. They are throwing a tennis ball against the garage door. They are not allowed to be doing that, but tonight you are content to let boys be boys.

3. Are you normally this accepting of events such as these?

   _____

   _____

   _____

   _____

   _____

4. If you were more relaxed would you likely be more accepting of events such as these?

_____

_____

_____

_____

_____

5. Would your coping strategies be less likely to be triggered if you were this relaxed?

_____

_____

_____

_____

_____

6. Would you be better able to observe yourself if you were more relaxed?

_____

_____

_____

_____

_____

7. Are you going to make time to learn how to better relax? Why or why not?

_____

_____

_____

_____

_____

_____

chapter twenty-five

THE FEEL, DEAL, AND LET GO PROCESS

Practicing this process facilitates a greater awareness of your coping strategies—unhealthy attitudes. More importantly, it provides a way to lessen the affect of your unhealthy attitudes—painful beliefs, negative emotions, and unproductive behaviors. It requires a commitment to change for it to work. A willingness to change will not suffice because people that are willing and not committed tend to be reactive rather than proactive. The Feel, Deal, and Let Go process, in order to be successful, requires a proactive approach. This method can be performed during a relaxation session or whenever you can quietly reflect. Until you are accomplished at this practice, it will take you a number of sessions to work through it completely.

To use this method, you will need to act in a conscious, accepting manner. Begin by opening your feeling nature and allow yourself to feel, as you consider an event that is troubling you. Re-create the emotions and physical sensations you experienced at the time of the event. Don't practice avoidance. If your coping strategies are triggered, don't allow yourself to subconsciously react and suppress your feelings. Instead, stay present-centered and focus on your feelings. Consciously attend to them. Ask yourself, "what am I feeling?" Encourage yourself to feel those emotions and physical sensations more completely throughout your body.

Once you are firmly anchored in your feelings, ask yourself, "as a child when did I feel this way?" Become receptive and allow yourself to perceive when as child you felt similarly. The emotions you experience allow you to transcend time and perceive your past because your emotions are closely tied to your memories. Give yourself time and be patient. If you are unable to perceive anything on a conscious level after a few minutes, practice relaxation. Ask yourself, "what am I avoiding?"

As your perceptions begin to unfold, perceive how your Rights were violated from your perspective as a child. Once you understand how your Rights were violated, ask yourself, "how would you have liked things to have happened differently?" Give yourself time to imagine how events could have been different. Clearly understand the occurrence. From your present-day perspective, develop a thorough understanding of the Basic Right violation that occurred, including the role that you played. Determine whether you continue to allow your Rights to be violated and/or whether you continue to violate another's Rights. Understand your payoffs and be accountable for your unhealthy attitudes. Envision a healthy attitude—belief, feeling, and behavior—and payoff that you can adopt in place of the unhealthy attitude.

With a complete understanding of the event, your role in its occurrence, any ongoing Basic Rights violations, and your payoffs, fully accept what has and continues to occur. Practice forgiveness towards others in your past and present if you have been violated and for yourself for your role to play. Release your unhealthy attitude and practice relaxation. Imagine adopting the healthy attitude you envisioned in its place.

In a future session revisit yourself, as a child in the past, and provide reassurance that future violations won't occur. Address yourself in the present and make a similar commitment. Strengthen your new belief and sense how that makes you feel and motivates you to act.

Partnering with your soul, as you work through this process, will enable you to better observe, forgive, and be compassionate. Have hope in the process and you will more likely succeed in transforming your reality, as your attitudes and payoffs evolve.

Personality: What if something comes to the surface that is upsetting during my relaxation session? Won't that disturb my relaxed state?

Soul: It may, but it need not.

Personality: How would it not?

Soul: It depends upon the level of relaxation you have achieved and are able to maintain when you become consciously aware of the event that precipitates the emotional feeling. Practice will enable you to develop a more stable state of relaxation both in your sessions and during your normal daily activities.

Personality: What if I can't stay relaxed?

Soul: How relaxed you remain when an emotional feeling emerges is not of importance. In time you will remain more relaxed as long as you practice. However, recognize that you are being presented with an opportunity to learn about yourself when suppressed emotions and memories surface. You can choose to take advantage of the opportunity or let it pass.

Personality: What kind of opportunity is that? I'm trying to learn how to relax more deeply and instead issues may erupt, which are likely to disrupt that process.

Soul: That is part of the process of learning how to relax more deeply.

Personality: Oh I see, I'm being tested to see if I can maintain a relaxed state in the face of adversity.

Soul: You are not being tested.

Personality: Then what is the point of it?

Soul: Suppressed emotions related to your coping strategies prevent you from relaxing more deeply until they are understood more completely. When you are more relaxed these feelings have a greater tendency to emerge from your subconscious. Once the feelings emerge and you deal with them more effectively you will no longer need to maintain greater vigilance to keep them in check. You will be able to achieve an even more relaxed state both in and out of your sessions.

Personality: What causes these feelings to emerge?

Soul: Life's events. As you move into a relaxed state and your mind drifts you may be re-minded of an event that has recently happened which caused you distress. The deeper feelings associated with past events that are related to this event, are able to emerge at that time. Or you may decide to proactively use your relaxation sessions to uncover your deeper feelings by purposefully reviewing a recent situation and your associated feelings and beliefs about it.

Personality: But I thought I was supposed to let my thoughts move away and not focus on any of them.

Soul: You certainly can do that when your intent is to deepen your state of relaxation or meditation. However, during some of your relaxation sessions you may wish to con-sider the thoughts and feelings that emerge. Let us leave the mental and spiritual prac-tices until later and focus primarily on the physical and emotional processes associated with relaxation.

Personality: I have so many thoughts. Do I consider each of them?

Soul: Consider those that seem the most important to you, but first learn to move into a state of greater relaxation. Focus on your abdominal breathing and imagine your breath moving throughout all of your body. Take note how your entire body feels even as thoughts emerge. Feel the rhythm of your breath and your body as it moves when you breathe. Feel your hands and feet and arms and legs. Work on trying to feel all of your body. At first you may not feel much, but over time you will be able to feel more. After you have achieved a more relaxed state during your session, then consider the thoughts that emerge or those that you wish to purposefully consider and periodically check on your breath and how your body feels.

Personality: Why do I need to check on my breath and feel my body?

Soul: You are learning what your body feels like as it becomes progressively more relaxed. As you become consciously aware of this relaxed state, you can reproduce it outside of your relaxation sessions so that you can feel more relaxed more of the time.

Personality: Why can't I focus on just how my body feels and learn how to relax more deeply?

Soul: You can, but thoughts will emerge that beckon your consideration.

Personality: You said that I could wait until I learn to meditate before I had to focus on mental processes.

Soul: The mental practices you will learn in meditation are different than those that you will experience during relaxation. In meditation you will learn to listen better by learning what it is like to have a quiet mind as you learn to better appreciate me.

Personality: I am more quiet when I listen to you now.

Soul: Yes you are doing better, but much of what I communicate to you does not penetrate your mind. As you consider your thoughts while relaxing I will be able to better communicate with you. That improvement in our ability to communicate will correlate with the degree of relaxation that you are able to attain. This is an example of how a relaxed state gradually develops into a meditative state.

Personality: So what do I do when a thought emerges that I want to consider?

Soul: Determine how you feel as a result of having that thought. See how your body feels in response to it. Allow your feelings to emerge and do nothing to hinder their flow. Do not suppress them or avoid them. Welcome your feelings and allow them to spread throughout your entire body. Do not fear them and instead observe them rather than judge them as bad and then avoiding them. Observing them rather than becoming caught up in them will allow you to remain more relaxed.

Personality: How am I not going to be afraid of fearful thoughts?

Soul: They will not hurt you. They are the feelings of your past, reminders of events that caused these feelings to develop in the first place. Feel them as completely as you can in the present moment knowing that you are safe.

Personality: For what purpose?

Soul: Allowing yourself to reexperience these feelings more fully assists you in recalling the events of your past that caused their formation and reinforced their existence. Your emotional feelings allow you to transcend time. This will allow you to understand the beliefs and fears that you have developed around those events.

Personality: And I'm really supposed to remain relaxed during all of this?

Soul: By having these feelings and thoughts emerge, while you are in a relaxed state and a safe environment, you are providing yourself the opportunity to remember events that you have been suppressing. If you wish to understand yourself better, then it is time to remember the events that caused you to reinforce your coping strategies. You may even be able to remember the events that caused their formation. The degree to which that upsets you is your choice. If you are willing to observe more than judge, forgive more than remain unforgiving, be compassionate with yourself and others, and be hopeful, then you will create an atmosphere of greater tolerance and understanding for yourself. The extent to which you do this is entirely up to you. The more you can maintain an attitude of greater observation, forgiveness, compassion, and hope, the more relaxed you will remain, and the more you will remember.

Personality: There is more to your method of relaxing than I am used to and probably more than I'm prepared to do.

Soul: Your idea of relaxation has been to lie down and take a nap. In that state only your dreams can help you to learn about yourself. Even then you would need to explore them in a more meaningful way to gain any relevant information.

Personality: What you are suggesting doesn't seem all that appealing especially when I'm just trying to relax and reduce my stress.

Soul: I am only suggesting that you assume a relaxed position, close your eyes, breathe using your abdomen, and surrender yourself to me.

Personality: That's not too hard, except for the idea of surrendering to you. Having to deal with my thoughts and feelings is another issue.

Soul: We have not even gotten to that point yet.

Personality: What do you mean?

Soul: Our focus has been on feeling them in preparation for dealing with them in a more meaningful way.

Personality: You're kidding aren't you?

Soul: You can learn to relax by focusing on your breath, learning to feel your body more completely, and dismissing every thought by returning your focus to your breath and body. Realize, however, that you are actively avoiding issues that at some time you will be required to face if you wish to develop yourself further. There is a reason that these issues are confronting you.

Personality: How much will I benefit if I only work on relaxing without dealing with my thoughts?

Soul: Over time you will learn to move more easily into a moderately relaxed state during your sessions. You will also learn to be somewhat more relaxed during your normal daily activities. You will have learned a new behavior that will allow you to feel better and act differently. However, the issues that fuel your tension and that are triggered by the stresses in your life will remain unresolved. As a result, you will not be able to relax more completely until you deal with them.

Personality: No pain no gain. Is that it?

Soul: You choose the degree of pain you wish to experience. You need not have any depending upon the attitudes that you adopt in this process.

Personality: Well go on and tell me how I can deal with these issues.

Soul: First you must appreciate them more simply.

Personality: How?

Soul: From the mind of a child.

Personality: You want me to discuss my issues with my children.

Soul: No. I want you to appreciate your issues from the viewpoint of when you were a child. That will help you understand them more clearly and allow you to better understand their origins.

Personality: How do I accomplish that?

Soul: It is very easy as long as you are feeling your emotions more completely. Having the same feelings now as you had then quickly allows you to review your past. All you need do when you are relaxed and feeling those feelings is to ask yourself, "when as a child did I feel this way?"

Personality: And then what?

Soul: Wait for an answer.

Personality: What if nothing comes?

Soul: You will always be given an answer, but you may not perceive it unless you are relaxed, willing, and open.

Personality: Why wouldn't I want to know the answer if I'm asking the question?

Soul: When you judge something as too painful you have a tendency to close yourself off from perceiving it. You must learn to remain the observer. Ask and then feel, listen, and watch. If you are truly open to receive it, you will.

Personality: Then what?

Soul: Understand the issue from that perspective because it still influences you. Whenever you respond using a coping strategy you are responding from when that coping strategy was formed and reinforced. The actions of your coping strategies are little more than childish responses. Try to understand them more simply.

Personality: Understand them in what way?

Soul: Understand what happened in reference to your Basic Rights. You either allowed your Rights to be violated or someone violated your Rights against your will. In either case you developed coping strategies to deal with future situations that you perceive to be a similar threat. After you have a more complete understanding of the events that transpired, and your role in their creation, you can meet yourself as the child who was violated. Provide comfort, as you would have liked another to do. Explain to that child that there is no longer a need to fear further violations. Be compassionate and lead with your heart in this process. You must also deal with your present-day self by becoming more accountable to yourself. Become aware of the payoffs that you presently derive from the use of your coping strategies. Be open to envision more desirable payoffs by acting in a more honest, straightforward manner.

Personality: With all of this thinking how am I supposed to be maintaining a relaxed state?

Soul: Spend less time thinking and more time being in a receptive state. You will receive answers to the questions that you ask. Maintain your posture of being the observer. As such, check back periodically and sense your breath and how your body feels and take a moment to deepen your state of relaxation. Then proceed by letting go of the thoughts and feelings after you have received all of the information that you think you will at that time.

Personality: Let go of what?

Soul: By employing your coping strategies you perpetuate an attachment to your fears and old beliefs that you have created in response to your past violations. Letting go of your fears and old beliefs will lessen your need to use these strategies. When you are free of them your perceptions will become clearer and your awareness will grow because you are no longer limiting what you are willing to believe, feel, and do.

Personality: How do I let go of them?

Soul: This process involves practicing forgiveness for yourself and others. The greater the forgiveness the more easily and completely you will be able to let go of your attachment to your old fears and beliefs. After you understand how your Rights have been violated you can more easily determine how to prevent it from happening again by acknowledging, claiming, and upholding your Rights. You can also more easily assess the damage that has been done, understand why it happened, and grieve the loss. Then you will be ready to pardon all concerned and more completely let go of the event in its entirety.

Personality: Many of these events happened long ago. Wouldn't it be better to simply let sleeping dogs lie?

Soul: They do not sleep. They remain fully active every time you use your coping strategies and they have been active since your early Rights violations. That is why you must approach this process through yourself as a child because that is when most of them were created. They have persisted from that time. In the present you simply reenact a strategy that was created then.

Personality: What if I can't remember the original violation?

Soul: You may never remember, but to the extent that you are able to effectively heal these Basic Right violations, even if you only identify reinforcing events, you will have less need to employ your coping strategies.

Personality: Do I do all of this in one session?

Soul: It can be done in one session, but as you learn the process, do it in stages. This process also can be done outside of your relaxation sessions, sitting quietly and relaxed when you are not likely to be disturbed. You do not need to approach this process alone. There are many qualified individuals who can help you sort through these issues. They can help you recognize some of your behaviors, feelings, and beliefs that you are less willing to acknowledge on your own.

Personality: Maybe I should focus on learning how to relax first.

Discuss and/or Journal

The Feel, Deal, and Let Go process can be divided into three parts—Feel, Deal, and Let Go. After completing the process it is helpful to reinforce what you have accomplished. During your relaxation sessions or when you are in quiet reflection, consider practicing these parts, one per session, in sequence. As you learn these procedures continue to practice only one part per session. Repeat the same part in subsequent sessions until you believe that you have fully completed it before moving onto the next part.

Feel: Open your feeling nature and allow yourself to feel, as you consider an event that is troubling you. Re-create the emotions you experienced at the time of the event. Ask yourself, "what am I feeling?" Encourage yourself to feel those emotions more completely throughout your body. Once you are firmly anchored in your feelings, ask yourself, "as a child when did I feel this way?" Become receptive and allow yourself to perceive when as child you felt similarly. Give yourself time and be patient. If you are unable to perceive anything on a conscious level after a few minutes, practice relaxation. Ask yourself, "what am I avoiding?" Repeat this part later until you perceive an event from your childhood.

Deal: Perceive how your Rights were violated from your perspective as a child. Once you understand how your Rights were violated, ask yourself, "how would you have liked things to have happened differently?" Give yourself time to imagine how events could have been different. Clearly understand the occurrence. From your present-day perspective, develop a thorough understanding of the Basic Right violation that occurred, including the role that you played. Determine whether you continue to allow your Rights to be violated and/or whether you continue to violate another's Rights. Understand your payoffs and be accountable for your unhealthy attitudes. Envision a healthy attitude and payoff that you can adopt in place of the unhealthy attitude.

Let Go: With a complete understanding of the event, your role in its occurrence, any ongoing Basic Rights violations, and your payoffs, fully accept what has and continues to occur. Practice forgiveness (assess the damage, who was responsible, prevent a reoccurrence, make reparations, grieve the loss, and pardon all concerned) towards others in your past and present if you have been violated and for yourself for your role to play. Release your unhealthy attitude and practice relaxation. Imagine adopting the healthy attitude you envisioned in its place.

Reinforce: In a future session revisit yourself, as a child in the past, and provide reassurance that future violations won't occur. Address yourself in the present and make a similar commitment. Strengthen your new belief and sense how that makes you feel and motivates you to act. Partner with your soul, as you work through this process.

1. Can you think of any events in your life or ongoing circumstances for which it would be helpful for you to practice the Feel, Deal, and Let Go process?

_____

_____

_____

_____

_____

_____

_____

2. Can you think of a coping strategy/unhealthy attitude that you have, that you would like to change using the Feel, Deal, and Let Go process? What healthy attitude would you like to adopt in its place?

_____

_____

_____

_____

_____

_____

_____

_____

_____

chapter twenty-six

MEDITATION

WHAT IS MEDITATION? It is a state of being. A state of being what? A state of being more consciously integrated with our soul and All That Is. Meditation tends to be practiced in discreet sessions to experience and enhance this state of being. With practice, the meditative state we are able to achieve can be experienced during our regular daily activities. In this way, our meditative state can become the way we are in life. To what end—what's the payoff? The payoff for our personality is a growing conscious awareness of our spiritual side and All That Is—living life in partnership with our soul and All That Is.

Soul: Have your relaxation sessions been relaxing?

Personality: I've been progressing quite nicely during these past months. I'm surprised how short each session seems and how my day seems to go better after having relaxed in the morning.

Soul: Have you been practicing the Feel, Deal, and Let Go process?

Personality: I've tried it a number of times with some success.

Soul: What has happened?

Personality: At first I would come out of my relaxed state when I felt strong emotions, but after I remembered to be the observer, I was able to better maintain a relaxed state. In later sessions I was surprised how easily I was able to perceive myself as a child after allowing myself to feel my feelings more completely. However, when I began to think rather than ask questions I couldn't remain as relaxed.

Soul: Staying in the role of the observer is important.

Personality: Why does that work?

Soul: Observing yourself causes you to change your reference point to me to a greater extent. In that way you begin to see yourself through my eyes. When you shift your reference point you are not so easily pulled into reliving what you are witnessing.

Personality: I'm not as afraid when I'm in the role of the observer.

Soul: When you are more strongly identified with me and not simply on a mental level, you will have much less fear.

Personality: But I still have a fair amount of fear, just less than I would normally have.

Soul: That is because you limit how closely you are willing to accept and identify with me.

Personality: But I have come to the conclusion that I'm willing to accept you more. You have continued to give me good insight and I'm learning to trust you.

Soul: You trust me more, but primarily on a mental level. You are still holding back considerably, both emotionally and physically.

Personality: I am not aware of that.

Soul: You are not consciously aware of the dynamics at work in your subconscious mind.

Personality: I guess I'm not that far along.

Soul: You need not be critical of yourself. Who are you comparing yourself to? Your progress has been considerable.

Personality: I would like it to be faster.

Soul: You are concerned about becoming different than you are right now. Focus on being what you are now. Practice the Feel, Deal, and Let Go process without concern for any specific goal other than simply increasing your understanding about yourself.

Personality: Why is it so important to practice?

Soul: Most people live their entire lives maintaining their old fears and beliefs. Practicing the Feel, Deal, and Let Go process in conjunction with relaxation or meditation is a fast way to sort through your subconscious fears and old beliefs. That will hasten your growth and enhance your conscious awareness because you will become less dependent upon your coping strategies. Your journey in life will be much more enjoyable as a result.

Personality: I think I'm ready to learn how to meditate.

Soul: Then learning to accept me to a greater extent will be an issue you should address sooner rather than later.

Personality: Why?

Soul: You will not be willing to surrender to me if you do not accept me.

Personality: But I am willing to accept you.

Soul: Only superficially.

Personality: How can I do so more completely?

Soul: Understand how you really feel about me.

Personality: How?

Soul: Practice the Feel, Deal, and Let Go process.

Personality: And think about you?

Soul: Determine how you feel about me. Take some time and become more relaxed. Focus on your breath and how your body feels. Feel all of yourself and intensify your level of relaxation.

Personality: I am very relaxed now.

Soul: How did you feel when you realized your son was not going to make a full recovery?

Personality: I was devastated.

Soul: Remain the observer. What do you feel in your body now when you allow that feeling of devastation to permeate throughout your entire body?

Personality: I feel hollow and empty, as though everything has been removed from inside of me.

Soul: As a child when did you feel this sense of loss?

Personality: I see myself all dressed up at my grandmother's burial. I am beginning to realize that her death means that she is not coming back. I am struggling with that understanding.

Soul: Your mind is oscillating between understanding the meaning of death with its ramifications and remaining in denial about death and avoiding your feelings of loss.

Personality: I don't want to believe in her death.

Soul: As you came to understand the finality of her death you were obliged to accept your loss.

Personality: I see myself several weeks later in my mother's arms. She is telling me that my grandmother is with God because God wanted her to be in heaven. She said that my grandmother is happy being there with God and that I should be happy for her.

Soul: Are you happy for her?

Personality: No, I want her to be here with me. Why has God taken her from me?

Soul: Why do you think God has taken her from you?

Personality: I must have been bad, but nobody yelled at me. Only God is making me feel bad because God took her from me.

Soul: If you were not bad, then why would God do such a thing?

Personality: I don't know.

Soul: What do you feel towards God?

Personality: I hate God.

Soul: Can you ever trust God?

Personality: No, never!

Soul: Remain the observer.

Personality: I can't. This was too upsetting, but now I understand why I feel the way I do about God.

Soul: Do you see how that influences your feelings towards me?

Personality: It now makes sense to me. I view you as being somewhere between me and God. Therefore the way I feel about God influences how I feel about you. That is why I've never been able to fully trust you.

Soul: Or anyone else for that matter. You believe that if you cannot trust God, then you cannot trust anyone.

Personality: That makes sense.

Soul: Realize how those beliefs that you formed at the age of five have influenced your life. Recognize that they still do.

Personality: It's alarming.

Soul: Do you fully appreciate how those beliefs have influenced you?

Personality: Probably not, but I can see that I don't trust very easily.

Soul: Which means that you are suspicious of other people's motives. It biases you towards blaming others rather than determining your own role in the creation of events. Do you see how that influenced you concerning the collision?

Personality: That's one of the reasons why I blamed the other driver for the accident. I also did not want to be accountable for any part of it.

Soul: Do you understand why it is difficult for you to forgive the other driver?

Personality: Only to some extent, but I do understand my payoff in maintaining an un-forgiving attitude. I still have a difficult time thinking that I shouldn't be judgmental.

Soul: If you were non-judgmental it would also be difficult for you to justify your lack of trust. Do you know why you wish to remain this way?

Personality: No, but I am willing to learn.

Soul: Try to deepen your level of relaxation. Again, focus on your breath and feel all of yourself. Feel yourself moving into a more relaxed state.

Personality: Okay.

Soul: How did you feel when you first realized that you could have prevented the collision?

Personality: I felt horrible and ashamed.

Soul: What does that feel like?

Personality: I feel sick to my stomach and I feel hot all over my face, neck, shoulders, and arms. I feel a headache coming on.

Soul: Remain the observer. As a child when did you feel this way?

Personality: My mother overheard me saying that I hated God. She came into my room and scolded me. She said that God always did what was right even if we don't under-stand it. She said that I was wrong to hate God and that I should be ashamed of my-self for doing so.

Soul: How did you respond?

Personality: If God was always right and God did something that made me feel this bad, then God must hate me.

Soul: How did that make you feel?

Personality: I felt no good and alone. Even my mother was on God's side.

Soul: Can you determine which Basic Right violations were reinforced due to this episode?

Personality: I can see how that would have reinforced my lack of self-acceptance and my ability to feel safe and secure. I can also see how that influences the way that I feel and express emotions and of course how that affects my beliefs.

Soul: How do you wish your mother had responded at that time, keeping in mind your Basic Rights?

Personality: I wish she could have comforted me and helped me to understand death in a different way. She could have accepted how I felt and even validated my feelings. She could have helped me sort out my beliefs.

Soul: What would you have said if you were in her place?

Personality: I would say that it's okay to feel sad and angry that your grandmother is gone. Although it hurts because she is no longer here, you will feel better in time. Always think of the nice times that you and she had together and remember those times when you think of her. Remember how good she made you feel. Understand that she would want you to feel as good now as you did when she was with you. She would want you to smile whenever you thought of her.

Soul: What would you have said about her death?

Personality: I would say that although her body has died, all the good that was inside of her still lives, but in a different way. In the way that she lives now, she feels love because she is with many others that love her as much as we do.

Soul: Take this opportunity and imagine telling this to yourself when you were five years old.

Personality: I feel it in my heart.

Soul: You have extended compassion towards yourself. Can you forgive your mother for how she handled the situation?

Personality: She did the best she could. She didn't mean any harm.

Soul: No doubt. So can you forgive her?

Personality: Yes I can.

Soul: Well?

Personality: What are you expecting?

Soul: Remember the process.

Personality: I understand why it happened. She was raised to believe what she believes and she was simply trying to instill those beliefs in me.

Soul: And reinforce her own beliefs for her own purposes.

Personality: I guess so.

Soul: Assess what resulted from the event.

Personality: It shaped and reinforced several of my own beliefs that I still hold about God, my worthiness, my sense of safety and security, and my feelings and how I feel and express them.

Soul: Maintain the role of the observer. Does that anger you?

Personality: Yes it does, but I'm feeling that a lot of my anger is self-directed.

Soul: Do you understand why?

Personality: No, I was the victim.

Soul: When you were five years old you did not have the reasoning ability, or the power or freedom that you have now. It was easy and reasonable that you adopted the views of your caregivers. However, you have been holding onto these views for many years, perpetuated by the use of your coping strategies. You could have reexamined and changed your beliefs at any time, but you did not.

Personality: And so I'm angry with myself for continuing to believe lies?

Soul: Your self-directed anger reflects your self-intolerant attitude. You are angry with yourself because in your mind you now realize you were wrong. You are dividing the blame between your mother and yourself.

Personality: Why?

Soul: It is what you do rather than simply accepting yourself and your circumstances because you cannot reconcile self-acceptance with being wrong. As you continue to forgive your mother consider forgiving yourself.

Personality: I will try.

Soul: What will you do to prevent a reoccurrence?

Personality: I will evaluate what others tell me more carefully. I will work to understand why I believe as I do.

Soul: Would you like to grieve your loss?

Personality: I'm afraid I don't understand what my loss was or is.

Soul: In talking about your parents you once said, "They could have done so much better. I would be a completely different person if they had raised me with more compassion . . ."

Personality: So I did.

Soul: Well?

Personality: My attitudes have shifted since then. I realize that they did the best job they could. I understand that I can be a completely different person whenever I make the choice to change. I have no need to grieve over this. I already have.

Soul: Then are you ready to forgive your mother?

Personality: Yes I am.

Soul: Hold all of these thoughts in your mind and body and feel all of yourself. Now feel me throughout and around you, supporting you in this effort. Release these thoughts and feelings and any ill will you have in regard to this event and all similar events. Pardon your mother and yourself and as I spread my love throughout your being, accept it and direct that love to your mother as well.

Personality: I have done so. Why did you include me in terms of accepting love?

Soul: You cannot give what you will not receive.

Personality: Are we done?

Soul: Not quite. Would you like to forgive yourself?

Personality: For what?

Soul: For not accepting yourself more.

Personality: That seems a bit foolish.

Soul: Why? This is something you have been doing to yourself for most of your life and it has significant consequences.

Personality: I have difficulty accepting myself more than I do. I've always been this way. I don't feel like I actively keep it going or that it is even of my own doing. It's more like a passive presence within me that has always been there and always will be.

Soul: It is easy to see why you approach this issue more passively, as though you remain victimized. However you are the one that perpetuates your lack of self-acceptance. Understand how this is affecting you.

Personality: I know that not accepting myself more is significantly affecting me. I look to others for approval, I never feel good enough, I am self-critical, and I am critical of others. I simply don't like myself that much, I don't believe that others really like me, and I feel that I will only like myself at some future time if I become a better person. To become a better person I feel that I must be right or at least, not be wrong, but yet I must be agreeable so that I can get along with others and they can like me. These attitudes have always been with me.

Soul: Continue to be the observer and try to increase your level of relaxation. Focus on your breath and your body.

Personality: Okay.

Soul: Do you understand why this has happened?

Personality: Why what happened?

Soul: Why you have developed and maintained a self-critical attitude.

Personality: I received a lot of criticism when I was young and I never reevaluated my beliefs and circumstances. I just wanted to prove myself right so that I could be seen as being right by others and myself. In that way I could believe that I was more worthy and I could accept myself more.

Soul: It is something more primary than that.

Personality: Help me to understand.

Soul: Your lack of self-acceptance is itself a coping strategy.

Personality: How can that be?

Soul: You use this coping strategy in your attempt to remain independent from me. It is an avoidance tactic, which allows you to focus on yourself as an independent entity. That is why you seek control. You do not wish to be reliant on me because you believe that I abandoned you. By focusing on yourself in your vain attempt to accept yourself more completely, in isolation from me, you have been seeking and trying to justify greater independence from me.

Personality: How did this happen?

Soul: When you were still very young you remained aware of me for a while. However, as you became more aware of your physical and emotional needs and the inability to have those needs met by me, your focus began to shift. You were angry with me because you thought I was not there to help you any longer. So you adopted coping strategies to have those needs met. Those coping strategies that you developed, in your early childhood and beyond, further constrained your ability to perceive me. Your memory of me became increasingly distant until I was no longer real to you. Deep within, you believe that I was not there to help you. You believe that I abandoned you. You developed a belief and a definition of yourself that excluded me in an effort to become independent of me. As a result, you have been working to accept yourself to a greater extent without me, but your attempt is futile.

Personality: Why is it futile?

Soul: Without me it is unlikely that you will ever deem yourself as good enough, because you will always believe that you can and should be better. By identifying with me and by perceiving yourself from my viewpoint, you can more fully accept yourself because then you will have greater awareness and understanding. Accepting me will enable you to accept yourself more easily.

Personality: I don't feel any sense of abandonment from you.

Soul: Yet you do not trust me completely.

Personality: I thought that resulted from my view of God.

Soul: That reinforced an earlier belief you held that is buried deep in your subconscious.

Personality: So this is why you have been trying to regain my trust by offering me all of this insight.

Soul: I have always been with you. You turned away from me when I could not meet the physical and emotional needs, which were not being met by your caregivers and the world around you. You chose to more readily identify with the physical world. I have never left you, but your awareness of me dimmed to the point that it seemed as though I was gone.

Personality: So again it was my own doing.

Soul: In a different era you would have been reminded about me in a more practical sense by your caregivers at a young age, but those teachings have not been widespread of late.

Personality: Everyone must suffer from this sense of abandonment and not even realize it.

Soul: It is very widespread, but more people are beginning to understand, just as you are now. It is time for you to forgive yourself.

Personality: I'm ready.

Soul: Hold all of these thoughts in your mind and body and feel all of yourself. Now feel me throughout and around you, supporting you. Release these thoughts and feelings and any ill will you have in regard to this event and all similar events. Pardon yourself and allow me to spread my love throughout your being, accept it, and accept me.

Personality: I will.

Soul: You will revisit these thoughts many times before you truly forgive yourself including me.

Personality: Why?

Soul: You must come to a greater understanding of the effect that these beliefs have had upon you. You must work through the grief and anger that you will feel. You must also learn how you plan to prevent a reoccurrence.

Personality: I think I know how I'm going to do that.

Soul: How?

Personality: I think I'm ready to learn how to meditate.

Soul: Even surrendering yourself to me?

Personality: I will view it as surrendering myself to me and something greater.

Soul: In time, as you learn to forgive and accept yourself more completely, you will have less of a need to control this process, but for now we can proceed.

Personality: Why can't I control this process?

Soul: Have you noticed that you become more relaxed when you practice allowance rather than control?

Personality: Yes.

Soul: Well the same applies to meditation, as it is a deeper form of relaxation.

Personality: So why can't I just allow the meditative state to develop rather than having to surrender?

Soul: You can, but it will have an affect on the quality of your meditative state.

Personality: What do you mean by that?

Soul: What are you trying to accomplish through meditation?

Personality: I'm really not sure.

Soul: Then why do it?

Personality: I just thought that I would be making more progress if I began to meditate.

Soul: More progress than what?

Personality: Than if I simply relaxed.

Soul: You can make excellent progress relaxing and practicing the Feel, Deal, and Let Go process. In fact, even after you have been meditating you can still practice relaxation to deepen your state of relaxation at the physical and emotional levels. This will provide a more stable base to operate from when you meditate.

Personality: Can't I do that when I'm meditating?

Soul: It all depends upon your intent. What is it that you are trying to achieve?

Personality: What are some goals I can work on?

Soul: Meditation is a state of being. In this process you can learn how to be. You may perceive that as a goal, but from my perspective it is nothing more than learning how to exist more as I do. As such, practicing meditation would be learning to accept me to a greater extent.

Personality: I expected that.

Soul: Because you are beginning to realize the importance of doing so.

Personality: I am beginning to recognize my desire to become more aware. How would you recommend I best proceed?

Soul: If your intention in meditating is to develop greater awareness, then what is it that you are trying to become more aware of?

Personality: I would like to become more aware of myself, my connection to all living things, and to All That Is.

Soul: Greater awareness of yourself and your connectedness begins with being able to perceive your vibratory nature because that helps you quiet your mind and perceive your connectedness energetically. You can learn to feel your connectedness through that medium.

Personality: Explain that to me.

Soul: In a more relaxed state you can perceive a finer vibration at the level of your skin first and with practice this can be felt deeper, throughout your body. When you are in this feeling state you feel your own energy system, which is that part of you that permeates and surrounds your physical body. Developing and deepening this finer perception is an important process, as it can be used as a form of feedback informing you of your level of relaxation. The more relaxed you are the better you can perceive this energetic aspect of yourself, and allow it to develop. Meditation is an excellent time to practice perceiving this vibration and in time you will be able to sense it more reliably during your normal waking state. Your finer vibratory sense is generally easiest to first perceive in your hands. It feels somewhat like static electricity around your hands. It may be associated with the sensation that your hands are full or puffy, which occurs as your awareness transcends the physical. You have already begun to feel this in your relaxation sessions. In time you will be able to perceive this vibration throughout your entire body. When you are not meditating and you can perceive this throughout your body you will be fully engaged in the physical and in the present moment, while remaining much more relaxed, but you also must learn to be better grounded.

Personality: Go on.

Soul: To facilitate the development of your feeling nature and to assist you in remaining present in your body it is helpful to learn how to ground yourself to the Earth. Imagine either roots growing down from your feet deep into the Earth or a beam of energy from the Earth penetrating the soles of your feet. In time you will be able to feel the same sensation in your feet that you can perceive in your hands when your finer vibratory sense is more active. When you can, allow this feeling to circulate throughout your entire body. Grounding yourself is very helpful at the onset of your meditation sessions. Remember you are the juncture of heaven and Earth. Grounding yourself allows you to close the circuit between your spiritual side and the physical realm.

Personality: What about my thoughts during meditation?

Soul: Focus on your feeling state, this finer vibratory state of being and as you have already done, allow your thoughts to drift away. As you begin to make progress, what you will sense is a widening gap, which develops between thoughts as you learn to release one after another. When you are in the gap, you are in a state of being, not thinking or doing. In time you can actively enter the gap by becoming adept at allowing it to develop more quickly. This process is facilitated by your ability to move into a feeling state at will. The learning process, however, is one of releasing or letting go of the thoughts and not one of actively searching for the gap. You will learn to gain control of the process only after you learn to let go of your attempts to control it.

Personality: Why do I want to learn how not to think?

Soul: This is how you learn how to listen and be in the moment.

Personality: Who would I be listening to?

Soul: To me for one. You can perceive me more clearly when your mind becomes quiet. Once you can attain a quieter mind, then you can ask a question and listen for the answer. You can learn to do this both within and outside of your meditation sessions. In time it will be easier for you to differentiate between my thoughts and yours and you will be able to perceive more from me. This will cause you to become more self-aware.

Personality: What about my desire to experience my connection with all living things?

Soul: You already can experience your physical, emotional, and mental connections.

Personality: I am interested in experiencing a deeper connection.

Soul: Your spiritual connection?

Personality: I guess so.

Soul: That can only happen with me.

Personality: Why?

Soul: Like perceives like. You are only like me to the extent that you identify more completely with me and even then you must learn how to elevate your vibratory nature as you continue to hold your conscious awareness. That is how you can perceive your spiritual connectedness to others and All That Is. I am your link.

Personality: How do I do this?

Soul: You must allow me to become more engaged in the physical in order to elevate your vibratory nature. I cannot do so without your permission.

Personality: What if I give you limited access?

Soul: Then the outcome will be limited accordingly.

Personality: I don't know how to proceed.

Discuss and/or Journal

Our personalities independent nature makes it difficult to create a practical partnership with our soul. With free will and the control that it has, our personality operates in the physical world as it sees fit. Because its awareness is generally limited, it does not appreciate the benefits that a spiritual partnership would confer. As a result, most people don't have a spiritual practice, such as meditation. By trying a spiritual practice we can begin to learn the potential benefits.

1. Do you have a spiritual practice? If so, what benefits do you hope to realize as a result of this practice?

_____

_____

_____

_____

2. What are your beliefs about your soul?

_____

_____

_____

_____

3. What are your beliefs about All That Is?

_____

_____

_____

_____

4. Do you wish to be more connected to others, your spiritual side, and All That Is? Why or why not?

_____

_____

_____

_____

chapter twenty-seven

LOVE, TRUTH, AND WILL

As we develop greater conscious awareness of our spiritual side, we face a choice. How much are we willing to embody or integrate with our soul? Do we choose to create a practical partnership? To do so, requires that we embody our soul by incorporating its values into our personality. This action is in conflict with our use of coping strategies.

Our coping strategies are born of fear, not love. Truth is the path that pure love takes. When we use our coping strategies we avoid truth. To fully embody and thus manifest love and truth we must be willing to shed our coping strategies.

Living in partnership with our soul and its values is a drastic departure from how we have been living our lives. For us to suddenly transition from our present personality-based state to a fully integrated state of being with our soul would require an act of Divine will. However, we have been endowed with free will. We have the Right to choose in the timeframe of our choosing. It is our personalities Right to determine when and how much it will incorporate love and truth into its life.

Soul: Developing a deeper spiritual connection is a gradual process. Be patient with yourself. It is a matter of small steps.

Personality: But I want it now.

Soul: Then take your first step.

Personality: In what way?

Soul: Towards me.

Personality: Why?

Soul: So that you can better know me.

Personality: How can I possibly come to know you when my perceptions of you are so limited?

Soul: You will learn to better perceive me through yourself.

Personality: How is that done?

Soul: You will begin to observe how you are different when you integrate with me to a greater extent.

Personality: How will I know when I embody you more?

Soul: You will know by how you feel and act.

Personality: So, when I'm feeling bad then I embody you to a lesser degree, is that it?

Soul: When you experience negative emotional feelings then you embody me to a lesser extent, because feeling bad is born of a coping strategy. My influence is reduced during those times because you engage me less, which reduces my access to you.

Personality: I'm not aware that I choose to engage you less. Why would I choose the discomfort of my coping strategy?

Soul: It is not in your nature to seek pain, but you frequently do so to avoid that which you believe will cause you greater pain. That is why you employ coping strategies.

Personality: Yes, I understand that, but why wouldn't I choose to engage you more, so that I can better observe myself and come to understand myself?

Soul: When you choose your coping strategies you react from your past. It is only recently that you have begun to acknowledge me. Your coping strategies have evolved from your desire to be in control, which causes you to operate independently of me. The attitudes of your coping strategies therefore reduce my access.

Personality: How do I do that?

Soul: Through your beliefs.

Personality: My beliefs are concepts that I hold in my mind. Can't you work around them?

Soul: Your beliefs are more like prison walls and I will not violate them, because they result from your free will. You have chosen to believe as you do and you must be accountable for the reality that those beliefs create.

Personality: I still don't understand how my beliefs limit your involvement.

Soul: Your beliefs define how you choose to engage and connect with the world around you. They consciously and subconsciously determine what you give and receive. Your perceptions are limited accordingly. When you operate from your coping strategies you narrowly define what is acceptable to you. When you choose your coping strategies you choose to limit how you engage me. That limits my access to you. When you embody me less you reduce my involvement in your life. It is the choice you make.

Personality: Does this stem from my being judgmental?

Soul: Many of your beliefs, particularly those that you hold about yourself and others, are little more than judgments. They are the likes and dislikes that you have formed based upon the successes that you have had in gaining control. For instance, you have learned that acting selfishly begets criticism and so you have formed a belief that it is bad to be selfish. Behaving unselfishly has been rewarded by praise and an attitude in others that is more likely to be compliant with your needs. This gives you a greater sense of approval and control, which is pleasing to you. As a result of your beliefs concerning selfishness it is difficult for you to accept and therefore perceive situations in which being selfish, as you define it, would better serve the common good.

Personality: I'm getting better about this.

Soul: How so?

Personality: I make time for myself to meditate. I never used to do that.

Soul: You make time for yourself by setting your alarm clock forty-five minutes earlier. You are depriving yourself of sleep rather than providing more time for yourself.

Personality: You said that when I meditate my mind stays awake and my body sleeps so I didn't think that I was depriving myself.

Soul: I know what you are really thinking. You are hoping that at the level of meditation you are currently practicing you will require less sleep. However, you have not yet achieved a meditative state that rejuvenates your body as well as sleep does. That is why you are sleeping longer on the weekends, to partially improve your sleep-deprived state.

Personality: I don't feel more tired.

Soul: That extra cup of coffee in the morning does the trick, at least during the day. Try not setting your alarm clock and see what happens.

Personality: I get the point.

Soul: Only the point about being sleep deprived, but what of shifting responsibilities to make more time for yourself. Some of your attitudes have changed on a mental level, but they are not materializing beyond that.

Personality: Are you saying that because of the way that I make time for meditation?

Soul: That is simply the result of how you feel and believe.

Personality: How so?

Soul: If you believe that you are deserving of the time to meditate you would make that time without compromising yourself. If you felt deserving then taking the time for yourself would not cause you to feel selfish. Your actions reveal your true feelings and beliefs.

Personality: Old habits die hard.

Soul: Because the old payoffs remain. That is why making changes in yourself is difficult. For you to relinquish the old payoffs you must be convinced that something better will replace them.

Personality: And what would that be?

Soul: Love.

Personality: You mean self-love, don't you?

Soul: Self-love is only one aspect. That is a reasonable place to start.

Personality: Why?

Soul: You cannot give what you do not have without sacrificing.

Personality: I must already have it because I am able to give it freely.

Soul: How so?

Personality: I treat those around me with love and affection.

Soul: And you expect love and affection in return.

Personality: Of course. Is there something unusual about that?

Soul: It is not unusual, but it is a limited version of love. For the most part, it is the love that one personality exchanges with another.   .

Personality: What other love is there?

Soul: The love that you can accept from me.

Personality: How does that differ from my love?

Soul: Your love is my love filtered through you. You attach other emotional feelings, beliefs, and actions to it. As a result, it is love that has conditions associated with it. It is less pure. If your spouse did not love you as much would that diminish the love you would give over time? When you give love to your children do you expect them to be more compliant with your wishes?

Personality: You get what you give?

Soul: And you give what you get.

Personality: From my spouse and children?

Soul: From me and through me from All That Is.

Personality: I thought you loved me unconditionally.

Soul: I do, but you limit what you will receive.

Personality: How?

Soul: By not accepting me more completely and engaging me more.

Personality: Would you not provide me with your love anyway?

Soul: Love is more than a word or a thought. Love is my reality—it is what I embody. Accepting and identifying with me brings my love to you.

Personality: Then how do you give love?

Soul: Fully and unconditionally. I do what love would do. I provide you with insight and assist with opportunity consistent with my love for you. I even infuse you with love when you allow it.

Personality: When does that happen?

Soul: Sometimes when you meditate you surrender to me. During those times you are willing to receive my love directly, but only to a degree. It registers in your conscious mind as a feeling of fullness or warmth in your upper chest.

Personality: Yes, I have noticed that feeling. Why do I feel it there?

Soul: It is our point of greatest attachment. If you allow it, that feeling can spread throughout your body and need not be limited to your meditation sessions.

Personality: I can't believe that I could hold that feeling during my daytime activities.

Soul: Then you will not.

Personality: Why not?

Soul: Because you believe that you cannot.

Personality: That's just an expression.

Soul: It is your reality. Your beliefs define and control your reality.

Personality: And your beliefs don't?

Soul: I have no need for beliefs and so neither do you.

Personality: That is the most preposterous notion that I can ever recall you saying. Our beliefs define us.

Soul: I know. That is why your reality is as it is.

Personality: If I had no beliefs then what would I be?

Soul: You would be left with me.

Personality: Why don't you have beliefs?

Soul: Because I am what I am. I exist in a state of being not believing. Your beliefs are mainly those of your coping strategies. You can perceive me as the love that filters through those beliefs. That is why your love and my love feel and behave differently at this time in your life. However, when you shed your coping beliefs then our love will be the same.

Personality: If I had no beliefs I wouldn't know how to act.

Soul: Your beliefs facilitate your decision making process with the intention that your actions will produce an outcome consistent with your coping strategies. If you discarded those beliefs you would have to make new decisions. You could use new considerations or engage your feeling nature or both. You could even ask, "what would love do?" I understand, however, that this is too much to ask of you at this time.

Personality: I have made progress, but I think that is beyond me at this time.

Soul: You are being honest with yourself.

Personality: And fearful.

Soul: With practice your fears will diminish.

Personality: What kind of practice?

Soul: Surrendering to me.

Personality: And where does that leave me?

Soul: Closer to me and deepening your connection to all things. That is what you want, is it not?

Personality: I did say that.

Soul: But did you mean it?

Personality: It is what I want, but I didn't realize that I would have to give up so much to get it.

Soul: What is it that you think you would be giving up?

Personality: It seems that I would be giving up a significant part of my identity.

Soul: You are beginning to realize how much your identity is defined by your coping strategies.

Personality: Considering this makes me feel that I'm nothing more than a bundle of coping strategies.

Soul: Do you wish to perceive the truth?

Personality: Yes.

Soul: Then allow yourself to accept it.

Personality: When I perceive the truth I accept it, don't I?

Soul: You must be willing to accept the truth before you can fully perceive it. Otherwise you will blind yourself to it with your filters, as you have been doing.

Personality: Is this your truth or my truth we're talking about?

Soul: There is only one truth.

Personality: Yours I suspect.

Soul: Truth is truth. Truth is the path that pure love takes. It is an expression of love.

Personality: But you said that your love and my love feel and behave differently.

Soul: That is because when my love travels through you it often deviates from the path that it would naturally take. The filters of your coping strategies distort my love in your attempt to accomplish a desired outcome.

Personality: Then my truth and your truth aren't the same.

Soul: Often they are not, but they are gradually becoming more similar as you engage your coping strategies less.

Personality: Overall I think that I am pretty truthful.

Soul: You rarely speak outright falsehoods, but you often allow for misperception and you commonly engage your coping strategies.

Personality: It's not my fault if other people interpret things the way that they do.

Soul: Everyone has that Right. However, when you perceive that others are being misled and you do nothing to correct their misperceptions, then you are allowing an untruthful state to develop or persist. It is no different than speaking a lie. You sometimes do it through omission or a misleading gesture, but it is still part of your behavioral repertoire.

Personality: I guess love wouldn't do that, but I don't see how using my coping strategies is a lie.

Soul: Your coping strategies are your means to keep your old fears and painful beliefs hidden. When you use your coping strategies you are keeping the truth about yourself hidden from yourself and others. You are maintaining a portion of your mind below your conscious awareness. Accepting the truth about yourself would allow you to explore and understand your subconscious mind. In so doing much of your subconscious would no longer exist in that way because you would be conscious of it. What do you want for yourself?

Personality: I would like to come to understand myself more.

Soul: Then accept yourself to a greater degree.

Personality: What part of myself?

Soul: Accept all that you are conscious of and be willing to accept all that you are not conscious of, including me. A willingness to accept me also means that you are willing to accept your subconscious fears and painful beliefs, since both of these aspects of you remain largely subconscious.

Personality: Why?

Soul: Acceptance is a manifestation of love. Love in the form of acceptance does not differentiate between those parts of your subconscious mind that you would consider good or bad. The path of love accepts both. That is the truth behind acceptance.

Personality: I had said long ago that I wanted to accept myself more. I never understood what that meant.

Soul: Now you have a better idea.

Personality: But I'm not sure how to proceed.

Soul: Summon your resources.

Personality: What resources?

Soul: Your will. It is up to you to choose your path and to take action accordingly. You have the ability to do so.

Personality: Of my own free will?

Soul: Of course. How do you plan to use it?

Personality: What insight would you offer me?

Soul: Begin by forgiving yourself. Accept who you are and your circumstances in life. Ground yourself in love and become more aware of what you are feeling, thinking, and doing. Claim and enforce your Basic Rights and respect the Rights of others.

Personality: What about relaxation, meditation, and practicing the Feel, Deal, and Let Go process?

Soul: These are methods for you to explore truthfulness, forgiveness, compassion, and hope.

Personality: And what about my relationship with you and All That Is?

Soul: As your self-exploration continues, you will develop greater sensitivity to all living things. A strengthening of the connection and communion between you and I and All That Is will result. By embodying love and truth your understanding, tolerance, and compassion of others will grow. When you accept what is, in this manner, you awaken to a life filled with possibilities and potential.

Personality: Insight and opportunity.

Soul: Yes, you awaken to me.

Discuss and/or Journal

Creating a practical partnership with our soul and All That Is, is what life is all about as human beings. It often seems that life's activities preclude us from walking this path, but that is not true. We have the ability to develop a partnership with our soul as we live our lives. Exercising our own free will in this regard is all we need do.

1. Do you wish to create a practical partnership with your soul?

_____

_____

_____

_____

_____

2. What steps are you willing to make?

_____

_____

_____

_____

_____

_____

_____

_____

_____

_____

_____

_____

POSTSCRIPT

Reading serves the intellect and aids in our understanding. It is a fine beginning, but only that. Absorbing the information contained in this book requires a departure from believing, feeling, and acting primarily from the perspective of your personality. It involves the ability to feel deeply the core of your being and to accept and identify with your spiritual side in order to practically integrate your soul and spiritual essence into your daily life. Replacing fear with love, ignorance with truth, and subconscious reactive patterns of behavior with conscious acceptance, understanding, forgiveness, and compassion leads to fulfillment and the attainment of your purpose. It is a path worthy of us all.

To learn more about One Red River and our mission, please visit us at www.oneredriver.com